SOCIAL SCIENCES

6/21/94 8/24/95 22T

12/98
25
9/98

Clockwise this page: Gertrude Atherton, Isadora Duncan, Sarah Winnemucca, Gertrude Stein with Alice Toklas.

Illustrations courtesy of Alma Lavenson, University of Colorado Medical Center, Nevada State Historical Society, Bancroft Library, Oregon Historical Society, and Franz Haufstaengl.

1/26

San Jose
Public Library

OVERTIME CHARGE IS 5 CENTS PER DAY

Careful usage of books is expected and any soiling,
damage or loss is to be paid for by the borrower.

Eminent Women
of the West

All mankind owes gratitude to the subject of this statue that stands in the United States Capitol at Washington and which here as frontispiece symbolizes the achievements of Western women of eminence. She is Colorado's Florence Sabin, the medical researcher whose discoveries paved the way to longer and healthier human life. (— *University of Colorado Medical Center*)

Eminent Women
of the West

by Elinor Richey

BERKELEY   Howell -North Books   CALIFORNIA

Printed and bound in the United States of America

Library of Congress Catalog Card No. 75-26293

ISBN 0-8310-7110-9

Published by Howell-North Books
1050 Parker Street, Berkeley, California 94710

Contents

For Frances

Acknowledgments

More than my previous books this one is indebted to libraries. Every biographer of a person of an earlier era owes much
to the adequacy of libraries and the skill of librarians. Because
my subject was outstanding Western women, a category much
neglected by biographers (unless the women made their mark
elsewhere, or were notorious), most of what has been written
about them reposes in libraries specializing in local and regional
history. Those are the ones which cherish such items as overland diaries, brochures of original land companies, menus of
long-vanished spas, and timetables of dismantled narrow gauge
railroads. They also preserve old letters, scrapbooks of flaking
clippings, and files of long defunct country weeklies. So imbued
with their sphere are some of their staffers, the biographer can
chat with them about his quarry as about some fascinating
mutual friend — no small assist in his lonely pursuit. Indispensable to me were the Oregon Historical Center; the Bancroft
Library; the libraries of the historical societies of Colorado,
Montana, Arizona, Nevada and California; the state libraries of
Oregon, California and Nevada; the California Rooms of the
Oakland and Los Angeles public libraries; and the Western
Jewish History Center in Berkeley. Among those librarians who
transcended their role, inspiring as well as fortifying, were
Frances Buxton, Irene Moran, Erma Davis and Mary Ellen
Bailey.

Invaluable also was another kind of history library: the
Regional Oral History Office, which specializes in recording
taped interviews with historical figures and their associates.

It is an adjunct of the Bancroft and ably headed by Willa Baum. After interviewing a number of persons connected with my subjects by birth or association, I learned Miss Baum's staff had tape-recorded interviews with several of my sources. Consulting their transcripts I was chagrined, yet pleased, to find their tapes had gleaned much I had missed. When a newspaper reporter, I cultivated the knack of keeping a news source on track, insistently tugging him back when he strayed from the question. This was fine for uncovering hard facts for an afternoon deadline, but subtlety and illumination were apt to slip the net. Those experienced oral librarians had permitted, even encouraged, their sources to digress, to meander off on side trips or detour up the back roads of their memories — and thereby uncovered exciting facts and anecdotes nobody would have thought to ask for. So I wish to thank Suzanne Reiss, Edna Daniel, Sally Woodbridge and Malca Chall for being wise enough to give their sources free rein while the tape recorder whirred on and on.

Still, I did gain much from personal sources, and am grateful to those who submitted to my less than expert interviewing: Imogen Cunningham, who received me at her studio on San Francisco's Russian Hill; Jeannette Rankin who though ill invited me to visit her at a Carmel retirement home, where she died weeks later; David C. Duniway, grandson of Abigail Scott Duniway; Rondal Partridge, son of Imogen Cunningham; Edna McKinnon and Harriet Huber, respectively sister and grandniece of Jeannette Rankin; Flora and Morgan North, niece and nephew of Julia Morgan; Dorothy Coblentz; Edna and David Daniel; Edward Hussey, Louis Schalk, and Margaret Wheat.

For the use of various helpful materials I thank Gae Canfield, Vivian Hallinan, Arthur Waugh, Therese Hayman, and the Oakland Museum. Much gratitude is due five friends, writers of taste and skill who read portions of the manuscript and supplied helpful criticism: Helena Lawton, Floyd Salas, Celeste McCloud, Irene Hilton and Tom Thomas; as well as Richard Bridgman, author of *Gertrude Stein in Pieces,* who offered valued pointers on my manuscript on Gertrude Stein.

Special acknowledgments are due my publishers, who have supplied indispensable materials and counsel throughout the writing of this book; to my husband Hill who patiently corrects my phonic spelling and assists in other ways; and to two gentle friends, Marie Underwood and Olga Pausch, for their wisdom and encouragement.

One more library note. I am an inveterate owl and prefer working nights, even Saturday nights. Quite happily I discovered the after-hours telephone reference service of the Oakland and Berkeley public libraries — that is, learned that nightly until midnight somebody was there to look up things for you. Whenever at some still hour paralysis seized my brain or the tree outside my window looked too melancholy, I would phone for some small fact I needed, because the answering voice was always welcoming, enthusiastic. And it always worked. Enthusiasm came bouncing over the electronic circuit recharging my limp brain waves. So my thanks to that unseen genie who responded at the touch of the telephone dial.

Several of the profiles which comprise this book appeared originally, in shorter form, in *American Heritage* and in *American West*. I am grateful to these publications for permission to reprint the material.

ELINOR RICHEY

Berkeley, California
June, 1975

Foreword

A few years ago when researching for another book in Oakland, California, I was interested to discover that four women who intrigued me greatly had all grown up there. These four, geniuses all but otherwise just about as different as women could be, were Julia Morgan, Isadora Duncan, Gertrude Stein and Lillian Gilbreth. They had been contemporaries, were born within six years of each other, between 1872 and 1878. I found it astonishing that these indubitably liberated women had grown up during the height of the high collar, high teas Victorian era, when the notion still persisted in many quarters that fragile womankind was better off without burdensome enlightenment. All that was really needed was knowledge of how to select and snare a husband — a good-providing one, of course. But these four women had contrarily pursued and snared knowledge and ideas. All but Isadora attended Oakland High School, graduated from college, and went on to higher study. By the time she was ten, the schoolroom could no longer hold Isadora, but from early childhood her appetite for music, dance and drama was insatiable.

It was with an electrifying thrill that I realized these women were not merely high achievers, but each had been an innovator in her field — an original creator. Julia Morgan, the first woman to graduate from the Beaux-Arts and first to receive national recognition as an architect, was also one of the innovators of the Bay Region Style of architecture. Flamboyant Isadora Duncan, by rebelling against the fixed disciplines of classical ballet, invented modern dance, while Gertrude Stein

10

became the most tradition-shattering writer in the English language. Lillian Gilbreth not only opened doors in engineering for women but was a pioneer efficiency expert. That she became a national authority on model homes and nurseries could not have been unrelated to the fact that she was also the mother of twelve, two of whom authored the popular book about their lively menage *Cheaper by the Dozen*. That all this originality should have gestated in one California town (the census of 1870 counted a mere 10,500 Oaklanders) was coincidence indeed.

At least I considered it coincidence then. But as historical research carried me through other Western states, I kept hearing of other female movers and shakers. Women of stubborn persistence had thrust back barriers of all kinds. In Wyoming, six-foot-tall Esther Morris, after getting herself elected the first female justice of the peace, lobbied through a legislative act that made Wyoming women the first in the country to vote and to serve on juries. Oregon's editor-reformer Abigail Scott Duniway led successful campaigns to bring suffrage and professional and property rights to women. But Western suffrage heroines are too numerous to name here. Suffice it to say that the first dozen states to pass suffrage acts were Western states.

Women also invaded medicine. Oregon's first doctor Bethenia Owens-Adair was almost tarred and feathered for daring to perform an autopsy on a male: later she shocked Victorian society by advocating birth control and abortion. Milicent Shinn came off a California ranch to pioneer in Child psychiatry. As superintendent of Stockton State Hospital, California's Margaret Smyth was the first woman to head a state hospital for the insane. Mariana Bertola's brilliant plan for infant and maternal hospitalization was widely adopted throughout the country. The feats of Colorado's Florence Sabin in medical research included original discoveries about blood and lymph that paved the way for monumental medical breakthroughs.

Women were no less a force in law and government. Arizona's Sarah Herring Sorin was the first woman attorney to practice before the Supreme Court of the United States, while California's Annette Adams became the first woman Assistant

U. S. Attorney General. Jeannette Rankin, after moving her
native Montana into the suffrage column, ran for office and
became the country's first Congresswoman. Teachers owe debts
to author Kate Kennedy, who championed equal pay for women
teachers, and to Utah-born Florence Prag Kahn, who fought
for teachers' pensions and professional benefits and championed
other reforms while serving for a decade as California Congresswoman. San Francisco's social worker Amy Steinhart
Braden was a leader and innovator in public child welfare. Arizona judge Lorna Lockwood championed legislation in mental
health codes and delinquency prevention.

Women shone in almost every field. San Diego's pioneer
horticulturist Kate Sessions introduced new plants to the South-
west. Los Angeles' Alice Stebbens Wells, a family connection
of the stage line founder, became the world's first policewoman
and founded and headed the International Association of Po-
licewomen. San Francisco-born Aurelia Reinhardt took an unknown little school and molded it into Mills College with a
world-wide reputation. Seattle's Imogen Cunningham was one
of a handful of pioneer photographers who elevated photography from an amusing curiosity to an art. Explorer Louise
Boyd of San Rafael, California made six expeditions to the Arctic which won her world-wide acclaim from scientists, foreign
decorations, and a namesake in Greenland — Miss Boyd Land.

Patently, there was something about the West that activated
this creativity, that stimulated women to transcend their customary roles. I knew now those four Oakland innovators were
no mere coincidence. The social climate of the West had somehow precipitated them. But how?

These defiant ones, I discovered, rarely came from the ranks
of pioneer women, those helpmates who accompanied husbands, dutifully or in protest, to places of male selection. The
roles of the new arrivals had, in fact, differed little, save in
degree of drudgery, from those of their Eastern cousins. No,
these bold innovators were the descendants of the pioneers —
the first generation Native Daughters.

Not that their mothers had lacked in courage or persistence.
But the pioneer women spent their fortitude in journeying out

and in civilizing their new homestakes. Theirs was the longest, most grueling migratory journey ever made in search of homes: they crossed the Indian-and cholera-plagued overland trails, braved the disease-ridden Isthmus of Panama, and chanced the perilous trip around the Horn. Some of them had been hand-picked as brides for their very stamina to endure that journey; fragile sweethearts were quickly abandoned by men who had set their eyes on the Western horizon. If these women did not set out with courage in their luggage, they found it somewhere along the way, through necessity. Persistence too they had and needed for cultivating the raw, wild, sometimes violent place they found. They insisted on houses with floors and windows instead of lean-to shacks, on roads instead of trails, on clearings, on gardens, on schools and stores and opera houses. Some of them even tamed the wild Spanish cattle into giving milk, although they usually had their husbands hold the horns. But it never occurred to them to establish *new* kinds of homes and schools; what they set their hearts on were houses and schools exactly like those left behind. They were not innovators, except as necessity dictated, but it was they who made the West habitable.They knew quite well the indispensable role they played in civilizing a primitive land, and they were proud of this mighty deed. They planted this pride in their daughters, along with their honed and tested courage.

But some pioneer women gave their daughters something more. Some uprooted women were cruelly disappointed by what they found when they alighted from a tattered Cone-stoga wagon or debarked from some stinking ship. What greeted them did not match their husbands' rosy promises, or their own personal dreams. For others disillusionment set in later in the face of unending pioneer hardship. Resentment smoldered within them. This too they passed on to daughters.

Still, it was a discontent infused with hope; it was never really defeatist. For in the West optimism was as ubiquitous as sunshine, was irresistibly in the air, linked with the rainbow myth of the pursuit of happiness. If Western women generally were less contented than their husbands, they were sanguine, nonetheless. Historians have observed that Western pioneer women were more cheerful than their counterparts of the earlier Midwestern frontier, who tended to melancholia and hopelessness. Western women found much not to their liking, but they looked to the future. This too they passed on to daughters.

If from their mothers these extraordinary daughters took courage and persistence and pride of sex and optimistic discontent, what got they from their fathers? Courage, too, of course. Men who caught the virulent Western fever tended to be specimens of rare bravery and endurance. And those who settled the stark, arid cattle ranges back from the Pacific Coast were a distinctive breed indeed, truly tough-fibered men of colossal stamina. Daughters drew sustenance from example, but they also gained something special via inheritance. A sizable proportion of male pioneers were descended from several generations of restless, critical, frontier-hoppers. Often the trek had begun in Europe, with each generation progressing farther west. Nervous restlessness was in their genes, and so in the genes of their offspring. Stranded on the Continent's farthest reach with no geographical frontiers left to conquer, their progeny were prone to slash onto the frontiers of scientific discovery, or social reform, or artistic innovation. With horizontal conquest at land's end, as it were, their quests turned vertical.

What did these exceptional daughters gain from over-all Western society? Unprecedented freedom and stimulus to develop their potential. An emphasis upon the individual, instead of on family or purse, encouraged originality in thought and deed. The economic risks of frontier society fostered this. In the frontier town of Denver, Colorado, one Count Murat, descendant of the King of Naples but down on his luck, trimmed the miners' hair, while his countess did their laundry. The panhandler and the banker might change places next year, and they knew it. As a result Westerners tended to judge each other fairly, male and female, and this attitude oiled upward mobility.

But the nudge to individuality was not merely economic. It was also romantic. The West had grown up on the strides of heroes and heroines, and still passionately believed in them. Pioneer parades long remained popular, and pioneer reunion picnics. Old-timers were coaxed to stand up and recount memories of the trail and early homesteading days. The younger generation might feign boredom and poke fun, but just the same they drank it in along with the pink lemonade. The promise was still persuasive that everybody was born to pursue adventure and attempt the incalculable.

To a small degree chivalry had something to do with the wider privilege Western women enjoyed vis-à-vis their Eastern sisters. Being scarcer in the West, they were valued higher, indulged more. Of the westward migration of 1849, only about ten per cent were women, and a diminishing disproportion continued for decades, although by 1870 it was down to roughly two to one. But gallant men tended to favor pretty women, leaving the rest of Western women, as elsewhere, on their own.

Probably more of a factor was the wider latitude Western women gave each other. They were less censorous of their sex than women elsewhere. Age had something to do with it. For several decades after the West was opened the percentages of women over thirty and over forty were appreciably lower in the West than in the East, and lower than in the United States as a whole. Older women were exceedingly few. Western women thus were largely removed from the influences and the criticism of the more cautious and conservative members of their sex. This made them more daring, more experimental.

Something else Western society bestowed upon its women was means to develop their potential. Women early were granted equal opportunity to higher education. From its opening day in 1850, the University of Deseret in Salt Lake City admitted women, as did all other territorial and state universities in the West, except the University of California, which went co-ed its second year. By the late 1860s descendants of the first pioneers were refusing to be shut out of men's professions. Moreover, they were demanding their professional rights. In 1869, women persuaded the legislature of Wyoming Territory to pass a law that "in the employment of teachers no discrimination shall be made in the question of pay on account of sex when the persons are equally qualified." It is believed to have been the first legislation for equal rights for women in the country. California followed suit with a similar law in 1872.

The census of 1890 reflected this feminine surge in the West. Whereas it showed only eight per cent of the female work force nation-wide to be in professional service, 14 per cent of the West's women workers were professionals. They were variously teachers, musicians, artists, actresses, physicians and surgeons, writers and scientists, lawyers and professors. Although it had only five per cent of the nation's population and about four per cent of the country's women, the West had 17 per cent of the actresses, 11 per cent of the women authors and scientific persons, 14 per cent of the women lawyers, 11 per cent of the women artists and art teachers, ten per cent of the women journalists, seven per cent of the musicians and music teachers, and five per cent of the women professors.

Clearly Western women had seized the brass rings granted by an exuberant democratic society, a kind of neo-renaissance sans Medicis. These daughters of the pioneers were given their heads as women had never before in history—or perhaps since—been given them. And they used them to rise to the greatest heights of achievement. Yet, this splendid chapter, in which Western women opened professional doors for their sex and through their innovations opened doors for all mankind, has been almost totally ignored. For all their glorious accomplishment, women have been virtually omitted from Western history — history, needless to say, composed by men. The textbooks on Western history scarcely give women a passing nod. Most of them dispense with the subject by devoting a few lines or a half page to "the role of women" in the West.

Hoping to correct, at least somewhat, this gross misrepresentation, I chose nine western women for profile treatment in this book. One was a remarkable Indian girl who, after attending mission school in California, returned to her Nevada tribe and, catching the spirit of the times, assumed a position of tribal leadership never before granted a woman. My roster of nine greats might not be your nine: but my nine were one and all, truly invincible spirits. And as such they worthily represent their other Western sisters, who made the most of the freedom generated by a unique, almost miraculous interval in American history.

Imogen Cunningham

Sure on the Shutter

WHEN IMOGEN CUNNINGHAM was asked in her ninety-second year — her seventy-fifth as a photographer — what she liked to photograph best she wouldn't be pinned down. "I'll photograph anything that can be exposed to light," insisted the bright-eyed, sprightly little woman. Nor could she decide upon her favorite of the many styles and techniques she has employed. Not even a favorite camera. All had interested her once. Still did. The world's most honored woman photographer, one of a handful of gifted practitioners who elevated photography from a curiosity to an art, remains as she began: an insatiably inquisitive, open-minded experimenter who "will try anything once."

Since her curiosity has led her to test or innovate all of the main movements that have shaped photography since she first pressed a shutter in 1901 in Seattle, her career story is a microcosm of the history of American photography in this century. Her photographs, which have been shown in every major museum and gallery in the world and are represented in all of the distinguished photographic collections are of an astonishing variety. Imogen, as everybody including her grandchildren calls her, has done it all.

Perhaps because she has slipped in and out of photography movements so effortlessly, she shrugs off credit for innovating this or pioneering that. For instance, by 1910 she was experimenting with nude compositions of women. After her marriage, she began using her undraped husband as model when summering on Mt. Rainier, thereby pioneering in use of the male form

17

as aesthetic material for photography. She may have been the
first woman to photograph the male nude. Today she views
this daring departure as merely an opportunity that presented
itself by the privacy of the setting. "Nowadays you wouldn't
be allowed to chase a naked husband around Mt. Rainier."

Although photography has always been her bread and butter, Imogen has always indulged in the luxury of photographing
exactly as she pleased. As in Seattle she risked losing her society clientele by making nude studies and exhibiting them, later
she infuriated traditional photographers by venturing into realism. Whatever interested her, she pursued it. For several years
she devoted almost full attention to making close-ups of plants
without a thought of whether anybody would look at pictures
of the leaves and buds and stamens she was bearing down
upon. To her, freedom has been as necessary as air — freedom
to experiment with her medium, or, as she puts it, freedom "to
monkey around."

There is no doubt where she got her independence. It was
from her father. Isaac Cunningham, a small wiry restless man
of Scotch descent, was a freethinker in religion, politics, health
practices and just about anything else that came down the
pike. Before pioneering in Oregon, he had briefly attended
college in his native Missouri, served on the Union side in the
Civil War and farmed in Texas, where he married and sired
three children. After his wife died, he brought his children
north to the busy river town of Portland. While working as a
grocery clerk he proposed by mail to a Missouri widow, who
promptly accepted and journeyed out with her one child.
Imogen, born April 12, 1883, was the first offspring of this
union. Bookish Isaac named her after Cymbeline's daughter.

Imogen was still a baby when Isaac corralled his brood and
took them to the growing lumber town of Seattle, but he soon
moved them on to a communal farm on the Olympic Peninsula.
After several lean years, it was back to Seattle, where they
lived in a shabby edge-of-town district and Isaac mended roads
to feed his family, now an even dozen.

Isaac Cunningham was too austere a man to be doting, but
his fondest looks were for his lively red-haired daughter Imo-

gen. The headstrong child awed her brothers and sisters and her mild, passive mother. She was far braver than most children. For instance, she wasn't afraid of turkeys even when their fierce-eyed pecking heads towered above her; she would pick up a stick and brandish her way through a gobbling flock. Only Isaac could discipline her, and he rarely did.

She was past eight when she entered school. A wood between their house and the school sometimes attracted bears, and it was feared the tiny child might march fearlessly into a confrontation. She was kept at home until there was a school-age brother to accompany her. Nor did she attend Sunday School. Agnostic Isaac did not forbid his progeny to go to church, but each Sunday morning he cooked up a batch of fudge, and its aroma usually overcame the Sabbath inclinations encouraged by the Methodist mother. Lacking other distractions, little Imogen spent her days drawing pictures, for which she displayed a decided bent. She demanded and got a box of watercolors.

School proved disappointing. It didn't teach drawing, and Imogen didn't like the other subjects and wouldn't pay attention. Her father coaxed her to study. It was his anxious wish that his children might escape the hard scrabble he had had. He was steering the Cunningham boys into printing apprenticeships, the girls toward nurses' training. The apple of his eye learned with dismay that she was to be a schoolteacher.

Still, when she couldn't be diverted from drawing, Isaac found the means to place her in a private art class that met downtown on Saturdays. The middle-aged instructress was a painter of huge portraits for Seattle's *beau monde*, and Imogen was bedazzled. After that, at school she did nothing but sketch portraits of her schoolmates, until her wise schoolteacher turned her passion to advantage. She let Imogen sketch all she wanted *after* she had completed her classwork, thereby turning the bright child, despite herself, into a first-rate scholar. Imogen's first fans were her schoolmates, although few volunteered as subjects: Imogen was too good at capturing quirks.

She was in high school when one day in the library she discovered her future in a copy of *Craftsman* magazine. Her eyes fastened upon some photographs by a New York woman, Gertrude Käsebier, a disciple of Alfred Stieglitz. They were filmy views of a mother and child in natural attitudes in a simple home setting. Imogen had never supposed photographs could be moving in the way good paintings were. To her photography was something that was done in a downtown "gallery" where individuals or family groups went to "be taken." Subjects were posed stiff as park statues in or around elaborately carved chairs under a swoop of drapery. The staring likenesses that resulted were pasted in fancy padded albums that reposed on parlor tables. Imogen had never given a thought to photography before, but now she longed to try it.

But how? Although photography was then 62 years old, Daguerre having discovered in 1839 a way to record an image cast by an illuminated object, only recently had cameras become available to ordinary people. Imogen didn't know anybody who owned one. Finally, she found an advertisement for the International Correspondence School in Scranton, Pennsylvania, offering a camera and a home photography course, both for $15.

She saved up and sent in her $15, and back came a four-by-five-inch glass plate camera and a book of instructions. When she showed her prize to her father he was even less enthusiastic than about her drawing. He said sadly that he never thought a daughter of his would want to be "a dirty photographer." But then he turned right around and built her a little darkroom onto the woodshed. He even piped cold water to a lead sink that drained outside. Imogen made a red oilcloth box and put in a candle for a safe light, and Imogen Cunningham, Photographer, was on her way.

That she "had the eye" was evident from the start. Photographs of family and schoolmates showed the same knack for characterization that her sketches did. She showed similar understanding of nature. One of her early pictures, a view of a swamp behind their house, today reposes in the distinguished George Eastman House collection.

Today many photographers never go near a darkroom, but at that time focusing a camera was only the beginning. When

Imogen set up her woodshed darkroom, photography was but recently removed from the wet plate process, in which plates were tinctured just before exposure. Imogen's camera used plates that came precoated, but the developing process was most complicated. Like all photographers then, she had to buy her own chemicals and prepare the mixtures. The fixing and printing processes were lengthy and tedious.

Since chemistry seemed so important in photography, Imogen determined to master it. In 1903 she matriculated at the University of Washington to major in chemistry, the first and only of Isaac Cunningham's children to go to college. By then, aided by the local boom sparked by the Alaska gold rush, he was operating a coal and wood business. The Cunninghams now lived in a modest house on Queen Anne Hill. Isaac was optimistic that his studious daughter would get over her photography mania and yet make him proud by becoming a high school chemistry teacher.

Imogen was a day student, riding to classes by trolley, balancing a mound of books, a lunch box and often her adored camera as well. Lively, blue-eyed and red-haired with a galaxy of freckles about her nose, she wore sensible loose clothes stitched up by an older sister, which quite concealed her shapely little figure. She was gregarious and well-liked, but she had few dates. While aspiring to a career considered bohemian, if not dissolute, she was probably the most straight-laced coed on campus, subscribing to her father's precepts of vegetarianism, temperance and social idealism. Besides which she was independent and hot-tempered. Boys were awed by her. She was always on the run. While pursuing top grades, she worked part time as a stenographer and made slides for the botany department.

By the time Imogen graduated from college her father realized the schoolroom would never confine his spirited daughter. But why, he wondered, would she choose to work for nothing as a darkroom drudge at Seattle's Curtis Studio? Imogen was that eager to learn the platinum process which Edward Curtis used. Developing paper coated with platinum salts lent a romantic soft-focus effect to photographs and was then much

favored by artistic photographers. Stieglitz and Gertrude Käsebier worked in platinum.

At Curtis Studio Imogen assisted a young woman who
applied the platinum solution, a tedious process and a responsible one, for platinum was expensive. Imogen assured her
father that her work was in the realm of chemistry not sensuality, and that her employer was no "dirty photographer" but
a scholar engaged in photographing vanishing Indian tribes.
Moreover, she soon was earning a salary. Five months after she
went to work, the young woman she was assisting quit work to
get married, and Imogen got her job.

She remained for two years, until she departed for Germany
on a Pi Beta Phi scholarship. She won the $500 study grant
offered by the national of her college sorority by submitting a
portfolio of photographs taken in time squeezed from chemistry. With her hands shriveled from immersion in caustic
solutions, she leaped to the conclusion that what she needed
was more of the same. Instead of using the stipend to study
under some accomplished photographer, she chose a year of
studying photographic chemistry at the Technische Hochschule
in Dresden.

The wonder is her talent did not drown in a sea of chemistry. The concept of photography as an art form was so new
there were no clear paths of cultivation. And that schoolteacher
who had forbidden sketching until homework was done had
planted the idea that art was a frill to be paid for with tedium.

Savings from her salary paid a spartan passage over. She
traveled from Vancouver to Montreal by rail in a crowded
hard-seated coach in which passengers cooked meals on a
stove at the rear of the car. Imogen dined on dark bread and
dried fruit fished up from her valises. Her most vivid memory
of the trip was of strewn orange peels. From Montreal she
sailed for Liverpool, from which it was on to London for a
whirl of the museums and art galleries before crossing the
Channel.

Imogen had scarcely to set foot in Germany when her
eagerness to try out her college German swept her into an
unlikely project. Pausing briefly in Berlin on her way to Dres-

den she became acquainted with a young woman, a dressmaker who specialized in a new kind of garment called "reform-kleider," a free-flowing dress worn by women who believed in "going natural," that is sans foundation garments. Imogen, who was five-feet-four and slim as an oboe never wore them. When she confided this to the dressmaker, the woman radiated interest. She told Imogen she would present a style show in Dresden soon and Imogen must attend. She must promise! She must be prompt!

On the appointed day, Imogen arrived at a Dresden address hoping to get a good seat. To her dismay she learned she was to be the model. She was hustled backstage, and before she could summon her German to protest she was thrust into a billowy costume and pushed onstage before a sea of plump *hausfrauen.* Crossing the stage, she was snatched back into the wings and whisked into another garment, repeatedly until all designs were shown. For her services she received not so much as a free reform-kleider. But she did profit from the example: Imogen herself became most adept at recruiting free models.

At the austere Hochschule where Nietzsche once taught philosophy, classes began at seven a.m. As a laboratory project Imogen experimented with using a green safe light and conducted a study comparing the efficacy of platinum paper and lead-coated paper. She wrote an article on the latter which a German journal bought for ten marks and an English journal pirated. During this time her budget was so tight she couldn't afford materials for photographing.

All that technology began to pall on Imogen — just as it had two decades earlier for Stieglitz while studying mechanical engineering in Berlin. She realized now that it was the aesthetics of photography that interested her, not its processes. Stealing time from books and laboratory, she began to sample Dresden's culture banquet. She haunted museums and the painting and sculpture galleries, attended lectures on art history. She would remember "going often to the theater, which was very cheap."

On her way back home, she paid a brief visit to New York to look up two of her idols. Gertrude Käsebier seemed delighted to talk to her young admirer and generously encouraged her. Imogen next called on Stieglitz at his famous "291" gallery, which he opened after launching the photo-secessionist movement for encouraging recognition of photography as an art. Imogen introduced herself to the formidable man and they conversed briefly. It was an exchange he would have forgotten when they met as fellow professionals two decades later.

By the fall of 1910, Imogen was back in Seattle, and for the very first time was free to devote full attention to taking photographs. She was then twenty-seven. For ten dollars a month she rented a little ivy-covered cottage on Terry Avenue not far from the hotels. It served her doubly as portrait studio and dwelling. When sitters preferred to be photographed at home, she trolleyed out with a straw suitcase containing her 5x7 camera, twelve plates and a folding tripod. In her absence her parents, having settled all their other children into nursing and printing, had retired to an apple farm in northern California.

From the time she hung out her shingle she had all the work she could handle. Which raises the question: Was her decade of chemistry an unnecessary detour? Would she have succeeded without it? Probably not as quickly. The timing of her studio opening was most opportune. The novelty of photography as a mere recorder of likenesses had worn off and the public was ready for something more creative. Seattle's accelerating prosperity had given rise to a leisure set of wives and daughters of lumber and shipping and mining magnates. Afternoons they departed their Gothic and classical mansions overlooking Lake Washington and glided about in their electric automobiles pursuing culture. They were delighted to discover a young European-trained photographer whose sign was imprinted with quaint German lettering. They might have overlooked a hometown product with only her talent to offer.

After she photographed the elegant Mrs. Elizabeth Champney, the celebrated author of *Vassar Girls Abroad,* Imogen became the latest vogue in Seattle. Everybody who was anybody found her way to the cozy little studio draped with delft blue, where a roaring fire crackled and tea steamed up from blue china teacups. The tea party craze was at its height, and young artists and writers formed the habit of dropping by Imogen's around tea time. By ember glow they read aloud romantic pre-Raphaelite poetry, lofty passages from Rossetti and William Morris' *The Wind and The Wood Beyond the World*. Morris' depiction of an idyllic medieval world of unspoiled woodland and noble people were for Imogen a creative suggestion. On weekends she took her friends to the country, garbed them in fanciful costumes, and photographed them in poses expressing the emotion of the poetry — love, supplication, renunciation, *auf Wiedersehen.*

Evenings she often joined her friends at a class in life drawing, and that too sparked inspiration. Why not pose nude models aesthetically in woodland settings? She photographed some of her young women friends in dream-like attitudes, and a young painter and his girlfriend were her models in a series of ethereal studies. Imogen later recalled of those exercises: "I liked to photograph people in the nude in strange and difficult situations, like standing around in pools of water, regular 'September Morn' stuff."

In 1912, a feature writer for a Seattle journal was sent out to interview the young photographer. The Society of Seattle Artists was sponsoring an exhibition of her portraits and dramatic studies (but not her nudes). The society, making an exception to their rule excluding photographers, voted Imogen a member. She was also making a national splash. A selection of her work had been shown at the Brooklyn Institute of Arts and Sciences, and her photograph "The Shipbuilders" had been included in the Annual of the Photography Association of America and reproduced with complimentary criticism in *The Camera* and *American Photography*.

In the view of that feature writer, Imogen's nature studies possessed "the charm and atmosphere that you find in the quiet, restful paintings of Corot," while her portraits captured "personality, spirituality, soul if you will . . ." She was surprised to find Imogen so unassuming. "There is something about Imogen Cunningham with her petite figure and the frank, sweet gaze of her blue eyes that reminds one of a jolly interest-

ing child. Unlike many artists she is not self-centered." She cited
Imogen's efforts for young artists. Imogen often invited young
painters and sculptors to display price-tagged works in her
studio to tempt her wealthy customers when they came for
sittings.

Unknown to Imogen, this generosity would shape her future. She had made friends with a tall, cultivated woman, a
Mrs. Partridge, wife of an impecunious astrologer and seller
of occult literature. Mrs. Partridge played piano at a Seattle
vaudeville house, supplying background music for acrobats
and dancing dogs, but the light of her life was her only child
Roi, then studying etching in Paris. When Roi mailed home a
sheaf of his work, Imogen saw it and liked it so well she offered
to hold a tea party sale. The sale was a big success. Imogen
mailed the proceeds to Roi, enclosing a letter expressing her
delight in his work. Back came a charming letter thanking her
for the check, which, he said, would enable him to extend his
studies.

Thus begun, their correspondence developed into a spirited
exchange. They were amused to discover that their departures
from Seattle had been but a few days apart, from the same
railroad station, and for almost the same destination. Roi had
studied for a time in Munich before going to Paris. What went
unsaid was the reason they had not met in high school: Imogen was a decade older than Roi.

Then suddenly Roi was back in Seattle. World War I had
erupted in Europe and the French government had advised
foreign students to leave. One autumn afternoon in 1914, Imogen answered the rap of the brass knocker on her cottage door,
and there was Roi, darkly handsome, superbly built, smiling.
Imogen was smitten. There had been boyfriends, but this was
different — this was love. Roi was as fascinated with her, with
her liveliness, her honesty, her assurance, her fire. And he
could scarcely have been indifferent to her artistic success.

Although both had moved in bohemian circles, they shared
a certain innocence. Imogen had been watched over by a protective father, Roi by a possessive mother. Neither had ever
had a love affair. Subconsciously Roi may have been seeking

release from his strong mother. Did he see in Imogen a surrogate — a mature woman who was also solicitous of his career? Her established situation made marriage possible. The winter holidays blew cheer and warmth on their romance. By February Roi and Imogen were man and wife.

They spent a long, happy summer vacation on Mt. Rainier, one of Roi's boyhood haunts. When Roi could be coaxed from his sketching, she photographed his undraped form beside lakes, on craggy peaks, in mountain meadows. Imogen was pregnant, happily so. Focusing on the beautiful body of her husband — Roi could have been a professional model had he wished it — she knew she was carrying a beautiful child.

That fall they were half of a four-man show at Seattle's Fine Arts Room, the other two participants being painters. The Partridges stole most of the attention. There was high praise for Imogen's dreamy woodland studies of costumed friends made on those early photographing treks into the woods. She had given them romantic titles: "The Offering," "By the Waters," "Voice of the Wood," "The Vision." One reviewer cited the poignancy of her work, commenting, "It is easy to understand why her work is given recognition in noted foreign salons when these compositions are studied." (Some of her work had recently been shown in London.) Roi was no less appreciated. His etchings, which included work done on Mt. Rainier as well as in Paris, were called charming and virile.

In their euphoria the Partridges decided on a daring venture. Imogen printed up her nude studies of Roi and gave them such titles as "Love" and "The Fawn." A place was found to exhibit them. All the nudes were discreet views and not the least erotic, yet they churned up a scandal in the realm of the arts such as Seattle had never known before. Angry letters flooded newspapers; ministers fulminated in their pulpits. The artist colony found the fuss amusing, as did Imogen and Roi, even while wondering how it would affect Imogen's portrait business. Actually, her clientele took it in stride.

During the following Christmas season Imogen gave birth to a son. Roi, delighted, gave him the name of Gryffyd, a tribute to his Welch mother. As soon as possible Imogen returned to her studio, for Roi's etchings brought little income. Roi set off on an extended sketching trip to Whidbey Island and other coastal points, leaving Imogen alone to cope with the demands of infant and clientele. Roi's parents had always humored his impulses, even to the point of letting him drop out of high school; he expected no less of Imogen. Upon filling his sketchbooks he returned to Seattle. When he departed next, this time for Carmel, California, to have a fling at painting with some Paris friends, Imogen was pregnant again.

Imogen adored little "Gryff" who had her red hair and Roi's handsomeness, but combining marriage with career which had seemed so easy that first year when she and Roi had worked happily side by side, now seemed to ask more strength than she possessed. Still, how could she possibly give up the work that had sustained her wholly until Roi came along? She panicked even thinking about it. Amidst this concern came a disrupting fire in her studio. The cottage was saved, but repairs were necessary. Roi returned from California to help out in the emergency, tanned, cheerful and enraptured with California.

Imogen reopened her studio and Roi returned to Carmel. But daily she grew heavier. Fatigue often forced her to cancel a sitting. Reluctantly, she faced the realization that with two babies she wouldn't be able to keep the studio. But how to support them? Then, mystifyingly, another fire broke out in the cottage. An emotionally-disturbed maid was setting them. At this point Imogen capitulated. Hastily she decided to go to San Francisco where one of her sisters worked as a nurse, and have her baby there.

But she was in her last month of pregnancy, and her doctor vetoed travel. Imogen was adamant. In her rush to vacate the studio she discarded her files of glass negatives, collected since her earliest camera work. Recklessly, she cracked them over the rim of a garbage can and tossed them in. Only by a fluke were a few of her early negatives saved, permitting prints from them to be viewed later in shows across the country and abroad. She had tied up some old negatives in brown paper to use as weights to flatten prints. The person who helped her pack supposed they had been packaged to ship, and thereby saved them for posterity. Imogen boarded a train under her doctor's stern order that should she feel birth symptoms she was to alight at the next stop and race for a hospital. She averted disaster by sheer force of will. Scarcely had she alighted from her train in San Francisco than she was rushed to the hospital to give birth to twin boys — two more redheads.

Now it was Roi's turn to face up to matrimonial reality. And he did, most honorably. The galvanizing news that he was the sole support of a wife and three infants brought the carefree painter scurrying off the Carmel beach to an emotional reunion with Imogen in San Francisco. Happily, they agreed on two more Celtic names, christening their twins Rondal and Padraic. The Partridge family would present spelling problems for others for years to come.

The delicate state of mother and infants required a hospital stay of three weeks. Imogen gave up her vegetarianism, the better to nurse her babies. Meanwhile, Roi found a house for them in San Francisco's Twin Peaks district; then he began to work for a billboard company doing advertising art.

Later, Imogen went to visit her parents at their Sonoma County apple farm, proudly carrying her infants. Isaac, a bearded gnome in faded overalls, had fashioned wooden cradles from apple crates for his twin grandsons. He admired his daughter's success with her studio and her professional honors, but both of her parents took for granted that her career was over. Her mother, who had always worried about her daughter's exposure to the knocks of a "man's profession," who had cried when Imogen left for Europe, who had worried at her tardiness in getting married, now beamed her relief that everything had turned out all right, after all. Susan Cunningham felt that her children were safe when they were "settled," and she now believed Imogen to be firmly settled into domesticity.

Imogen, beginning to revive, believed nothing of the sort. She had no intention of settling into anything. Rather, she was determined to find a way to fit the indispensable parts of her life together. She wanted domesticity too, and so had given it the precedence it momentarily demanded, but already she was scheming to put it in tandem with photography.

For the present she was tethered to her bustling duplex on Twin Peaks, to a regimen of spaced feedings and household tasks. Clearly, if any photographing were to be done it would have to be done on the premises. So she photographed her wriggling red-haired babies and sent her work out for printing.

She was still using a five-by-seven camera, but new sheet film recently had become available. New photographic material always fascinated her, and she eagerly tried out the new film. She found it more sensitive to light, a quality which permitted more detail. This pleased her. Like any doting mother, Imogen was not interested in blurring the images of her offspring, but in capturing them as vividly as possible. With the aid of the new film she dispensed with soft-focus effects. Her work took on a sharper, more defined image.

Meanwhile, Roi was not pouring all his creativity into advertising. Work done in after hours sold in a San Francisco gallery, and it was his etchings, not his billboards, that brought him to the attention of Mills College, the select Oakland girls school that nestled in a vale of the Oakland hills. Then awakening intellectually, Mills soon would be called "the Vassar of the West." In 1920, Roi joined the faculty as head of its art department.

The Partridges moved into a big shingled house in a hilly district not far from the campus. Imogen was glad to get her children into a leafier setting and thought, "Now, I'll have room for a darkroom again." The darkroom was not immediately forthcoming, however. Three days after they moved in, their well ran dry, and water had to be hauled uphill and used sparingly.

Imogen's toddlers spilled happily over their big backyard and the adjoining vacant lot, and as she darted around after them she became interested in the unfamiliar plants that grew in the dry soil. Upon inquiring, she learned they were cacti and other succulents. So as well as photographing her children, she began photographing the plants. Just as she had never focused on large groups of people, she gave her plants and trees and blossoms individual attention, either in entirety, or in part as she might frame a person's face or hands. She gave these studies the same sharp-focus definition she had given her children.

The result was some astonishingly distinctive photographs — Agave spear tips against a geometric background, so sharp you could feel them prickle; a magnolia blossom soft and languid as a tropic night; sycamore trunks that look like spotted legs; water hyacinth leaves glossy and veined, resembling wet lips. She gave some of her plant studies the sort of precision that documentary photographers later would confer on industrial subjects. Yet for all their concreteness, these images in their own way were as poetic as her earlier romantic studies.

Soon she was into portraits again. After the water problem was solved, she set up a darkroom, and before long found room for a studio. Word of Imogen's talent had reached Mills, and both students and faculty clamored for sittings. Roi dubbed her student business "The Acne of Perfection," because so many negatives had to be retouched for freckles and pimples. One young college employee was the subject of some superb nude studies in Imogen's new style. One nude as clean-lined as a Brancusi sculpture, dubbed "Boyer's Bottom" by intimates, later was to become both an exhibition favorite and a World War II pinup.

Roi and Imogen were a popular faculty couple, and their comfortable home became a drop-in point, much as Imogen's Seattle studio had been. More often than not there were guests for dinner to linger over Imogen's good cooking and the always spirited conversation. The precocious Partridge boys, who called their parents by their first names, were included in the intellectual talk. Everybody joined in to analyze the versatility of Leonardo Da Vinci, the forces of the Renaissance, the theories of color. Studious quiet Gryffyd was an urbane charmer like his father, but the impulsive twins were prone to puncture the opinions of their elders. In the neighborhood the pranksome twins were known as "the little Partridge devils."

For all the apparent togetherness of the Partridge menage, Roi and Imogen clashed often. These two talented people were basically different personalities, and the gulf was widening. Roi had always inclined toward elegance and propriety, and the affluent atmosphere of the fashionable girls school and the adoration of his students reinforced it. His quasi-bohemian dress and talk gave way to sartorial splendor and precise diction. Meanwhile democratic Imogen changed not an iota from her plain-spoken, carelessly-dressed, freckled-nosed self. They disagreed on nearly everything, including child-raising. Roi was strict with the boys, Imogen indulgent. Roi's attitude may have held a touch of resentment that Imogen's devotion to the boys subtracted from the bolstering she gave him. She willingly cooked for his colleagues, helped set up exhibits in the college art gallery, and poured tea for show openings. But now she reserved part of herself for her sons and her creativity.

While Imogen was focusing sharply on her backyard plants, stripping her techniques of unessentials, elsewhere several other inventive photographers were working along similar lines. Abandoning the pictorial tradition, they were making clear images of everyday objects and settings, exploring their forms as ends in themselves. In those years painting was going in the other direction, moving from representational into abstraction. Some art historians believe abstract came about because artists realized the camera had surpassed them at capturing reality. Certainly, a few photographers were capturing reality as it had never been captured before. In New York City Paul Strand was recording the plain truths of city life. At his vacation home on Lake George, Stieglitz was focusing on ordinary rural objects — details of houses, barns and trees, wild grasses, cloud formations. In Germany, Albert Renger-Patzsch was giving plants almost the same kind of scrutiny that Imogen was.

One gifted photographer whose images began to sharpen concurrently with Imogen's was Edward Weston. Small, restless Weston had come to California in 1909 on holiday from his native Chicago and stayed. Around the time Imogen was opening her Seattle studio, he was opening one in Glendale. During the 1920s Weston made his headquarters in San Francisco, and he and Imogen met and examined each other's work. He praised her plant studies and encouraged her to place them with an agent. Imogen was thrilled to find a talented photographer who shared her views.

Weston in turn was stimulated by Imogen, and like her he began using plants as subjects. He made squash, cabbage and peppers the focus of stunning close-up compositions. Peppers became a favorite study with him: he was to write of them, "Peppers never repeat themselves: shells, bananas, melons, so many forms are not inclined to experiment — not so the pepper, always excitingly individual."

Imogen's plant and flower studies appeared in and on covers of American and European camera and nature magazines. A close-up of a full-blown magnolia would become one of her most popular prints. A half century later she would be filling orders for it at the rate of $100 a copy.

Slower to appreciate her new style were West Coast photography salons, still in thrall to the pictorial tradition. Imogen's and Weston's work was frequently excluded from shows during this period. The shy Weston brooded silently over this prejudice, but Imogen freely spoke her low opinion of judges who banned her work. However, one of her flower prints, a detail of the striped glacial lily that comes out of mountain snow in early spring, was accepted for a traveling "International Salon of Photography." Weston caught the show when passing through Los Angeles and mailed Imogen this note: "I went out to the museum today . . . to see the 'International Salon of Photography.' As usual, most of it was rubbish, although several Japanese had fine things, but I had one thrill, and it was your print, 'Glacial Lily.' It stopped me at once. I did not note the signature until I had exclaimed to myself. 'This is fine!' It is the best thing in the show, Imogen, and if you keep up to that standard, you will be one of a handful of important photographers in America — or anywhere."

In 1929, Weston was asked to select the work of outstanding American photographers for an international exhibit in Stuttgart, Germany. He chose eight of Imogen's plant studies. They drew enthusiastic reviews and Eastman Kodak Company purchased prints of all eight entries for their Eastman House Collection. Today these studies not only repose in museum collections, but remain very much in the mainstream of photography; they are so contemporary that six of the prints were

selected by West Coast Airlines (now Hughes Airwest) for
their 1967 calendar.

The same year of the Stuttgart show, a Berkeley bookstore,
the Sign of the Palindrome, a mecca for Bay Area intellectuals,
exhibited Imogen's plant photographs in its small art gallery.
They provoked much talk. To many, her plant close-ups were
in both subject and style queer photography indeed. But to a
small coterie of experimentally-minded photographers, Imogen's work brought high excitement. Among her cheering section were Willard Van Dyke, John Paul Edwards, Mary Jeannette Edwards, Henry Swift, Weston, of course, and his new
partner in a Carmel studio, Sonia Noskowiak. Afterward these
like-minded camera devotees kept in touch to compare prints
and discuss methods.

They began meeting informally in Van Dyke's Oakland
studio with Imogen an enthusiastic participant. In 1931, the
group gained a stimulating new member, Ansel Adams, a stocky
San Francisco-born photographer who couldn't get enough of
photographing his beloved Sierra Nevadas. Just recently Adams
had met Paul Strand, whose prints so impressed him that he
promptly abandoned his hazy pictorial effects and went simon-
pure. Soon after Adams joined them, the group decided to
become better organized, the better to promote their theories,
which in a nutshell were that the aim of photography was to
present reality in a wholly honest manner. Artifice was taboo;
vision was all. It was Van Dyke who suggested they call themselves the "f/64 Group." They were all dedicated to the sharp
image, and the lens opening f/64 provided the ultimate in
resolution and depth.

They never did get around to electing officers, or even
holding regular meetings. But they did produce an event that
was to change the course of West Coast photography and
strongly influence camera work throughout the country. In
November, 1932 they presented the "Group f/64" show at the
M. H. deYoung Memorial Museum in San Francisco. Detailed
explicitness was the common denominator of the otherwise
varied exhibit of eighty photographs. Among them were veined
and warty plants, faces with highly textured complexions, sen-

sitive studies of Negroes, farmers and workers, and all manner of sharply visualized outdoor scenes.

The controversy the show churned up lasted for months, years even. The f/64 show was to photography what the New York Armory show of 1913 had been to painting. Both dealt traditionalism a mighty blow. Pictorialism was put to rout. Its devotees fought back furiously with articles and letters to newspapers and magazines. They claimed the f/64 purists were simplistic fadists, soon to be forgotten. The attack gave the f/64 group an opening to expose the pictorialists' reliance upon retouching, distortion, cropping, texture screening and sensational subject matter.

The deYoung show hastened the rise of its four stars — Imogen, Weston, Adams and Van Dyke. Imogen subsequently was invited to present one-man shows in San Francisco and at the Dallas Art Museum. She, Adams and Weston had begun their solid rise to the first ranks of still art photographers, while Van Dyke soon would turn to making distinguished educational films for schools and television. Today copies of prints from the deYoung show are in the collections of many museums; the San Francisco Museum of Art owns all eighty prints.

The depression was at its nadir, but for Imogen, at least, honor was crowned with coin. *Vanity Fair*, the journal that wittily monitored society and the arts, invited her to join its distinguished photography staff that included Edward Steichen. Based in San Francisco, she was to be on call to make personality studies of celebrities, especially the Hollywood crowd.

On the surface she seemed to have succeeded wonderfully in commingling marriage and career. She and Roi appeared gayly together at each other's show openings. But in fact during those years when her career had blossomed, her marriage had been deteriorating. Her son Rondal would recall, "The marriage had become so strained it came as a relief to us when our parents finally split up." Gryffyd was studying architecture, while Padraic had decided to become a mining engineer. Rondal was already a skilled photographer. Instead of college, he took a job as assistant to Dorothea Lange, then beginning her documentary studies of migrant farm workers.

But for Imogen, who had always been in the bustling center of a big, busy family, adjustment did not come easily. A close family friend recalls that the separation when it came in 1934, quickly followed by divorce, was "awfully hard on Imogen." She remained alone in the big house in Oakland, commuting to her *Vanity Fair* assignments with overnight bag and bulky 8x10-inch camera.

Imogen was now ready for her long love affair with people that has been her great career in portraiture and art photography. Again all the ingredients for success were present. She was well seasoned in portrait work; she had her stunning new style perfected; she had both personal freedom and professional opportunity. And there was an aching void in her life to be filled by hard work. Up until then her portraits had been seen only by the friends and families of her subjects. Now they would have a national showcase.

Early in her association with *Vanity Fair* an editor asked if she had a preference in subjects. Her reply was, "Oh, yes, ugly men." She explained she liked to photograph ugly men because they weren't preoccupied with facial aspect. Just as she scorned photographers who retouched the reality out of their portraits, her greatest vexation with sitters was with those who fretted about presenting their best side to the camera. For her aim was to capture their inner selves and to record her response to their character, and that process was thwarted if the subject was in love with his shell.

So she was handed the assignment she called her "ugly men series"— doing personality spreads on James Cagney, Wallace Beery, Spencer Tracy, and Warner Oland, who played Charlie Chan but was really a Swede. She got along fine with all four, and her photographs bristled with exuberance and vitality. She found Cagney "red-headed and a mass of freckles, just exactly like my kids." He was then playing a prizefighter, so she photographed him in outdoor sunshine in his boxing trunks. He complimented her for being "the only photographer who hasn't blown a fuse at my house." Beery flew to his appointment with her in his private Ballanca plane. Alighting smiling at the Burbank airport he presented himself for her camera wearing spotted gray flannel slacks, dirty leather jacket, an elegant silk scarf, a big diamond ring and patent leather evening pumps. "He had also brought a toothache," Imogen remembers, "but he behaved very well . . . I believe I got it all in."

But women, some of the world's most beautiful, also faced her searching camera. She frankly found beautiful women difficult to photograph; women interested her more when their looks were not so perfect. Accordingly, when she photographed Joan Blondell she insisted that she remove her false eyelashes. The blonde actress had not faced a camera without them for years, but awed by the determined purist, she obeyed.

Assignments now flowed in from *Vogue* and other magazines and from book publishers. In 1937 Imogen was asked to photograph Gertrude Stein during her much-publicized American tour with her inseparable companion, Alice B. Toklas. Imogen found Gertrude an ideal subject. "Only once in a great while do you get a person who is completely natural, but Gertrude was." She recalls of the photographing session, which took place in a suite of San Francisco's Mark Hopkins Hotel, "I'd have had rosy going, but for that manager of hers."

Alice fluttered impatiently over the sitting, hurrying things, disconcerting Imogen who always gave infinite patience to a sitting and demanded no less in return. After photographing her subject indoors, Imogen asked Gertrude to step out on the balcony to gain natural light — and hopefully to lose Alice. Gertrude cheerfully followed and propped her monumental girth against the balcony rail. But very quickly Alice stuck her head out and said, "Miss Cunningham, I'll give you three minutes more." Imogen stopped in mid-focus. Glaring her fiercest, she snapped, "Miss Toklas, the sitting is over!" Thereupon she hastily exited, leaving Alice in open-mouthed surprise, Gertrude posed pointlessly against the San Francisco skyline. She collected all her plates, of course. One of them had recorded the famous view of Gertrude, shingle-headed and wise as a sphinx, sporting an elegant brocade vest. The photograph gazes out from many of the books about Gertrude and reposes in the Stein collection at Yale University.

Most sitters for portraits are acutely self-conscious, Imogen has found. "Most people assume an unnatural look . . . You can break them down in some way, seduce them." Anna Freud was such a case. While attending a psychiatry enclave in San Francisco, she was brought unwillingly by colleagues to be photographed, and at the outset Imogen was almost as unenthusiastic as Miss Freud. "She was wearing a pale yellow sweater and no brassiere — all wrong! I asked her, 'Have you got a dark sweater?' She had, and I buttoned it up to her neck. She still wouldn't unbend, so I suddenly threw a whole pile of Navajo jewelry into her lap." It didn't work. The sitter protested, "You treat me like a child." So Imogen had to resort to her ace-in-the-hole method. She told the daughter of the "father of psychiatry" that she believed "most psychotherapy is nonsense." At that Miss Freud quite forgot herself and gratified her photographer with an expression of alert concentration.

Many another sitter, celebrity and otherwise, has had his or her apparel vetoed by the uncompromising Imogen. If the clothes the sitter arrived in seemed out of character or too trendy, she asked for a change, or blanked them out in some way. She kept a length of black cloth handy to throw over shoulders for a quick transformation. Some sitters have been cloaked in her own severe black cape that along with her peace symbol pendant in later years became her trademark.

When her work was exhibited in the major cities, critics praised her portraits for their backgrounds as well as facial aspect. She put her skill with nature and still life to work in characterization. She led the painter Morris Graves into his leek garden and snapped him framed between two heaven-pointing pods. Ansel Adams was captured in a heroic stance on a mountain top. She did a striking study of fastidious Edward Weston with his cats — all 23 of them. Herbert Hoover is firmly gripping the collar of his police dog in her study of him made in his later years. Hoover liked it and ordered a print.

When the subject is famous, a photographer can plot characterization ahead, but in private practice characterization is harder to come by. Yet, Imogen gained a reputation for recording trait in subjects of whom she knew nothing but their name before they arrived at her door. She once wrote as her credo: "The portrait photographer must be able to gain an understanding at short notice and close range of the beauties of character, intellect, and spirit so as to be able to draw out the best qualities and make them show in the outer aspect of the sitter."

Her method is to settle her subject in a chair in her studio and circle round, sniffing out character, scrutinizing, asking subtle questions. The sitter mustn't know what is happening, so simultaneously, she is tinkering with equipment and making small talk to put the sitter at ease. "I suffer the whole time I am doing it," she has said; "I don't believe people know how much a photographer gives out during a sitting." When she believes she has found the salient characteristic, she begins focusing her camera. Probably her singular skill is the ability to select the critical moment to record that characteristic — a skill possible only to one with profound insight into human nature. Although she and her subject have brushed sleeves but briefly, Imogen has gained a portrait with depth and intensity. Not surprisingly, there are times when her depth sounding dredges up a dominant trait not wholly admirable, and being the true artist that she is, she is irresistably moved to record it.

Some of her most sensitive portraits were studies of her twinkling-eyed father. Over the years she photographed him in his overalls in humble farm settings. In his ninetieth year she recorded him perched on a large pile of cordwood he had just sawed and split. This remarkable man, who in his retirement years studied higher mathematics through University of California correspondence courses, was never ill until his death at ninety-eight from hardening of the arteries.

Of course, Imogen never restricted herself to mere profit-making. Whatever face or object or idea moved her always exerted more pull on her attention than any mere assignment. Her energy spilled over into monkeying around — with still life, with nudes, with nature studies, with documentary, with surrealism, with abstraction. She did playful studies of legs and arms and hands. She photographed wooden fences. She did a series on dolls which *Life* magazine featured in 1972.

Nor did f/64 principles confine her. She was too much of a pragmatist to swallow them whole, as did some members of the movement, to their detriment. She never scrupled at tinkering with multiple images, negative prints and all manner of other experiments, nor did she hesitate to apply them to portraiture. For instance, she used double images that watched each other to suggest the psyche of artist James Broughton.

Through the decades she grew wiser, but seemingly no older. Her sense of wonder remained pristine. What most attracted her and her camera were the young. She frankly preferred the company of youth. Not merely the previous generation — she enjoyed running with the twenties and thirties crowd, especially those involved in the arts. And they delighted in Imogen. "People my age talk about their arthritis," she complained. Her affinity for youth led her to teach photography at several Bay Area art schools and colleges. Once when she arrived at Humboldt State College to teach summer session, she was disappointed to find herself quartered in a hotel. "Is there any reason the students don't want me in the dorm?" she asked plaintively. Into the dorm she was moved.

During World War II she photographed her young friends in their uniforms at the studio she shared with a San Francisco photographer. In 1947, she moved into a cottage studio on Russian Hill. Roliflex swinging from her neck, she often walked the distance to North Beach and visited the coffee houses, haunts of the crowd the press dubbed the "beat generation." Later she photographed young activists at their peace rallies and marched in their parades. In the late 1960s her elfin figure in flying cape and embroidered pillbox hat could be glimpsed about the Haight-Ashbury district, mecca of the "flower children." Many of her vivid youth studies succinctly sum up their era.

In April, 1973, several hundred of Imogen's friends from over the decades gave her a rousing ninetieth birthday party in San Francisco's Golden Gate Park. Simultaneously birthday restrospective shows opened in several museums around the country. Her New York exhibitors, the Witkin Gallery and the Metropolitan Museum, particularly wanted her on hand. But she told them she couldn't miss her party. She was a little late for it, however, arriving in cape and ripple-soled shoes after completing her regular morning darkroom stint. Her 1970 Guggenheim award and the shows it precipitated had stepped up demand for her prints; she could scarcely keep up with orders. There was a mound of birthday gifts, including a Nepalese fur hat which she promptly applied to her crown. There were champagne toasts and games of frisbee. The photographers present got in their inevitable spate of shop talk — none more eager and inquisitive than Imogen's.

On a sunny San Francisco afternoon late in 1974, this writer climbed Russian Hill via cable car to look up Imogen Cunningham. What would she be doing and thinking as she approached her ninety-second birthday, after all her one-man shows, her top professional laurels, her honorary degrees?

Directions led to one of the less fashionable streets on the hill's west slope, to a block of mostly chunky stucco apartment buildings set flush with the sidewalk. Her house was set far back on its lot and screened by foliage. One entered a click-latched front gate, climbed cement steps and followed a crooked gravel path through a deep garden. Desultory plantings of succulents recalled Imogen's plant studies. There, nearly hidden behind a huge, bearded Washington palm, perched her neat frame cottage.

My doorbell ring brought not Imogen but an amiable young man. Imogen would be back soon, he said; he was helping her get out some prints. In the living room I sat down to wait on a hide-a-bed sofa overspread with a Navajo rug. The smallish room was spare of furniture but crammed with paintings, metal and ceramic sculpture, wood carvings, plants, books, magazines, mementos, and of course photographs.

Soundlessly Imogen materialized, whisking off her cape and pillbox, greeting me with a crinkley-eyed, wide-mouthed smile. Not yet settling, she darted about like a water bug, inspecting the young man's work, scanning her mail, checking phone messages. Then suddenly, she was facing me in a rocking chair, her hands cupping the arm rests, her legs dangling below a youthful flared skirt. She was all electric attention with a hint of feistiness in the set of her head.

The lifelong experimenter in photography, it turned out, had returned from an acupuncture treatment. She was confident the series she was taking would cure the vertigo which slowed her mornings. She was anxious to correct it, as every minute counted these days when there were so many demands on her.

Mornings went to darkroom work. Orders for prints arrived daily, and there were commitments for future shows. Almost every afternoon she had to see somebody. Or be somewhere. She had been filmed twice recently for television. Also she had played a bit part, in a friend's underground movie, wearing a victorian nightie. Often there were journalists to talk to, students with lists of questions and tape recorders. Colleagues dropped by as did old friends, new friends, her sons and her nine grandchildren who liked to bring their friends over too.

These days there just wasn't enough time for taking pictures and she didn't like that. The photographs she had managed to take two weeks before she hadn't found time to print. And now she must drop everything to go to Santa Barbara. The museum wanted her down there for the opening of an exhibit of her photographs, the ones from her latest album. Earlier that year her work drew big crowds at the Oakland Museum. Her 1917 Korona View 4x5 camera is exhibited there, and she has promised to will them her other working tools. Her eyes sparked fire as she told me that some foolish reporter (clearly a warning) had written of her that "Imogen keeps busy." She sniffed indignantly, "I don't *keep* busy. I *am* busy."

But just that week she had arrived at a long-postponed decision: to have others handle her print orders. She would entrust her tens of thousands of negatives of pictures she has taken since 1906 to a skilled professional who would process prints and handle their mailing. She admitted it went somewhat against her grain, for unlike most photographers of stature, she has always shunned assistants, preferring to handle every detail herself. But darkroom work had been pushing out camera work, and she couldn't have that.

"I want time to monkey around," she said. "There are lots of pictures I want to take. And I'm only going to photograph faces I like — I'll choose my own subjects. There's new equipment I want to try. For one thing, I'm going to try out a smaller camera." Her blue eyes lit up with anticipation.

As it had in that other cottage studio 65 years before, what interested Imogen Cunningham most was the work she would do tomorrow.

Imogen Cunningham in the 1930s when on the staff of *Vanity Fair*. (— *Alma Lavenson*)

Florence Sabin in her laboratory at the Rockefeller Institute in New York. (— *The State Historical Society of Colorado*)

Florence Sabin

Exploring Inner Space

Peering modestly from a niche in Statuary Hall in the nation's capitol, the solemn corridor where states boast of their most famous sons and daughters, is a dumpy, round-faced little woman who would escape notice except for the microscope incorporated into her life-size likeness in bronze. Florence Rena Sabin represents her native Colorado, but she also symbolizes those most selfless of modern heroes, the white-coated medical researchers who spend their lives perched on high stools in obscure laboratories questing for a healthier, longer existence for mankind.

A pioneer in her chosen profession, Florence Sabin was in the vanguard of those who opened the way for the monumental medical breakthroughs in our time. If the big thrust of science in the last half of the 20th century has been the probing of outer space, for almost a century preceding, man's most urgent mission was spelunking within his own body, prying out with newly available means and instruments the vital secrets locked so long inside his skin. Unlike our flamboyant astronauts, these battlers against disease lived lives of quiet self-abnegation, merging themselves in an anonymous procession which pressed on doggedly with minimal recompense and public recognition.

Their heroism lay in their incredible patience — patience far transcending the usual human persistence — to endure physical restriction and mental monotony. Fixed to one place, to one strained position, they concentrated for years, decades even, on one small segment of the human body. Florence Sabin spent most of her life focused upon the body's smallest units,

45

the cells of the blood and of the lymph canals. Her investigations carried her into many a blind alley, but in time she dispelled mysteries that had baffled medical men for centuries and which brought her a dazzling succession of professional honors. But she also won stripes in the feminist brigade. She did much to open up the jealously restricted medical profession to her sex. The door she had sidled into with difficulty changed under her influence into a proven field for women.

This laureled blazer of medical and professional trails was an offspring of that most storied kind of pioneer, a gold prospector. Horace Greeley's famous mule-pack reporting trip to the Colorado gold strike and his ringing exhortation to young men withered the plans of a young Vermonter to become a country doctor. Instead, small-statured George Sabin, a descendent of Huguenots, followed his itching feet with difficulty and vexing delays cross-country to the craggy ore fields around Central City. Alas, Greeley's assessment of the district as "the richest square mile in the world" had proved exaggerated. By the time Sabin arrived, in late 1860, the surface "blossom rock" had vanished, leaving deep-running veins to be mined with difficulty. Sabin made no strikes, but his round honest face won him a post as mine superintendent, and he stayed.

About that time, elsewhere in Vermont, dark-eyed Serena Miner likewise was pining for adventure. An advertisement for a teaching position in the Deep South bestirred her to set off by sailing ship for that romantic place. But Serena's dream collapsed too. The Civil War broke out, leaving her stranded among political foes. Cut off from returning to Vermont, she journeyed to Colorado and found a teaching opening in the graceless mining camp of Blackhawk, twin settlement to Central City. And there, in 1868, she met and married George Sabin.

Florence Sabin was born November 9, 1871 in Central City in an odd little house but one room deep and propped against a hill so steep a bridge led from the top floor to the back yard, where grazed the family cow. Florence was the second child, and from her first consciousness seems to have felt overshadowed by her sister. Mary, two years older and decidedly prettier, was an extroverted chatterbox. Stubby, moon-faced Florence was painfully quiet and shy. She crept diffidently behind bold Mary as the little girls explored the dingy slag piles and the crooked streets and watched the water peddler delivering water from his wagon with a long snakelike hose. While highly admiring and dependent upon her sister, Florence nonetheless resented Mary's bossy ways. Occasionally, she would plant her plump feet firm, clamp her thin mouth into a line and stare her sister down. And for a moment Mary would be the cowed one.

When Florence was four, George Sabin moved his family to Denver. Denver in the 1870s was no more impressive than Central City, but it was closer to a mine in which he had acquired an interest. They rented a modest box-like house on Wasoola Street, now part of Denver's downtown, and from its porch the children watched with awe the frequent procession of painted Indians walking single file to the trading post. Florence followed her sister into the Broadway School, where she was not noticeably precocious. Nor in her early school years did she demonstrate any bent toward science. However, the family remembered how gravely she reacted to her mother's shock at seeing some children drink from a common dipper. Afterward, no matter how thirsty, Florence wouldn't drink a drop of anything except from her very own cup.

Another thing she was indubitably instructed in in Denver was the frailty of human life. The arrival of a baby brother set the little girls floating in happiness, until the infant's sudden death when but a few months old. Mary protested that it wasn't fair for God to take their only baby brother, until her father had to admonish her. Florence's reaction was to sob silently to herself for days. When their mother told them another baby was coming they hoped for another boy, and joyfully it was. But their mother remained in bed after that confinement, and their father cautioned them to talk quietly. On Florence's seventh birthday there was neither cake nor presents; late that day her mother died.

George Sabin, whose multiplying mining interests kept him much on the road, was obliged to place his daughters in an Episcopal boarding school in Denver. In the proper, impersonal

atmosphere of Wolfe Hall the children suffered agonies of
loneliness. Mary schemed unsuccessfully to draw attention,
while Florence burrowed into a shell and barnacled herself to
her authoritative sister. Their trips out the big iron gate were
few; they were even marooned there during summer vacation.
Mary chafed and fumed and predicted they would be stuck
there all their lives. At night Florence sobbed into her pillow.
Even on those cherished times when their father came for
them, Florence was too shy to talk much. The sad little girls
fastened their hopes on a scheme involving their baby brother,
who had been bundled off to an aunt. They would bring him
to Wolfe Hall and take turns looking after him and taking care
that he didn't disturb the school. While waiting to broach their
project to their father, they learned the baby had died.

Their Uncle Albert rescued them. Their father's brother
offered to make them part of his small family, and they
throbbed gratitude on their cindery train ride across the plains
to the comfortable Sabin home in the Chicago suburb of Lake
Forest. Mild-mannered Uncle Albert seemed to understand
Florence better than anybody. He didn't call attention to her
crying spells nor command her to be cheerful; he recognized
her marked need to envelop herself in something. During his
after hours from schoolteaching he liked to play piano, and he
sparked in his shy niece an interest in music. Happily she sat
beside him at Saturday afternoon concerts. Soon she was taking
piano lessons, devoting every possible moment to rigorous practice. She was also much taken with a framed motto Uncle
Albert gave her. It read: "Jehovah never did a finer thing than
when he turned Adam and Eve out of the Garden of Eden and
said, 'Children, get busy!' "

Their Chicago cousins were boys, and Mary remained the
only child Florence felt really comfortable with. She was always
diffident, vaguely anxious. Her letters to her father were full of
self-reproach: She had broken two of her aunt's favorite teacups; her pet bird sang too much and disturbed the household;
she had made taffy but measured wrong and it had turned to
sugar. So low was her self-esteem she sometimes signed her
given name minus a capital letter.

The next few years, while bringing no cataclysmic changes, still lacked in permanence. On trips West to visit their father, he talked disturbingly of entering them in a Vermont boarding school. With Uncle Albert they traveled to Vermont and got to know their Sabin grandparents, a smiling pink-cheeked pair in a white clapboard farmhouse. At the end of one visit, it was decided that Florence would remain — probably an adult scheme to break her dependence on Mary. Florence delighted in her grandmother's bottomless cookie jar, having her crinkly hair combed into ringlets, and being the pampered center of attention on her first New England Christmas. But the unexpected death of her grandmother in January sent her back to Chicago. Throughout this period of her life, she clung to her piano practice as to a rope on a gale-tossed ocean liner.

The fall Mary was a high school senior and Florence a sophomore, the girls entered Vermont Academy, a small but excellent preparatory school. Mary fluttered contentedly into campus life, but Florence hid in her music practice room, thumping out scales for hours on end. Later in the year when Florence was asked to play a duet with another student in a school program, she accepted with gravity. She was overjoyed by the routine report in the school paper: "The piano duet by Misses Tester and Sabin was listened to with the greatest interest by the entire company."

That fall in Chicago as Mary packed her trunk to enter Smith College, Florence balked at returning to Vermont Academy alone. Why couldn't she just stay at Uncle Albert's and take music lessons? Her uncle had a gentle talk with her. Perhaps alarmed at the gap between her meager talent and her monumental absorption, he persuaded her to return to the academy and prepare for college. Thereby he propelled her, at 17, toward a crucial turning point.

Back at the academy, lost without Mary, Florence clung ever more tenaciously to practice, to the point that the other girls made fun of her. One afternoon as she bent rigidly over the keyboard, twanging out a monotonous finger exercise, two classmates passed by her piano. "Play a piece," one said scornfully. "Why do you have to play those awful exercises?"

Florence kept her eyes on the music. "Because I intend to make music my career," she said airily.

The other girl giggled. "Oh, don't take yourself so seriously, Florence. You'll never be anything but an ordinary musician — no matter how hard you try."

Feigning deafness, Florence repeated the exercise again, pounding fiercely. Then suddenly she slammed down the lid and fled from the room. She ran from the building and along a campus path. But she didn't cry. She was thinking hard and fast and clear. Maybe she *didn't* have any talent. Maybe that was why Uncle Albert urged her to prepare for college. And if she wasn't talented, then she wasn't going to be a musician. Not an *ordinary* musician. Not an ordinary anything! She would be great . . . at *something*. She knew she would. She'd just "get busy" and search out what it was to be.

For the next three years, until she "sugared off," as Vermonters called high school graduation and during her first two years at Smith College, she busily searched. Sweeping music to the side and grinding away at her academic courses, she pulled up her middling grades enough to graduate with honors. She matriculated at Smith without a major, but her fellow freshmen remembered her as the girl who wrote so vigorously and long on her entrance exam.

Again Mary gathered her baby sister under her dominant wing. Disappointed to find Florence had turned bookworm, she urged her to make a little social effort. Mary moved in a platoon of girlfriends and on weekends sometimes had a date from Williams College. Florence's characteristic social attitude was to stand stolidly in her flat shoes appraising everything through her gold-rimmed spectacles. She hadn't an ounce of small talk, and when she did rarely open her mouth there was no predicting what she might say. Her crinkly brown hair was parted mid-center over her button nose and combined with her stocky build to make her look even shorter than her five feet two inches. As an adult she was to bear a striking resemblance to Carry Nation. Smith girls had a tradition of studying outdoors on spread shawls on fine days, but rain or shine Florence wouldn't budge from her heaped study table. Nor would she engage in the popular campus sport of tennis; the dust that collected on players' skirts was unhygienic, in her opinion.

After winning her Smith diploma, Mary began teaching high school mathematics in Denver. And Florence still hadn't decided what she wanted to be. Her freshman year she had liked her science course best, but was fascinated too by philosophy and her professor's emphasis upon "the true philosophic spirit — the wish to know." As a sophomore, chemistry was her favorite, and she even loosened up at the chemical tea parties in the Physics Library, sipping tea from beakers, stirred with test tubes. In her junior year she became enamored of zoology, marveling at the complexity of the frogs and starfish she dissected. Long after the others had gladly escaped the smelly formaldehyde, she remained intent over her assignment. Should she teach zoology? But high school teaching didn't have appeal.

She was past twenty when she finally decided, toward the end of her junior year at Smith. It was the night of the big spring reception, and nearly all the girls had gone. The second floor was pin-drop quiet. Florence wondered: Was she the only person left behind? No, Dr. Grace probably hadn't gone — Dr. Grace Preston, the admired college physician who lived in her building. But everybody else would be there in their party dresses, and she could visualize the engaged girls proudly propelling their fiances about. With her own plans so up in the air, she envied them their settled futures. Yet, she didn't envy them married life; she had long since faced the fact that inasmuch as she hadn't ever had a date, it was unlikely she'd ever have a husband either. And she hadn't faced it bitterly. Having been so beholden to others ever since her mother died, she looked forward to having freedom, economic and all the rest of it. Freedom like Dr. Grace enjoyed. Dr. Grace hadn't married, and she didn't feel that life had passed her by. On the contrary, Dr. Grace seemed as contentedly occupied as anyone she ever knew.

By the time the other girls returned, laughing and whispering, she had made up her mind to become a doctor. And once she had decided, it was as though deep down, she had known all along. It seemed only natural that she would choose a career

that ran in the family — both her Great-uncle Levi and her
Uncle Robert, her father's youngest brother, had been doctors,
and her father had wanted to be. She lay awake all night too
excited to sleep, for in the morning she was going to ask Dr.
Grace to tell her how to prepare to become a doctor.

When Florence, eyes glinting behind her spectacles, announced her intention to practice medicine, Dr. Preston had
to conceal her dismay. In terms of prospects, a girl could
hardly have chosen a more unlikely field. The young doctor
had never seen Florence so animated, and she hated to puncture it. Choosing her words carefully, Dr. Preston explained
that for a woman becoming a doctor was a hard, uncertain
fight. It required four years of medical training, plus one of
internship, and none of the university medical schools would
accept women. There were a few women's medical colleges,
but it was most difficult for their graduates to obtain intern-
ships. Further, the public just wouldn't accept women doctors.
Some druggists wouldn't even fill their prescriptions. She herself had been lucky to be able to return to her college alma
mater as its first resident physician, but such openings were
few. Seeking a medical career, she emphasized, might bring
Florence great hardship and disappointment.

Florence's father and sister were no more encouraging when
she unwrapped her bright plan for them that summer in Denver. Her father said little, but Mary pronounced the idea foolish, hairbrained. Doctoring was no profession for women, Mary
declared with finality. Later, Mary told her there was another
reason why studying medicine was out of the question: their
father's mining interests were not prospering; he couldn't afford
to finance more schooling. Mary advised Florence to be content
with teaching school in Denver, like she was doing. Florence
listened Mary out, reflecting that though she loved her sister
dearly Mary was and always had been bossy. Moreover, Florence realized she no longer required Mary's approval; she had
become her own woman. As for the money, she would earn it
herself, some way.

Four years later finds Florence, over Mary's protests, on an
eastbound train on her way to enter medical school. It is 1896

and she is now 25. In her purse is a checkbook on a substantial bank account saved from two years teaching at her old school Wolfe Hall, one year substitute-teaching at Smith College, and summers tutoring a Denver banker's offspring. It is no woman's medical college she is headed for, but the medical school of illustrious Johns Hopkins University in Baltimore, Maryland, where she will study alongside men.

Since Florence's night of decision at Smith, something had happened in medicine that was part of the feminist surge across the country. Women had already won the vote in several Western states. Eastern women were finding suffrage more resistant, but they were thrusting levers under other rights. In Baltimore, two imbued young women had, in effect, pried the "men only" sign off the new medical school. Their lever had been money. The University had recruited a fine medical faculty, only to have its financing source dry up. Two daughters of Hopkins trustees, Carey Thomas, later to become president of Bryn Mawr College, and railroad heiress Mary Garrett, glimpsed opportunity. They decided to organize a Women's Fund Committee and raise the money and offer it on condition that women be admitted. Wealthy feminists across the country opened their purses and with a hefty assist from Miss Garrett the sum reached half a million dollars. The trustees reluctantly accepted the tempting offer, over the protest of President Gilman, who argued girls couldn't possibly keep up with male students.

Florence was part of Johns Hopkins' fourth class of medical students, one of fifteen "hen medics" who set their sails to keep up with the thirty men who matriculated with them that October. After unpacking her serviceable wardrobe in her assigned room in "hen house," the women med students' dormitory, she began attending classes in the stolid red brick buildings of the graceless utilitarian campus. She plunged into dissecting pickled piglets in Anatomy I with all the pent-up avidity of her four-year wait. Yet, no matter how vigorously she scrubbed up afterward, she squeamishly eschewed touching food in the dining hall and restricted her diet to what she could convey mouthward via fork and spoon.

As fascinated as she was with anatomy, it paled beside histology, the study of cells and tissues. With histology it was instant love! She lived for those hours spent in the spotless, odorless histology lab with its rows of microscopes and racks of glass slides. Histology presented a breathtaking world of marvelously matched particles, groups of cells of similar size and shape — variously round, flat, elongated, spindle-shaped, or branched, each characteristic of a body part or organ. With infinite care, she would mount a tissue specimen upon the antiseptic glass and, deftly training her lens upon it, make it her all-absorbing sphere of existence.

For the hen medics there were weekend divertisements provided by the Women's Fund Committee, an avid cheering section for "their protegees." Over luncheon souffles and during intermission at musicales, the women applied some rather burdensome, if velvety, pressures. They impressed upon the young women that the world was watching them. They expected their girls not merely to keep pace with male students but to hand a rebuke to President Gilman by surpassing them. Further, one of the first three hen medics to be admitted had left an embarrassing deficit to be evened. Not only had the girl fallen in love with a professor but had forsaken her ambition and married him, causing it to be bandied that "33 and one-third per cent of the first group of hen medics dropped out." Also wanting vindication was the snide remark of the head of the Department of Medicine, Dr. William Osler, that "Human beings may be divided into three groups — men, women and women physicians." So it was incumbent upon them to be ladylike at all times. Florence took these obligations most seriously.

Nonetheless, her life held more pleasure, warmth, even relaxation, than during her college years. Schoolteaching had cracked her shell. At Wolfe Hall her ability to kindle enthusiasm in her students had surprised her. She delighted to find that the plain, colorless, nearsighted Florence Sabin had the power to inspire. Further, she discovered that the act of transmitting intellectual fascination from the depth of one human being to another tied giver and receiver to one another in friendship. Likewise at Johns Hopkins the enthusiasm she radiated before her favorite subjects brought her friends. While her prime love affair was with the world opened by the microscope, human companionship had become important in her life.

Her cerebral radiance also brought her into the rarified orbit of Dr. Franklin Mall. The small, brilliant head of the anatomy department, who had trained under the most eminent medical professors in Germany, at 31 was already a name in medical research. But to his students, Frankie Mall, as they called him behind his back, was either demon or diety depending on how he looked at them. When displeased or indifferent his looks could wither. Expecting nothing less than total dedication from his students, he treated them as fully responsible adults who had to work out their own salvation. He flung challenge upon the waters and if a student didn't seize it, he was left to flounder alone. In Mall's opinion, assistance deprived a student of the thrill of discovery. Once noticing that a student in his laboratory was doing nothing, he inquired acidly what was the matter. When the lost young man replied he didn't know what to do, the professor reached for a broom and handed it to him.

Florence was surprised to learn that this stern, small-statured man was the romeo who had charmed that early hen medic into forsaking her goal. But soon she discovered how blissfully favored, almost annointed, one felt at melting the frost on that summit. One day in the anatomy lab he paused before her work on the zinc table. Florence held her breath as he prolonged his pause. Even in a routine lab assignment, she had displayed an originality that arrested him. At length, he articulated the word "nice" and moved on. Florence blushed with pleasure. Soon he was according her work compliments of more than one syllable. Scarcely believing, she found herself on friendly terms with the awesome professor.

This development was no less noticeable to her classmates. It was well known that Franklin Mall did not bestow his enthusiasm upon any run-of-the-mill student. Indeed, he had been quoted as stating that from ten thousand students there might be one thousand who were highly intelligent. Out of this thousand perhaps five would start in research. All five would

be able to prepare slides, but only one would become a true
investigator. All wondered: "Would Florence Sabin — a hen
medic — be that one?"

With the approval of Dr. Mall in her pocket, she sidled further out of shyness. Her confidence swelling, she even became
something of a class leader; her impressed classmates tapped
her knowledge, begged her opinion. She was whisperingly
pointed out to visitors as "a brain." Much envied were her
powers of observation when working with scalpel or microscope; *nothing* escaped her eye. Admired too was her cool
detachment before physiological specifics. Some of the women
bristled when professors told anatomical jokes to illustrate a
point.

Toward the end of her first year she wrote as a routine
anatomy assignment a paper on nerve tissue that was published in the Johns Hopkins Hospital Bulletin. Such publication
by a student was rare and brought congratulations from her
classmates and the Baltimore Women's Committee. But the
paper also drew praise from the faculty for its original observations. Not long afterward, Dr. Mall paused at her laboratory
position and asked if she would care to undertake an independent laboratory project, a rather long-term one. It would
involve preparing a model of the brain stem of a new-born
child. A thrill went through her as she realized the import of
his words. She happened to know that a model had never been
made before and such an instructional aid was much needed
by medical schools. She, a student, was being trusted to do it.
Gravely, she accepted.

Thus, almost from the outset of her medical study, she
slipped into a vital role in the field of medical research. One
marvels at the astuteness of the young professor in selecting
precisely the right person for that formidable project. The utmost precision and patience were required for constructing a
model of that intricate lower brain area where the spinal cord
widens into a mass of nerve fibers and blood vessels and contains the seat of control of breathing and circulation. It called
for painstaking dissection of brain tissue, preparation of slides,
drawings, incisings on wax — infinite repetitions of these steps,

before the model could be made. And of course the project had to be sandwiched between heavy course work at one of the toughest medical schools in the world. But here was a task into which she could really burrow. Weeks stretched into months, then into years. When in her senior year she completed her model, neurology experts credited her with shedding new light on how the brain is formed. So faultless was her model, Dr. Mall decided it must be manufactured in Germany for worldwide distribution; he also set her writing a manual to accompany her creation. Both model and manual were to find their way into medical schools everywhere. Some of them remain in use today.

Despite all the time and hope and energy diverted to her exacting brain project, she ranked third in her class when, in spring, 1900, she won her M.D. degree. In long black robe with green reefers, she claimed her diploma on the stage of the old Academy of Music. Her rank entitled her to that rarity for a woman, a precious internship at Johns Hopkins Hospital. An internship was what she had prayed hardest for when she matriculated four years before, but now enamoured of medical research, she hesitated. In the end she accepted it, prodded by the other hen medics, who couldn't imagine anyone passing up the envied brass ring.

So she put on a white coat with stethoscope in pocket and walked the drab halls of the hospital endowed by a Quaker merchant for the "sick and indigent of Baltimore." There misery in the raw presented an almost infinite variety of disease. She swabbed throats, dressed wounds, examined sputum, and one day diagnosed in a young woman a case of fatal arterial disease — one of only five such cases then so far reported in medical history. Dr. Osler was greatly impressed — that same Dr. Osler whose comment on women physicians had so incensed the Women's Fund Committee. He told Florence she could have a brilliant future as a diagnostician.

She was not swayed. By then she knew it was medical research for her. How she had missed it! For what had most impressed her about medical science was not its powers but its limitations — how much remained unknown. The baffling mysteries of disease and bodily processes tantalized her curiosity. And besides there was no denying that her fastidious nature preferred her germs trapped on a glass slide in a spotless lab.

But where would her lab be? George Sabin's death had released her from her vague plan to return to Denver and make a home for him. Mary, who had not married for all her beaux, exhorted Florence to come West and live with her. But Florence, having painfully achieved independence, now guarded it. As medical research was then pursued only in conjunction with college medical instruction, she told her friends she would seek a position in some medical school — some *other* school, for Johns Hopkins held firm against women faculty.

Her fans, the Women's Fund Committee, intervened. Reluctant to lose their shining example and encouraged by Dr. Mall, they financed a research fellowship in the Department of Anatomy specifically for young Dr. Sabin. Despite its small stipend ($75 a month), nothing could have been more to her liking. She was back in her favorite lab, back in the stimulating wave length of her mentor.

And how very pleasant not to have to leave her Baltimore circle of friends — more friends than she had ever had before. Now, she could take an apartment and repay some of the hospitality that had warmed her during her salad years. Dr. Mall and his lively wife Mable, "the drop-out," had included her in the activities of their young family, as had the Hookers, another medical couple. She reveled in these associations, exchanging professional talk with the doctors, suffrage talk with their wives. And she positively doted on their children. The Mall and Hooker children always remembered her for her frequent gifts of exactly the right book and her grave insistence upon their washing their hands before dining and after patting the family dog.

While there was never to be the slightest romance in her life, she was popular with classmates of both sexes. They had enlisted her in their after-hours romps. She had a standing invitation to the perpetual open house kept by the gregarious Steins, Gertrude and brother Leo, fellow Westerners enrolled respectively in medicine and biology. With a substantial allowance from their family's San Francisco streetcar business, lanky red-haired Leo and mushroom-contoured Gertrude bountifully dispensed gourmet snacks and culture. Vehement talk of art, literature and opera reverberated always in their red brick row-house. Leo usually had a new Japanese print to show and pontifically discourse upon. Indeed, the expansive brother and sister, who were to make art and literary history, both departed Baltimore sans diplomas.

Florence's hostessing style was different. Frequently, it took the form of a bustling steak supper in her sparse dust-free apartment with everybody energetically pitching in to assist. One crew armed with long-handled forks and stopwatch squatted before a low grill tending thick Western-style steaks. At Florence's direction, each sizzling steak was speared and turned precisely every 180 seconds. Afterwards, all helped scour up the kitchen, vigorously scrubbing pots and scalding dishes and cutlery with quantities of boiling water until the kitchen gleamed like a laboratory.

Knowing the potency of her curiosity, Dr. Mall had a truly challenging assignment awaiting his new research fellow. It was to investigate the lymphatics. Those minute vessels that carry lymph fluid throughout the body had baffled medical science for 200 years, blocking progress in numerous diseases. Where did they originate? What was their function?

Delighted by the size of her task, Dr. Sabin began her sleuthing with pig embryos. The main roadblock, she quickly ascertained, was lymph's colorlessness which rendered the vessels invisible. But what if she colored the lymph fluid? By a painstaking search, she pinpointed a lymph sac in the pig tissue and succeeded in injecting ink fluid into it. Now she could follow the dark flow through lymph channels hitherto invisible. In this way she ascertained the lymph vessels were not an independent system, as had been believed, but budded out from veins. When, in 1902, she published a paper announcing her discovery it set off worldwide excitement in scientific circles and brought her a $1000 prize from the Naples Table Association (now the Association to Aid Scientific Research by Women) for work "embodying new observations and conclusions."

Of course, this initial finding only spurred her along the trail. Much was still obscure. With Dr. Mall's avid approval, she continued to follow the little capillaries with scalpel and microscope, until they yielded up their function. Her observations established that the vessels after sprouting from veins reached toward each other, uniting to form channels that found their way to arteries. En route from vein to artery they cleansed the tissues they passed through, carrying away cellular waste and bacteria, thereby fighting infection. Thus in her very first assignment as a professional medical researcher, she cracked a major medical mystery.

She also sparked a major controversy. Her conclusions met roars of objections from those whose theses she had punctured. The attack revealed a new fighting Florence Sabin. Gone was the timid self-doubter. Sure of her ground, her retorts to critics were bold and spirited. In one paper defending her work, she declared: "The facts are correct and have been verified, the reasoning was correct and has been justified." And so they proved.

During these years she was also gaining fame as a teacher. Her dazzling medical breakthroughs had inspired the University to quietly lift its ban on women faculty. Dr. Mall succeeded in installing her in his department, first as an assistant professor, then, in 1905, as an associate (she would become a full professor of histology in 1917).

Students quickly found the new "hen professor" to be no easy mark. In her studies under Dr. Mall she had found that his teaching philosophy suited her exactly — he hadn't prodded nor breathed down her neck, but had left her on her own. Now, he became her model. Assuming her students to be as committed as herself — that is to say, totally — she dealt formidable assignments. She delivered her lectures with machine-gun rapidity, disdaining to repeat for sluggish ears. There was no nonsense, no mollycoddling, no excuses.

A minority fell behind, grumbling. But to the rest she was the most fascinating of teachers. Her lectures were fresh, full of surprise. She tore up her notes after making them, so that she would have to prepare new ones next term. The cerebration vibrating from her classroom often drew upperclassmen and faculty, just to listen. She threw herself into her laboratory demonstrations with such absorption that it became a standing joke, even to her.

Her examinations were no less original than her lectures, if not always as appreciated. Once in an anatomy exam, she presented the task of identifying all the tissue in a stained cross-section cut through a mouse. It was no ordinary mouse: she had removed its innards, cut them up, stirred them, and stuffed them back into the body cavity before slicing the baffling cross section.

Nighttime passersby the medical school glimpsed her framed in light, bent over her microscope. Did she, some wondered, sleep there? Her research began when classes ended, and occasionally when a piece of work wouldn't wait, she did actually spend the night at the lab. Such was the night when she observed the growth in culture of the chick blastoderm — that little speck in the yoke of an egg. First, she watched the blood vessels form and lengthen. Finally, came what she later described as "the most exciting experience of my life," the beginning of the first heartbeats.

That observation was part of her research into how blood originates. To pursue it, she developed a means of keeping bloodcells alive for several hours' observation, also a method of staining that permitted the different types of cells to be distinguished. These techniques, which were quickly adopted in laboratories throughout the world, made possible her original studies on how the red corpuscles develop, observations which proved a powerful stimulus to hematology. They also permitted her to determine which blood vessels will grow back after destruction and which ones will not.

Lab and lecture hall — these were her main habitats. Still, she packed more into her Hopkins years. Doting almost equally on baseball and opera, she attended each in its season. After her friend Edith Hooker became chairman of the National Woman's Party, she helped stage suffrage pageants, marched in parades, and edited copy on the party's journal *Equal Rights*. She called her Franklin touring car "The Susan B." Feminist ardor throbbed so hard for a time, she wouldn't let men hold doors for her. On summer vacation trips to Colorado, she humored Mary's passion for camping. And there were trips abroad with Mary, sampling London theater and Paris shopping. Once Florence remained for a stint of study in Germany.

Sometimes she had to exchange her lab coat for a ceremonial gown. Honorary degrees had begun to fall on her, the first from her proud alma mater, Smith College. The presidency of the American Association of Anatomists was thrust upon her. When Madame Curie, discoverer of radium, visited these shores, Dr. Sabin was chosen to make the address of welcome in New York. She elated feminists by becoming the first woman to be elected to membership in the prestigious National Academy of Sciences in 1925. All the publicity heaped upon her as a "woman scientist" rather irked her. Why not just call her a scientist?

While she was quietly chalking up professional and scientific firsts, another kind of ground had been broken. Medical research had emerged as a bona fide field of its own. No longer was it restricted to what medical faculties could accomplish between lectures. John D. Rockefeller, seeking the best buy for his philanthropy dollar had endowed the Rockefeller Institute for Medical Research to find disease cures. Most particularly, the New York-based Institute was to draw a bead on "the microscopic enemies of mankind." There full-time researchers, the best that could be found, were set to work in the best-equipped laboratories in the world.

Dr. Sabin's blood cell investigations had been closely watched by the Institute's brilliant director, Dr. Simon Flexner, a former Hopkins professor. Dr. Flexner had decided that his erstwhile associate was exactly the person to head the Institute's new department of cellular studies, which had been created to make a concentrated attack on tuberculosis, that most widespread of serious diseases. Would she accept the challenge? The chance to track that deadly bacteria certainly held appeal, as did the opportunity to integrate the all-male Institute staff. Yet, moving to New York meant pulling up roots again. Had Dr. Mall been living she probably would have rejected the offer, but his untimely death had left a gap in her life. In the spring of 1925, after twenty-nine packed years, and not without a tear, Florence Sabin cut her Baltimore ties. At 53, she was then midway in her career.

The tuberculosis bacillus had been discovered in 1882, but the virulent bacteria had proved highly resistant. The standard treatment remained the "rest cure," actually no cure, merely an arrest. Long rest and good care sometimes, but not always, caused the body to seal off the infected masses, which might or might not stay arrested. In her Baltimore investigations, Dr. Sabin had established the existence of several types of white corpuscles, some of which fought on the side of germs, some on the side of the body. One large variety which she called monocytes, seemed to help arrest the tubercle bacillus. But just how was the arrest accomplished? And why did it sometimes fail? If nature's slow, sometime remedy could be completely understood, then arrest might be induced by chemical means.

Dr. Sabin cast her net for understanding in her new well-equipped laboratory in the Institute's four-story limestone building that overlooked the East River at 66th Street. With rigid requirements she assembled her staff of graduate scientific investigators, laboratory assistants and technicians. But her authority deployed much wider. In a project set up by the National Tuberculosis Association, she was also to direct and integrate tuberculosis studies under way at universities and pharmaceutical companies. It was the largest cooperative medical research study yet undertaken.

If the largest research project did not awe her, the largest city did. On Saturdays she tripped along the crowded sidewalks munching popcorn, admiring everything. Nowadays an avid talker, she queried passersby, learning her way about. With shyness gone, she was enjoying a kind of belated youth. She devoured theatre news, became stage-struck and was as wide-eyed as any schoolgirl when friends took her backstage to meet Helen Hayes, Catherine Cornell, Grace George. In baseball she switched from the Orioles to the Brooklyn Dodgers.

She could not believe that she too was a celebrity in that celebrity town. Not merely in academic circles — the public

had discovered her. *Pictorial Review* Magazine chose her as its
"Woman of the Year" for making "the most distinctive contribution to American life." *Good Housekeeping* included her in
its "Twelve most important women of all time." The press habitually referred to her as "the foremost woman scientist in the
Western Hemisphere." Through it all she remained her plain,
unpretentious self, and when reporters came to interview her,
she, bedazzled by big city newsmen, besought to interview
them. Of course, she went where she was bid, to receive the
medal, the degree, the award, changing from cotton housedress
covered by a long lab coat to her "dress-up clothes," plain shirt-
waist dress of crepe or wool, lisle stockings and black patent
leather pumps. But she was less impressed by the distinguished
personages who made the presentation than by the personalities who shared the honors — the likes of Amelia Earhart,
Madame Schumann-Heink, Henry Ford.

With just a tinge of gloating she described it all in letters
to envious Mary back there in Denver, pouting because she had
to live alone. Mary was even treated to a description of the
White House, when Florence was included in a group of scientists invited to dine with Herbert Hoover. But "the most exciting thing that has ever happened to me," she assured Mary,
was sitting beside Albert Einstein at a dinner party at Princeton
University. She was flabbergasted to find that the world's foremost genius could chuckle. "His laugh rings out and makes
everyone around him happy," she wrote Mary.

Nonetheless, her prime excitement always was there in her
quiet, spotless third-floor lab. She was the busiest of her busy
team, the first to arrive each morning, the last to leave. Investigating the mechanism of tuberculosis involved the most monotonous of tasks, counting cells in microscopic specimens. Observe and record, observe and record, over and over again. And
it is the nature of basic research that most work leads to dead
ends, but when a killer disease is being stalked, the smallest
headway is a triumph.

Relentless scrutiny of the bacillus at length yielded its
chemical formula. Then, each chemical component was injected
into test animals and a study made of its effect upon body

tissue. It was found that the body's power to arrest the bacillus depended upon the amount of corresponding chemical already in the body; body chemistry varies from person to person, and some bodies found the bacillus more foreign than others. This and other discoveries were correlated with findings being made in laboratories elsewhere. During the thirteen years Dr. Sabin was with the Institute, small pieces of the puzzle were patiently, persistently fitted together. Thus was laid the groundwork for determining the drug and healing methods by which tuberculosis finally was brought under control in the 1940s. This vital work, which would benefit populations throughout the world was accomplished by a woman who in the words of one Institute staffer "always wore the air of a grandmother who had just put some cookies in the oven."

Since Mary's retirement in 1931, she had written almost daily, asking when Florence was going to retire and come home. They hadn't eaten Thanksgiving dinner together in 44 years, she complained. To receive her city teacher's pension she had to live in Denver, so she felt Florence ought to make the move. But Florence wouldn't budge; she couldn't abandon research still unfinished, she insisted. Her 65th birthday came and went and she remained happily perched on her high stool before her microscope.

Then, something unexpected happened. In a change of policy, the Institute announced it was enforcing retirement at age 65; the ruling affected five of their top scientists, including a crestfallen Dr. Sabin. After a flurry of packing, sad goodbyes to friends and co-workers, and a solemn presentation of her fine Spencer microscope to the Institute, in December, 1938, Florence found herself in Denver rather dazedly sharing Christmas dinner with a delighted Mary. At 67, years of unaccustomed leisure appeared to lie ahead.

Mary bubbled with plans for them. After they settled down in a roomy apartment near Chessman Park and Florence had hung her Japanese prints and arranged her books in her new bookcases, she pliantly and hopefully joined in. They took automobile trips in their Auburn touring car; they camped out and cooked over campfires; they donned bloomers and climbed mountain peaks; they took a boat trip to Alaska and climbed a glacier. In between, Florence filled speaking engagements and took trips back East to meet with this board and that committee. Time never hung heavily, yet something lacked. Unlike her meticulously planned laboratory projects, it all seemed to be drifting aimlessly in no direction. She lacked a *goal*.

By a fluke she found one. It was the wartime year of 1944, when across the country politicians were trying to regenerate interest in local issues by concocting plans for "a better postwar world." Colorado Governor John Vivian had conceived of a Post War Planning Committee and selected a roster of prominent Coloradans to grace it. In his Statehouse office he proudly unveiled his list for Denver *Post* reporter, Mrs. Frances Wayne, who perused it while he leaned back behind his polished desk, awaiting congratulations. The seasoned reporter scanned the list of personages who were to head subcommittees on mining, on labor, on tourism, on finance, on aviation, on industrial expansion. Finally, she asked, "Why isn't there a subcommittee on public health?" Before the governor could answer that, she complained again. "You haven't named a single woman." Crestfallen, the governor asked if she had any suggestions. Mrs. Wayne thought an interval. "Why not Dr. Sabin — Dr. Florence Sabin, the medical researcher? She'd fill both omissions."

The governor took the precaution of consulting his political friends. Would Dr. Sabin kick up a fuss, did they think; would she want to spend money? They assured him she was a quiet little lady with her hair in a bun and a friendly smile who, after all, was 73 years old. No, she would hardly be a boat-rocker. An invitational letter was mailed, an acceptance was promptly received, and the governor, having added Dr. Sabin to his list, put the matter out of mind.

In her sixth year of retirement the governor's new appointee was a coiled spring of thwarted drive. Of course, she knew nothing of political committees, nor of figureheads. As she saw it, she had been handed the grave responsibility of planning the health of her fellow citizens. As always when approaching a new project, she boned up. Emersing herself in a mountain of literature, she swiftly became knowledgeable on

matters of sanitation, on milk production, on sewage disposal.
She read the state's rudimentary health code and learned there
had been no new health legislation since 1876 — the year her
mother had encountered that school dipper! Several official
studies had pointed up shocking health conditions, but all had
been pigeonholed by apathetic legislators. The governor's new
committeewoman thought the situation disgraceful! How could
Colorado call itself a health resort?

She said as much publicly to whomever would listen. To
find more ears she set out on a trip around the state, spreading
alarm at the state's high death rate from preventable diseases,
its dearth of controls, while calling for sweeping health reform.
Also her eye was out for good committee material. But she
knew she would need outside help as well. If the state legislature ignored state health studies, then only some prestigious
national survey would make it sit up and take notice. While the
American Public Health Association was equipped to conduct
extensive health studies, their fee was high. By persistent in-
quiry she turned up an Eastern foundation that had sometimes
funded health investigations, but only when convinced their
findings would be acted upon.

Genuine indignation is contagious. Easily she enlisted a
capable committee composed of doctors, dairymen, sanitary
engineers, health officers and veterinarians, all sold on reform.
With this support in her pocket, she called on the startled governor and asked him to seek the foundation grant to finance a
health study. Governor Vivian was scarcely anxious to bring in
outside critics. But faced with her defiant zeal and assured it
would cost Colorado nothing, he reluctantly acquiesced. However, his letter of application was so lukewarm that the foundation people concluded the survey wasn't wanted and Dr. Sabin
had to apply urgent persuasion to convince them that it was.

The grant brought west the Association's brilliant Dr. Carl
Buck, geared to conduct a year-long study of Colorado's health
needs. When state officials repeatedly threw obstacles in his
path, he too decided the study would be futile. But with Dr.
Sabin and her committee running interference, he managed to
complete his investigation and return East to assess it.

His report was grim indeed. Coloradans were dying much faster than the national average. Thirty-four states had better records for disease control. Contagious diseases had killed more than three times the number of Coloradans killed in the war. Infant mortality was among the highest in the nation. Milk production went largely uncontrolled. Raw sewage polluted streams that irrigated farm produce. Buck minced no words in pointing blame: Colorado was spending less than ten cents per person on public health, and the Division of Health was a political football.

Here was a lever to wield on the legislature, if the public would help apply the pressure. Dr. Sabin took the precaution of having thousands of copies mimeographed. "We heard that the Buck Report was going to be put in a desk and locked up," she said. "It's hard to get a thousand copies into a desk drawer." The medical researcher was rapidly gaining insight into politics. Her committee, further imbued by the Buck Report, set to work hammering out health bills designed to roust the shameful statistics. Then, the governor's most avid post-war planner set out to stump the state and win converts.

Traveling at her own expense, she presented herself to her fellow citizens, a bifocaled, chubby woman in a too-long dress and ground-gripper shoes, but with a twinkly glow about her and a platform voice of surprising resonance and authority. She spoke wherever permitted — to lodges, churches, service clubs, PTA's, granges, women's clubs. She kept her dates through all weather, including blizzards. Just when a program chairman decided she couldn't make it, she would tool into view and rapidly alight, red-cheeked, glasses frosted, head bound in wooly muffler, legs encased in arctic boots. If it was handy, she was pleased to thaw herself out with a cup of hot buttered rum. But no matter, she always brought the power to astonish, to appall, to arouse. Did they know that babies were dying from tainted milk? That milkmen set their pails down in dirt? That rats and prairie dogs were spreading bubonic plague? "What are we going to do about it?"

As it happened, there was a possible course of action right at hand. Campaigning had begun for the 1946 state elections, and voters aroused by the plight of sick babies and infectious prairie dogs passed the challenge to the candidates. "What's your position on the Sabin Health Bills?" None was permitted to duck the issue, nor to forget it. When the votes were counted in November, those who failed to endorse the bills, or failed to endorse them loud enough, in nearly all cases went down to defeat. Among the fallen was the Republican gubernatorial candidate endorsed by Governor Vivian, who had been less assuring than the Democrat candidate W. L. Knous that Dr. Sabin's appointment would be continued.

All wasn't blue skies, however. The election alarmed those who had a vested interest in health non-regulation, of whom there were considerable numbers, and who up until then had assumed the new health bills would go the way of all the others. Now came attacks by arch conservatives who sniffed socialism in meat and restaurant inspection, by chiropractors and barbers who feared interference, by cattlemen and dairymen who feared controls. These joined forces to block the mischief in the legislature.

Through necessity, Dr. Sabin now found herself boning up on the art of lobbying. She spent weeks in the Statehouse buttonholing in the corridors, testifying, monitoring hearings, marshalling data, and rallying adherents for the vote. Said Governor Knous admiringly, "There isn't a man in the legislature who wants to tangle with her. She's an atom bomb."

And in the end they passed — four separate bills that provided for reorganization of the state health department to take it out of politics, doubling the state appropriation for health care, setting up county health departments, and increased assistance for the medical school. The only Sabin measure to meet defeat was part of a provision on Bangs disease control, and she got that through a later session.

This time there was no pretending she would enjoy leisure. She knew she wouldn't. Mary knew it too, and scarcely demured when Florence, her state bills now signed into law, trained a captious eye on the state of health in Denver. It was one of the over-25,000-population "home rule" cities exempt from state health regulations. Soon, by appointment of the

mayor, she was the new manager of Denver's Division of
Health and Welfare with a new set of goals. During the three
years she held office, she waged war on rats, dirty restaurants,
trashy alleys, and open garbage dumps. She introduced hair-
nets for waitresses and free chest x-rays for everyone. She saw
to it that no unpasteurized milk could get into the city. And she
virtually eliminated her pet abomination: straight-up bubble
fountains "where the germs bounce at the top like ping-pong
balls in a garden hose."

A month short of her 80th birthday, she resigned to take
care of Mary, now chronically ill. While watching her night and
day, Florence listened to baseball on the radio and caught up
on her reading. She enjoyed the latest book of her old friend
Leo Stein, whose writings she preferred to Gertrude's, although
she staunchly defended Gertrude against deriders. Soon she
grew impatient with aimless reading and decided on a literary
research project. She would read all of Shakespeare and sift for
clues that indicated whether Shakespeare really wrote his works,
or whether they had been written by another, as some savants
believed. She cleared the room of all reading but Shakespeare,
stacking books beside her like microscope slide racks. Occasionally, she was called out to collect yet another honorary
degree (she was to receive fifteen in all); and she was national
news again when named winner of the coveted Albert Lasker
Award for her public health accomplishments.

In the fall of 1953, under the strain of nursing Mary, Florence caught pneumonia and found herself in a hospital bed.
Mary had to be removed to a sanitarium. When Florence
returned home, she was in the care of a nurse. On October 3,
1953, the World Series was being played — her Dodgers against
the Yankees — and she listened raptly to her bedside radio.
Between innings with the Yankees ahead, she got up to take a
stretch. Midway across the room, she tottered and fell, victim
of a heart attack. Moments later she was dead at 81.

Her last project, deciphering Shakespeare, remained unfinished, and thorough sleuth that she was, with evidence still un-
sifted, she had reserved opinion. But she had completed almost
everything else she had set out to do, and if in heaven she

encountered Uncle Albert, she could answer yes, she had kept busy. In doing so she had left the world a far less precarious place than she had found it.

Abigail Scott Duniway when schoolteaching in Oregon at age twenty-eight. (— *David C. Duniway*) After a lifetime of campaigning for women's rights, she registers to vote in Portland, right. (— *Oregon Historical Society*)

Abigail Scott Duniway

Up from Hard Scrabble

"MAN IS, OR SHOULD BE, woman's protector and defender. The natural and proper timidity and delicacy which belongs to the female sex evidently unfits it for many of the occupations of civil life." Thus spake the United States Supreme Court in 1872 in upholding an Illinois statute barring women from practicing law, which a feminine aspirant to the bar had dared to challenge.

A few months before, in Oregon, a young overworked farm-wife turned editor had undertaken to shatter both of the time-honored premises upon which the tribunal based its decision. Abigail Scott Duniway, who as a teenager had tramped West from Illinois with her family over the cholera- and Indian-plagued Oregon Trail and later helped her husband tame a wilderness farm, knew *she* was neither timid nor delicate. And so far as she could see, man was less defender than exploiter, and woman had no choice but to submit. What unfitted woman in Abigail's opinion was not God-made emotional and physical characteristics, but man-made legal hobbles — hobbles man had applied for his own benefit.

Unhobbling the women of her adopted region so they might defend themselves was the goal of her bristling Portland-based weekly newspaper *The New Northwest*, launched in May, 1871. Simultaneously she pried three other levers under her "defenders": suffrage organizing, lecturing, and lobbying. But she had to assume one task she hadn't counted on. To her exasperation, she discovered that most women still imagined themselves protected. While shaming men into surrendering purloined rights, she prodded her sisters to look up from their dishpans "at which they were protected without wages" and from the ironing boards "where they are shielded without salaries" and see they were besieged not only from without but from within.

Optimistic by nature, Abigail predicted victory would come in five years. When it resisted, when opposition rose and grew and hardened, she revised her estimate but never her aim. Despite setbacks, defeats, financial crises and abuse, she kept on shaming and prodding for forty years. And they were forty satisfying years, for she thrived on contention and uproar. Moreover, they were years of steady gains, not only for suffrage, but for a train of other rights — changes that revolutionized the status of women throughout the Northwest. And because her feminist victories generally preceded those won elsewhere, they were a spearhead glinting across the Rockies and influencing the entire nation.

Abigail's drive and durability were inherited from four generations of restless, combative, adventure-seeking pioneers. Her great-great-grandfather James Scott, after emigrating from Scotland to Virginia in the early 1700s, moved on to South Carolina. In turn his progeny picked up and bushwhacked to North Carolina, to Pennsylvania, to Kentucky, to the Territory of Illinois. There in 1830, Abigail's father, Tucker Scott, married Anne Roelofson, daughter of a Danish-English family, which had been frontier-hopping since debarking at New York. By the time a treaty with Great Britain made Oregon the newest American Territory, Tucker had already sired a family, but that didn't stop him from striking out for that primeval place. It is not surprising that his daughter Abigail, stranded on the continent's farthest reach with no geographical frontier left to conquer, slashed into the frontier of women's rights.

Conditioning for her role began back in Illinois, near Peoria, on Tucker Scott's succession of debt-ridden farms. Hard times stalked the tall, eagle-visaged man, who could never stick to anything. He moved from farm to farm, tried sawmilling, returned to plowing. Whimsical himself, he was strict with others, haranguing his peers on the efficacy of teetotaling and

barking orders at his stair-step brood. "Work never hurt anybody," was his refrain. Being a girl, the third of nine children,
didn't excuse Abigail from hoeing corn and chopping wood,
even though work ever awaited at the dishpan and washtub.
One of her earliest memories was "washing dishes while standing on a chair to reach the table." Her small, overworked, ailing
mother was meekness itself, having had it drummed into her
by her pious father. He had denied her schooling on the
grounds it might enable her to sign her future husband's name
and withdraw from his bank account. Abigail resolved to
escape her mother's fate and wondered if she might do it
through her knack for making rhymes. She detested farm work
and whenever possible laid down her hoe to perfect her verses,
some of which had been printed in the country weekly.

The main trail to Missouri — the starting place for Oregon —
passed near the Scott farm. Tucker Scott was endlessly fascinated with the motley throng and their talk of Oregon's leaping salmon and tall timbers. One day, just as his wife had
feared, he announced the Scotts were going too. Her tears and
protests were futile. After selling the farm and purchasing
draft oxen and five covered wagons, Scott enlisted thirty other
victims of "the fever." On April 2, 1852, their wagon train
began rumbling westward over still frozen ruts. Mindful of
the error of an earlier migration from their region, the ill-fated
Donner party, they were allowing ample time to make Oregon
before winter.

Abigail, then seventeen, kept the trail diary. Her father,
who was party captain, assigned her the task and encouraged
it (she said) with an occasional box on the ear. Nightly she
scribbled amid the furore around a campfire redolent of the
"buffalo chips" that served for fuel. Her entries reveal a relish
for the excitement of the trail. They tell of breakfasting in
a snowstorm with "victuals crusted not with sugar but with
snow," of billowing dust that hid "wagons, teams and roads
entirely from our view," of perilous river crossings, scary, skid-
ding descents down mountain sides. The party watched appre-
hensively for "Pawnees who are reported as being rather hostile
and very thievish" and shunned trail parties of ruffians who

boozed and brawled and sometimes murdered. There was the "sharper," who tried to extract $10 from them for permitting their oxen to graze on the open prairie, "but we knew what we were about and saved our money." Her later libertarianism was foreshadowed in her comment on the slaves she glimpsed toiling in the Missouri fields: "May none of *us* ever be guilty of buying and selling the souls and bodies of our fellow creatures."

While noting the number of graves passed, Abigail optimistically attributed them to carelessness in food and drink, which prudent folk might avoid. But when they were passing through the Black Hills of Dakota, Mrs. Scott, who had stood the journey poorly from the start, fell ill of cholera and died the same day. The family was stunned. Later, two young men of the party died, and in August, after they had reached the fringe of the Oregon Territory, the youngest Scott child died of dysentery. Abigail recorded: "Last night our darling Willie was called from earth to vie with angels around the throne of God . . . He was four years of age and possessed an uncommon degree of intellect, a kind disposition and agreeable manners."

During the final month, as they crossed the Cascade Mountains to reach the land claim of an uncle in the Willamette Valley, Abigail's diary is tinged with disillusionment. We hear of broken bolts and wagon tongues, lost cattle, hunger, dirt, and "hard-looking" villages. On September 28, they reached the settlement of French Prairie, near Salem, ending their 2400-mile journey of five months and twenty-six days, but Abigail's perfunctory final entry lacked the slightest note of triumph. "We found them all [her relatives] in good health and well satisfied. They were of course glad to see us."

Disappointment was common among female newcomers to the Oregon Territory. Trail diaries tell of women who rebelled out on the trail. Suddenly, they would feel they had reached their limit of danger, dust and discomfort, and they would remember they had had no say in coming. Something would snap. One woman set fire to the wagon; another sat down on a bank until beaten and thrown aboard; one shot her husband and tried to kill her children; another went insane. The most common expression of women upon alighting was, "Well, we finally got to the jumping-off-place!" For there was an eerie strangeness about the towering trees, torrential rains, and cougars crying in the night. The clearing villages with their grizzled men and shacks amongst tree stumps had a heathen air.

But, no doubt about it, Oregon offered singular opportunities. Foremost was free land. The Donation Land Act of 1850 gave a man 320 acres; twice that to a married couple. Even before staking his claim, Tucker Scott profited from the commercial boom. Down in California gold rushers were demanding lumber, fish, and farm products, and money was jingling in Oregon's new farm towns. Renting a flimsy structure in Lafayette, Scott turned it into a going hotel by the mere act of calling it one. So desperate were bachelors for a place to lay their heads, he was able to demand total abstinence of his guests.

Another advantage was that in such a polyglot society nobody questioned credentials. There were no checkpoints on the Oregon Trail, and the prevailing attitude was that it was better not to pry. Abigail, who had less than a sixth grade education, passed herself off as a schoolteacher and was snapped up to teach at nearby Eola. She reported confidently for duty, after brushing up by studying an elementary spelling book she had stowed in the covered wagon.

Crowning that, she suddenly found herself a belle. Back home she had been a tart-tongued stringbean of a tomboy, but in the woman-scarce territory, where a wife was a prime status symbol, she was besieged by suitors. Bronzed ranchers, lumberjacks and teamsters begged her hand. And under such attention she blossomed. She filled out and became downright pretty, with a mane of light brown hair, even features, and flashing blue eyes. But she knew what she was about. A rumor that donation claims might be abolished had precipitated a frenzied scramble for brides, with bachelors galloping about rapping on doors and proposing to any female who opened one. Abigail did not conceal her contempt for men who pressed matrimony upon "tearful widows of a fortnight and little girls making mud pies."

Cautiously, she settled on a young man of similar background. Tall, mild Benjamin Duniway, four years her senior, had come out from Illinois in 1850. After a stint in the Jacksonville mines, he had ridden north to select a land claim and found Abigail as well. When they married in August, 1853, the eighteen-year-old bride, remembering her obedient mother resting in the Black Hills, purged the wedding ceremony of the word "obey."

And now little more than a year after escaping a bleak Illinois farm, Abigail found herself stuck on a backwoods farm in the wilds of Oregon. For Ben Duniway had chosen poorly. His tangled tract on the fringe of the tall timber required constant defense against the wild evicted animals. Ben was cheerful and willing, but that was part of the trouble. Because of it, Abigail staggered under an extra burden: neighboring bachelor farmers formed a habit of dropping by the Duniway's split-log cabin around mealtime, sniffing for chicken stews and pies. Amiable Ben always invited them to stay. In the lean-to kitchen, stirring pots with one hand, pacifying baby Clara with the other, Abigail vented her resentment by concocting names for their establishment. "Hard Scrabble" was her name for the farm, while their cabin was "Free Hotel." She also raised chickens and pigs and pieced out their income by selling milk and butter and making soap and candles for market. Ben genially delivered her products in his handsome buggy and as genially pocketed the proceeds. Reasonable in most ways, he held finances to be the exclusive province of men.

Eventually Ben conceded the battle with Hard Scrabble and, in 1857, acquired a tamer tract near Lafayette. Abigail, who had rejoiced to shake the bachelor freeloaders, now found herself cooking for a flock of hired hands, part of Ben's ambitious project to start an apple orchard. Chained to brainless tasks and to childbearing (one every other year) she began rhyming again. She mailed some verses to the weekly *Oregon Argus* with disappointing results. The editor printed one with the mortifying comment: "We publish the following to please the writer." He suggested she try prose. She obliged with a strongly-worded piece painting women the "victims of wrongs condoned by law," which drew letters expressing sympathy for "the writer's hen-pecked husband."

Undaunted, she attempted a novel based partly on her trail diary. Assembling a diverse group of overlanders, she stalked them like a captious schoolteacher across the plains and through their initiations in Oregon. Each learned his lesson — the efficacy of good health habits, education for women and stick-to-itiveness, or the folly of unpreparedness, procrastination and child marriage. The book's sole virtue was a lively style. Thus began a chapter concerning land brides: "Gustavus Willard must have a wife. That was settled. If he couldn't get *somebody*, he must take *nobody*, or her sister. A squatter lived three miles from his bachelor's ranch. He had a daughter 13 years of age. Verdant as the grass she trod, more thoughtless than the cows she milked . . ." In 1859, a Portland printer risked running off a small printing of the indiscretion titled *Captain Gray's Company*. This, the first novel published in the Northwest, lost money after unanimously bad reviews.

Abigail's plunge into the world of literature coincided with a family crisis. A crony of Ben's persuaded him, over Abigail's objections, to cosign a loan for a milling venture. "You needn't worry," Ben assured her; "You'll always be protected and provided for." After faring badly, the mill floated away in a flood. The Duniways were in trouble. As Abigail recalled it: "One busy day, when I had added to my other duties several rapid hurries down the hillside to scare the coyotes away from the sheep, and just as dusk was coming on — my husband having been away from home all day — the sheriff came to the house and served summons on me for those notes! Now, observe that when that obligation was made I was my husband's silent partner — a legal nonentity — with no voice or power for self-protection under the sun; but when penalty accrued I was his legal representative."

There was nothing to do but sell the farm and pay the notes. In 1863, a chastened Ben moved his family into Lafayette. The Duniways were now seven; little Clara had four stairstep brothers. There Ben took up teaming and hauling, but his team bolted, threw him under a wheel, leaving him a semi-invalid.

Abigail, who had been told not to bother her head about money, suddenly found herself forced to. By hanging muslin partitions, she converted their attic into a dormitory and ran a small boarding school for girls. Cramming before classes, she kept one jump ahead of her scholars, while Ben turned his hand to housekeeping. Within a year she had saved enough to shift the Duniways to the lively town of Albany, where she opened a millinery and notions shop. Abigail blossomed under responsibility. She would have been the last to will misfortune upon well-meaning Ben, but she could not conceal her happiness that farming was put behind. And she loved being in the driver's seat.

While fitting hats with her mouth full of pins, she heard out many tales of domestic woe, many focused upon family finances as administered by high-handed husbands. Women complained their husbands took their egg and butter earnings and spent them on fancy horses and rigs. Some said they had to steal from their husbands' trousers to clothe the children. Shop browsers wistfully fingered items on the notions counter, then put them back sighing, "I'll have to ask *him* first." Those tired farm women worked as hard as their husbands — didn't she know! — yet, they were treated like children.

Her shop became something of an underground feminist propaganda center where she encouraged women to demand their rights. But women's rights, she discovered, were practically nonexistent. The husband of one faded mother of six sold all of the family furniture and disappeared. Abigail persuaded a businessman to lend the woman money to buy more furniture and open a boardinghouse. But after the boarders moved in, the husband returned, repudiated the note and sold the new furniture. In the eyes of the law what he did was perfectly all right. It was his wife who had misbehaved, by signing a note without his consent. Abigail helped another needy woman by advancing supplies to stock a shop in another town. One day a stranger appeared with a judgment against her husband on a debt contracted before their marriage. While a man's property was indubitably his own, what was his wife's was his too. The creditor seized the stock, and Abigail was out her advance.

Even after death the husband could wield the baton. One of Abigail's customers was kept in constant turmoil due to the condition of her late husband's will. The estate, which the wife had helped accumulate and included property she had inherited, was left so permanently tied up she couldn't so much as buy a pair of shoelaces without making application to the judge-administrator. Abigail went with the woman to beseech the judge to make a sensible relaxation, but to no avail.

Abigail brooded over the injustice of it all. Why couldn't women control property and support their children when husbands failed to? Why couldn't they file lawsuits to protect their interests? Women even lacked power to control their children. One night at the dinner table she asked Ben how the law ever got so one-sided. To her surprise he had an answer. Laws were one-sided, he said, because men made them — through their voting power. Naturally, they made the laws to suit themselves. If women helped make laws, they'd be different. Abigail laid down her fork. She had been brought up to believe that women who asked to vote were eccentric man-haters. Her hopes took a mighty leap as Ben continued mildly. "It will never be any better for women until they vote. Some day a woman will start something." He didn't know what he was saying. Merely the thing that would change Abigail's whole existence and his along with it.

That was the spring of 1870 and Abigail was thirty-five. Having beheld the comet, she swiftly maneuvered into its train. She boned up on the suffrage movement from its *kaffeeklatsch* beginnings in upstate New York in the 1840s, through the formation the year before of the ambitious National Woman Suffrage Association. Two victories already had been won. In the fall of 1869, women in the rugged Wyoming Territory had coaxed the vote from their tiny legislature. Three months later in the Utah Territory, Mormon women, who had always had a say in church affairs extended their equality to the voting booth.

Soon Abigail was conducting meetings of a group she called the Oregon State Equal Suffrage Society. Appointing herself a delegate, she boarded a stage for Sacramento, California, to

attend a regional suffrage convention. There she made a peppery talk that drew much applause and was respectfully mentioned in the press. Much exhilarated, she stopped in San Francisco on her way home to visit the office of *The Pioneer*, the
West Coast's first suffrage newspaper. She decided on the spot
that she was going to have a newspaper too.

Within a year she was publishing *The New Northwest*, a
weekly newspaper with offices in Portland. Portland was an
energetic, mushrooming town of 8,000 with rows of pitch-
roofed frame houses climbing uphill behind the false-fronted
stores that skirted the Willamette River. The Duniway family,
which now included five boys, lived in the first floor of a $40-a-
month house, whose upper story accommodated the publishing operation. Clara, now seventeen, kept house, while Ben
tried earning again, a light clerical job having been provided
by Abigail's brother, Port Collector Harvey Scott. The older
boys helped the printer run off the paper. The Duniways were
a frank-spoken, joking lot. The children called their parents
"B. C." and "Jenny" (for Abigail's middle name Jane). No
disciplinarian, Abigail was instead the chief cutup, coming in
from her rounds with hilarious anecdotes and at night thumping on the battered organ loudly singing "Charming Billie" and
inviting the rest to join in.

The target area for *The New Northwest* was Oregon, Washington and Idaho. From its first edition, on May 5, 1871, it
stood out from other ax-grinding journals by being entertaining.
Remembering her own early resistance to suffrage, Abigail
knew better than to bait all her lines with women's rights.
Reports of crime and political scandal bolstered her editorials,
which held society to be corrupt for the reason that "the virtu-
ous, the refined, the sensible, the noble mothers, wives and
daughters of the nation do not assist in the national housekeeping." Her exclusive exposé of shady goings on in the Multno-
mah County Court House Ring made exciting reading in 1872,
and the following year she scooped the daily press with her
revelations of a schoolbook fraud. Work strikes or protests by
women anywhere in the world received ample space; they
echoed her editorial position that all working women were

exploited, but that with the vote they might demand and get equal pay for equal work.

Serial fiction, which she wrote herself, pointed up the hobbled state of women in a man's world. Her heroines resembled those of today's soap operas in the relentlessness of their travail. But instead of suffering in sleek suburbs, their milieu was farm or small town, and their circumstances were always straitened because of male incompetence or injustice. These victims endured nobly, rising above adversity like lilies from a scum pond.

In *The Plain Story of a Plain Woman,* her protagonist struggled under the burdens of farm work, child care, and schoolteaching, while her doltish husband, a hunting buff, attended his guns and hounds. In *The Old Woman,* an aging widow is left dependent on selfish children as a result of her husband's hamstrung legacy. Another heroine, a mother of fifteen, several of them defective, had her house sold at auction as her husband lay in bed whimpering, "Give me rum, or I shall die." Whether the reader placed herself in the miserable pair of shoes or blessed her escape from them, she was exposed to the idea that change was in order.

Abigail understood the reader appeal of conflict. She culled anti-suffrage statements from other publications and printed them with her rejoinders. One editor argued: "Men do not oppose woman suffrage because they respect women less, but because they love their families more." Asked Abigail: "Is this what prompts them to sanction customs that, were death to overtake them, would condemn their daughters to labor for half pay, or to perpetuate laws that compel widows to humiliating conditions in control of what is of right their own?" Stated another male of suffrage: "I detest and scorn it. It comes intuitively to every lady of the land to oppose it and her feelings recoil from it." Abigail said he seemed to possess an "excessively delicate temperament. We think he . . . should be placed in a dainty bandbox, scented with lavender and laid among catnip and dried clover."

She noted that some Washington, D. C., government wives had signed a petition condemning votes for women "because

Holy Scripture inculcates a different and for us a higher sphere, apart from public life" and because they were unwilling to bear burdens "unsuited to our physical organizations." Abigail editorialized: "We toiling and tax-paying women, but reading and reasoning women, who stay at home while these parasites upon the public bounty are flirting at the capital, do not care a single straw if they do not vote. A sensible exercise of their inherent right of franchise is doubless 'unsuited to their physical organization.' We do not wish to abridge their privileges, but we most emphatically deny their right to interfere with our prerogatives."

She waded fearlessly into the journalistic sport of name-calling. She dubbed one editor a "tender-pated popinjay" and hailed "poor vapid Luce of the *Independent* who is in danger of being suffocated by the reeking fumes of his foul imagination." Of another adversary she noted, "We feel over this fight with the *Statesman* just as the lion did when compelled to whip the skunk." She goaded one sparring partner: "Now, Billy, stop blubbering and look here." If her epithet elicited another she was delighted and printed it no matter how stinging. The only thing that truly distressed her was to have her name and activities barred from a newspaper, as did two piqued Oregon editors bested in an exchange with her.

In her correspondence column she dispensed sympathy and sound advice. Subscribers were invited to write her their problems and they did, prolifically. To "Nervous Sufferer" she urged: "You need *rest*. Get your decaying teeth extracted. Let Molly's face go dirty and John's knee peep out. These things will surely happen when you are dead and gone." But she discouraged wallowing in self-pity. She advised one Niobe: "Your revelations are sacred, but we feel it is not good for you to indulge in them." She also advised on such practical matters as how to make a waterproof cloak and a way to eradicate corn grubs.

Once, apologizing for a delayed answer, she detailed the demands on her attention: "A lady from the country wants a shade of silk matched. A philanthropic gentleman has a scheme for the reclamation of fallen women and wants our co-operation in giving him the address of such as may wish to reform. A lady desires us to procure the photograph of a deceased friend. A woman whose husband is in prison wants help in obtaining a railroad pass to go visit him. A man wants to borrow money. A child wants to sell matches. A poor woman who doesn't know how to do anything wants employment. A sick woman wants us to go with her to see the doctor. Some ladies made a fashionable call. The typos want copy. A formidable pile of exchanges await attention, and our youngest hopeful wants help in mastering his geography lesson." Her agenda must have made Nervous Sufferer feel almost leisurely.

Always on the alert for the feminist angle, she found it in the most unlikely places. After monitoring a class at a medical college, she reported that the lecturer "when speaking of fretful and disagreeable patients always used pronouns 'she' or 'her,' thus implying what every woman knows to be contrary to the fact that sick women are more irascible than sick men." At the state fair she took in a sideshow that featured a contortionist, had a chat with the performer and reported: "Madam Forestelle, the contortionist, performed her wonderful and dangerous feats every day and evening. The husband who 'supports' her by getting men to tie her up on the stage with a fifty-foot rope from which she magically frees herself in a box; by causing her to twist herself in every imaginable contortion for the vulgar gaze of the curious; by taking a sledge hammer and breaking a 300-pound rock upon her breast; and then squanders her money thus earned at the peril of her life at the saloon or gaming table, can not keep 'wool over eyes' much longer. There's just rebellion brewing in that kingdom."

In a day when few reform papers were self-sustaining, *The New Northwest* returned a modest profit. Abigail held advertisers by exhorting her readers to patronize them and to boycott businesses which wouldn't place an ad. For a time she was plagued by men canceling their wives' subscriptions, but she scotched that by identifying one man and threatening to publish a blacklist of such offenders.

A few months after starting her newspaper, she launched her campaign to organize the Northwest for suffrage, using as her trial balloon none less than Susan B. Anthony. Miss Anthony journeyed up from California, where she had been conducting suffrage business, lured by Abigail's offer of steamboat passage to Portland and a lecture tour of Oregon and Washington under her management. Abigail had some reservations about presenting the spinsterish Miss Anthony, but she found her not at all the man-hater she had expected.

It was a dry spell and traveling the dusty roads by stagecoach, they arrived everywhere looking like bright-eyed ghosts. The churches they had hoped to lecture in were closed to such a radical cause as women's rights. They had to speak in seedy hired halls; in Walla Walla they were obliged to orate in the back of a saloon, thereby providing a topic for pulpits the following Sunday. In one town a woman offered her parlor, but her husband arrived home unexpectedly and expelled them.

Nonetheless, Abigail counted the tour a success. Miss Anthony's lectures gave her a thorough grounding in the movement, and she picked up scores of subscriptions. Further, she took a measure of her territory and decided that while suffrage was far from popular it had potential. Everywhere she recruited soldiers — not leaders. Indeed, she would have been dismayed had someone emerged waving the standard, for she intended to carry that herself.

After that there was no shaking the dust from her shoes. For years she was to spend at least half of each week on the road, waving her banner and conferring smaller banners upon promising protégés. She wrote on the move, mailing copy from stage and steamboat stops. Her following grew, but so did resistance, as men ruminated her message and realized its threat. Former speaking places were withdrawn, but she always spoke somewhere, in a barn if necessary. Once when she was addressing a meeting in an unfinished school, the floor collapsed; she just picked herself up and led her audience to a sounder spot. Often she was interrupted by hecklers, sometimes had to dodge eggs and fruit. None of which disturbed her greatly; she knew the nourishing effect of persecution upon a new movement.

Besides, she could hold her own with hecklers. The same one rarely heckled twice. In Gervais, Oregon, an Irish jokester rose and regaled the audience as he depicted women trying to occupy lawyers' offices and judges' chambers, leaving their husbands home to quiet the babies with "rubber substitutes." Arms folded, he concluded: "I have often known a hen to try to crow, but I've never known one to succeed at it yet!" Abigail just smiled her brightest. "The gentleman is right," she conceded. "I have myself discovered that peculiarity in hens. But in the poultry yard of my friend, Colonel Thompson I once saw a rooster try to set, and he made a failure too." On another occasion, when an elderly gentleman rose and expressed contempt for women's rights, she invited him to tell why. He said he didn't really know *why* he opposed them, but he always had and guessed he always would. Abigail's quick-as-a-flash response was, "I've always heard the difference between a man and a mule was that a man could change his mind."

Once when approaching Yakima, Washington, in a stage, a man twitted her about suffrage to the merriment of other passengers. "Madam," he blandished, "you ought to be at home enjoying yourself, like my wife's doing. I want to bear all the hardships of life myself and let her sit by the fire toasting her footsies." Inside the town the driver stopped to let the man off at his front gate. There in the front yard was his wife chopping away at a pile of snow-covered cordwood. As the man leaped out, Abigail called after him, "I see your wife is toasting her footsies!" Thereby gaining him the nickname around Yakima of "Old Footsie Toaster."

But she never picked fights with men. Instead, she tried to win them with reasoning and flattery, never forgetting they would have to yield ground. She frequently called on them in their stores and offices to invite them to her meetings, and many came. Shrewdly diplomatic was her appeal: "Gentlemen, in our demand for the ballot, we are not seeking to rule over you . . . we recognize your right to liberty. We only ask for our enfranchisement because we desire freedom for ourselves."

Her writing and organizing were underpinning for her primary thrust — political action. She had assigned herself that task as well. Optimistically, she predicted the women of the

Northwest would be liberated by their state legislatures within five years. In 1872, she went down to Salem and did her first lobbying. She found quick rapport with the lawmakers, mostly men from farms and small towns who already knew her through her newspaper. Not only did she get a suffrage bill introduced, but she was permitted to address the legislature in joint session. She committed the *faux pas* of alluding to a legislator by name rather than by county, for which she was called to order. But she gained points with her apology: "Gentlemen, in years past when most of you were studying parliamentary law, I have been rocking the cradle."

The bill failed to pass, but as a consolation prize the legislature passed the "Sole Trader Bill' she had advocated. The statute enabled a woman engaged in business to register the fact with the county clerk, thereby protecting her tools, furniture, and stock from seizure by her husband's creditors. Further, if abandoned by her husband, a wife might obtain the court's permission to sell or lease property, collect money due him, and make contracts, all binding even if he returned.

Thereafter, she pursued the legislators by name through her columns, flattering the favorables, prodding neutrals, excoriating the opposition. Her suffrage bill failed again in 1874, as did her efforts to get the legislature to approve a state referendum on suffrage. But another rights bill was forthcoming. In 1878 came passage of a statute enabling married women to sue to protect their rights and property and to receive and hold in their own right the wages of personal labor. Another measure passed that year enabled tax-paying women to vote in school elections.

Without knowing what she was wandering into, Abigail welcomed the temperance movement that swept over Oregon in the mid-1870s. Temperance fervor had risen from the Midwestern prairies to crystalize in the founding in Cleveland, in 1874, of the Woman's Christian Temperance Union. Abigail despised the saloons that had siphoned off her millinary customers' butter and egg money. Moreover, she envied temperance. The churches, which had snubbed her cause, embraced temperance as if it were part of the Trinity, and she hoped to tie suffrage and temperance together and thereby slide suffrage in through the church side door.

She made haste to affiliate with a temperance society that met in a prosperous Taylor Street church. But its pastor, the Reverend Izer, hovered possessively over meetings, and Abigail's strategy of getting in a few words for suffrage at meetings annoyed him. Repeatedly, he cut her off, but she persisted. One night when she rose to speak, the minister raised his hand — a signal. Instantly, the congregation began to sing, drowning her out. When they finished, she resumed. They sang her down again. The vocal skirmishing continued until the minister closed the meeting.

When the next meeting began Abigail was seated in the front pew. Sermonettes, testimonials and hymns alternated in close succession. But midway there was a momentary lull. Abigail, who had been waiting, sprang to her feet and intoned, "Let us pray!" Thereupon she delivered her speech as a petition to the Almighty. She prayed that every yoke might be broken and the oppressed go free; that the "mother sex" might be freed from servitude without wages; that press, public and pulpit be led to realize that political freedom for women could no longer be denied. And finally, concluding her twenty-minute prayer, she implored that society be freed from the bigotry and tyranny of the pulpit as well as from the vice and tyranny of the saloon. When at last she spoke her "Amen," Reverend Izer leaped to his feet and shrilled for the Doxology.

Abigail shifted her allegiance to another temperance group, where treading cautiously she found more reception for the idea that suffrage and temperance might march forward hand in hand. But it wasn't long before her eyes opened to the danger of such a marriage. Initially, the temperance movement had confined itself to encouraging self-control; pledge-taking was the thing. But talk had turned to the goal of legal prohibition and of a prohibition party, and these advocates were eyeing suffrage as a short-cut to prohibition.

Abigail became alarmed. Suffrage had made headway in the West because of the libertarian spirit; men who enjoyed liberty were willing to share it. But men might think differently about giving women liberty if they planned to use it to curtail theirs. Further a third party would upset her political strategy of pursuing suffrage through a two-party system by shifting backing from one candidate to another according to their suffrage stance. She couldn't gamble on a separatist party that might not succeed.

She never let pride keep her from making an about-face if her cause required it. So, she a teetotaler from a long line of teetotalers declared herself opposed to a prohibition party. In her speeches and editorials she hammered away at the risks, pointing out the failure of third parties elsewhere. Besides, prohibition wouldn't prohibit, she argued; the drinker would find his draft. "We might as well try to prohibit sex on the grounds some are prone to break the laws of chastity." She proffered her own temperance plan: Curb drinking by regulation, taxation, education and ostracism. She recommended school instruction for inculcating abstinence. If the young transgressed, she offered parents two remedies. One was to empty a cask of whiskey before the imbiber and let him see the horrid dregs at the bottom. The other was to "overdose" young tipplers until they imagined they were throwing up "the very soles of their feet."

It didn't go down with temperance zealots. They said Abigail had come out for alcohol. Rumors painted her a closet drinker. Many temperance zealots withdrew from suffrage, undercutting her efforts to launch a suffrage referendum. Her oratory had made her a star at national suffrage conventions, but when she rose at a convention and urged against commingling suffrage and temperance, she was rebuked, even by Miss Anthony.

Later she would compare the havoc temperance raised to that kicked up in Chicago by Mrs. O'Leary's cow. The suffrage referendum she had sought finally was set for 1884 and Abigail lined up her followers to conduct a "still hunt" campaign. She wanted a quiet canvassing that would not arouse the liquor interests to pit their affluence against the referendum. But up to Oregon came Frances E. Willard and a flock of other WCTU speakers. They deployed over the state urging, "Vote for suffrage and pave the way to prohibition." As Abigail feared, the liquor interests moved in with money and workers, urging men to oppose suffrage and save drink.

At the height of her campaign Abigail held a rally in Salem's Marion Square. Politicians who had promised to share the rostrum changed their minds and sent excuses. But on the roccoco band platform among the tall fir trees, she radiated optimism. One observer described her as "large, fresh and handsome," noting she spoke with a "masculine emphasis." She told the women that politically they were "classed with lunatics, idiots and criminals." She reminded them that even the lowest bum could vote, but they couldn't.

As the crowd seated on the plank benches savored that, she fastened her eyes on a small boy hunched under a ragged sunhat and demanded, "Don't you consider your mother as good, if not better, than an ordinary Salem saloon bum?" Her surprised target started under the flurry of attention, but managed to get out, "Sure I do." Later, to the customary male ploy that since men had to do the fighting, they ought to do the voting, Abigail gravely rejoined: "Life's hardest battles everywhere are fought by the mothers of men in giving existence to the race." No male ever countered *that*. Right up to election day Abigail gave her all. But the liquor forces had been equally busy. The referendum failed.

Meanwhile, the movement was faring better in the Washington Territory. There, seekng enfranchisement by an act of the territorial legislature, Abigail wangled an invitation to address the body. Her witty, dramatic appeal won applause and resulted in a suffrage bill that nearly carried. She continued her politicking in the corridors, and during the next session of 1883 the measure passed handily. However, a little later temperance fervor swept into Washington when it was shifting from territorial government to statehood, and as a result woman suffrage was left out of the new constitution.

There followed what was for Abigail a quiet decade. She decided not to risk another suffrage defeat in Oregon until, as she put it, "temperance had sobered off." Family concerns also influenced her change of direction. The Duniway boys had plunged hopes and cash into homesteading in southern Idaho land near a projected railroad line that was expected to inflate property. Ben was ailing again, and Abigail recently had lost her daughter and her father. After getting married, Clara had contracted tuberculosis that proved fatal. Tucker Scott had come to his end after a pampered old age with a second wife.

In 1887, Abigail surprised Portland by selling her newspaper and going to Idaho. There they joined their sons on a site almost as primitive as their honeymoon farmstead. Abigail hoped the country air would be good for Ben. Also she planned to help the boys get started, while she moved Idaho into the suffrage column.

The Duniways returned to Portland in the mid-1890s, the land venture having proved disappointing. But Abigail came home with a suffrage victory in her pocket. Thanks to her appeals to the Idaho legislature and her thorough canvassing of the potato towns, Idaho was now a suffrage state, via a constitutional amendment gained by referendum.

Alas, prohibition hadn't sobered off in Oregon. White boutonniere ribbons still fluttered everywhere. But Abigail had returned with a scheme of stealthy infiltration. Her plan was to convert the women's club movement, then growing fashionable across the country, into a vehicle for suffrage. Women's clubs would be organized around cultural interests, but these would have suffrage women running things and quietly spreading the word. A state federation would link the clubs, while also welcoming existing women's societies of all kinds.

To throw temperance people off the scent, Abigail did not even appear at the well-attended first meeting in a Portland hotel that launched the ambitious project. At the second meeting, she took a modest role, and only gradually revealed her strong rein. She was now a widow, having lost her ever-faithful Ben in 1896, and gave almost full time to the cause. Soon culture groups were sweeping over Oregon like leaves before a wind. Suffrage talk on the floor was taboo, but woman's handicapped position in society was much discussed. Emphasis was placed on the political technique of nominating, caucusing and voting, to plant the idea of political capability.

Thus when Abigail went down to Salem and arranged another suffrage referendum, it was small work to enlist a majority of the clubs into her vote-canvassing effort. Unlike during earlier referendums, the press was generally favorable, with the notable exception of the Portland *Oregonian,* which was edited by Abigail's brother Harvey Scott. He strongly opposed suffrage on the grounds that there was already too much uninformed voting, which would be aggravated by female voters. The referendum was held in the fall of 1900 and very nearly carried. The men of Oregon voted 26,265 in favor, 28,402 against.

Far from being downcast, Abigail felt victory was certain to come in the next referendum. Her role in the club federation — she had been elected state president — had transformed her public image from that of radical to cultural leader, almost a *grandame.* She alternated her two hats with the utmost aplomb and confidence. So much confidence, in fact, that she took the chance of pushing suffrage to the fore. In 1904, she authorized Oregon delegates to the national suffrage convention to invite the women to hold their next year's convention in Portland during the Lewis and Clark Exposition.

In April, 1905, coat-suited suffragettes from across the country converged on the flag-bedecked world fair city and took up headquarters in the fashionable First Congregational Church. Miss Anthony came although ailing, accompanied by her protégé, the bosomy Dr. Anna Shaw, who to Abigail's regret had been elected national president the previous year. Miss Anthony had recruited Dr. Shaw, a licensed minister and spell-binding orator from the top hierarchy of the WCTU. Abigail felt, and said so, that Dr. Shaw was mixing suffrage affairs with temperance to no good end.

Although dismayed, Abigail was still determined to pursue her plan to further suffrage through Oregon's new constitutional amendment which provided that referendums might be called by public petition. She set her clubwomen circulating petitions for a suffrage referendum at the fair and was jubilant when her ladies succeeded in collecting enough signatures to place the measure on the 1906 ballot. It never crossed her mind that Dr. Shaw would elect to remain in Oregon and run the campaign. Unfortunately, Abigail had put herself in a position where she was powerless to prevent it; she had resigned as state suffrage president so as to be free to run the campaign herself. Her successor was too awed by Dr. Shaw to decline her offer.

Over Abigail's objections Dr. Shaw brought the "white ribboners" into active participation, and they moved from platform to platform, painting suffrage as the prelude to prohibition. Again the liquor interests were aroused, and their ample resources were thrown against suffrage. If that weren't trouble enough, the campaign was plagued by a strong anti-woman's suffrage effort. A professional "anti" from Massachusetts arrived and marshaled a vocal group of Oregon women. They bombarded the newspapers with letters declaring women didn't want the vote, that only a disreputable fringe desired it.

Abigail kept her typewriter hot, clicking out missiles of rebuttal. One "anti" averred that women didn't need the ballot to make their way in the world. Abigail submitted that if some women wished to build a bridge for their accommodation, "has anyone the right to say the bridge must not be built lest a few women who preferred to wade would be compelled to cross dry shod?" Another writer expressed fear that suffrage would "turn women into men." Mock-seriously Abigail agreed, lamenting what already had occurred in neighboring suffrage states. "Look at Wyoming: There hasn't been a woman within her borders since 1869; no man has had a button on his shirt or a baby in his house for 35 years. Look at Colorado: Not a woman in the state; no man in that woman-forsaken land has had a darn in the heel or toe of his sock for 13 awful years. Look at Idaho: Not a woman to be seen. Look at Utah: Polygamy is doomed."

In the midst of the trying campaign came one of her greatest honors. Any doubt that she had entered the ranks of the esteemed was dispelled with the proclamation of a special "Abigail Scott Duniway Day" at the world fair. It was the first such honor ever conferred on a woman outside of royalty by the head of an international exhibition. The announcement,

which called her a "most honored citizen" stated: "It is directly
through her agency that many of the laws tending toward
equity and justice for women have been passed in the various states of the Northwest. On Abigail's grand day October
5, 1905, Oregon women vied for positions in the splendid
ceremonies.

Then it was back to the battle. With Dr. Shaw's and Abigail's alienated forces working at cross-purposes the campaign
went badly and the balloting worse. When votes were counted
suffrage had been overwhelmingly routed by more than 10,000
votes. Charged Abigail bitterly "Dr. Shaw and her hired auxili-
aries . . . swamped and wrecked us."

It was a weighty blow. Abigail's lieutenants were demoral-
ized. Her treasury was empty. Rumor said she was finished.
Instead, at 74, she announced she was launching a non-stop
campaign until victory came in Oregon and Washington. She
regrouped her forces, salved egoes, spread optimism. Part of
her scheme was a public relations program to convince the
liquor interests that prohibition was not a suffrage goal. She
culled statements and clippings which bore this out and chan-
neled them to liquor executives and their journals. At the same
time she turned out a barrage of articles and letters-to-the-edi-
tors designed to convince men that women did not wish to vote
in order to rule them, but to keep in step with them.

She lost another Oregon referendum in 1908, and another in
1910; but that year the state of Washington voted suffrage. In
November, 1912, a few days after her 78th birthday, victory
finally came in Oregon (bringing the number of suffrage states
to nine — all of them in the West). Four decades at the barri-
cades had taught her patience. When the polls closed on that
last referendum, she announced that should the measure fail,
another campaign would start at once. Instead of staying up to
await returns, she serenely went to bed. Later, a newspaper
reporter went out to learn her reaction and found her "not in
the least excited — simply peacefully contented."

After the returns had been certified — 61,265 for, 57,104
against — Governor Oswald West announced he was inviting
Abigail Scott Duniway as "the architect of woman's suffrage in

Oregon" to inscribe the official proclamation of the constitutional amendment. Governor West had long been a fan of hers. Ever since that day in a Salem park when she nudged him into taking his first political position, by gazing down at him from the bandstand and asking if he didn't think his mother was as good as a saloon bum.

Now came an avalanche of newspaper editorials all over the nation extolling her. She had become the "Grand Old Woman of Oregon." Her transition from obloquy to veneration amused her. The day she presented the proclamation to Governor West for his signature, she twitted her new image by showing up attired in lavender and lace and drapped with a crochet fichu.

During her last campaign she often said her one remaining wish was to "enter heaven a free angel." But after that seemed assured she remembered something more. She had always meant to write her memoirs. Finally, she had the time. Her grandchildren remembered her seated amidst a heap of scrapbooks and old newspapers, alternately wielding a pair of shears and punching at a monstrous old Smith-Premier typewriter that had eight rows of keys.

In 1914 came publication of *Pathbreaking*, a rambling chronologically-scrambled and casually-documented volume that nonetheless was both informative and entertaining. One might have expected its 80-year-old laureled author to have mellowed. While writing it, she was always being interrupted to receive yet another honor. And the sons her critics had said she was "raising for the penitentiary" were succeeding in law, editing, education and business. She might have looked back mistily, all benign, all forgiving. But that wouldn't have been Abigail. She hadn't altered her opinion that anything less than passionate partisanship was dishonest pussyfooting. Old bones were disinterred, old battles zestfully refought.

Her book kicked up a fuss, as she had intended. She spent the final months of her life gleefully retorting to critics. On October 11, 1915, eleven days short of her eighty-first birthday, she died in her sleep of blood poisoning brought on by an infected toe which, independent to the end, she had tried to cure herself.

Gertrude Atherton

The Flappers Were Her Daughters

LONDON IN THE 1890s was gay, gregarious and agog over the arts. Literary figures shone with especial brilliance amidst the pomp and plush of fashionable drawing rooms then vibrating to their roofs with avant-garde ideas and challenged taboos. Moving with cool assurance through those scintillating gaslit throngs was a handsome California widow. Blond, svelte with big level-gazing blue eyes, she provocatively combined an aristocratic air with spade-calling talk.

She was Gertrude Atherton, whose novels were being published in rapid file by a London house to appreciative reviews and brisk sales. Although followed by a trail of dazzled suitors, she showed no inclination to cash in her laurels for a titled husband, and frustrated her admirers by always slipping away to the countryside to dash off another book.

Despite a prolonged sojourn in England, she had no intention of forsaking her native heath. But she *was* picking a bone with it. Her own country had spurned her talent in no uncertain terms. Her London success had come as a pretty surprise, but she considered it her rightful due, and it was now her burning purpose to blazon her name so vividly upon the English literary firmament that Americans would be forced to accept her. Her bone-picking was especially directed at New York and at her home town of San Francisco. New York had called her writings raw, cheap, obscene, and "stupidly immoral," while branding her heroines farfetched, freakish, and the "daydreams of a shop girl." And her hometown and the haughty California family she had married into would scarcely have ostracized her more had she done a belly dance at the winter cotillion.

And for what? For doing the same thing that had brought London to her feet. For writing novels about independent young women who flouted Victorian mores, pursued the men they wanted, enjoyed sex in and out of marriage, and held give-and-take discourses with their brain-mates. These flinty heroines moved in an action-packed locus awash with lechery, suicide, alcoholism, adultery, and an infinite variety of sudden catastrophes.

Of course, the reason the English so readily accepted all these defiant females and their gritty American backgrounds was precisely because they *were* American; such conduct and standards seemed to them entirely appropriate for parvenues. If there was anything the English could not tolerate in those days of waxing American power it was Americans who presumed to act like English gentry. Mrs. Atherton, as perceptive as any of her coolheaded heroines, was somewhat suspicious of her London vogue, but she wasn't above using it to make her countrymen eat their words.

She had been genuinely puzzled by the American response to her writing. Farfetched? Unreal? Her writing did not seem so to her. Indeed, it was the tenor of the criticisms that had seemed farfetched. Prior to departing New York she had wondered publicly in an interview why it was that she "could not write an article for a newspaper, much less a novel, without throwing the entire United States into a ferment."

Gertrude Atherton could not believe her heroines farfetched and unrealistic because she, like many writers, created her heroines from the psychological ingredients of her own character. They were all, at least partially, herself in various disguises. Likewise, the trials she maneuvered them through were equivalent in degree, if not in specifics, to those she herself had weathered. Being highly self-centered, she had assumed her experience to be the way life was, and accordingly had written what seemed to her were everyday character traits and events. Actually, both real life and its translation were highly atypical — anything *but* everyday. Gertrude Atherton's Cali-

fornia childhood and young womanhood had been an unending
series of catastrophes and crises, occurring almost with the reg-
ularity of horror tableaux in an amusement park tunnel-of-love,
with the most hair-raising horror of all saved for its end. In
adjusting to her life-quakes she had acquired remarkable resil-
ience and toughness; and her blue eyes had acquired their cool,
unwavering gaze.

Symbolically, her birthplace, in 1857, was on San Francisco's Rincon Hill, which later would be leveled to accommodate a factory district. Change, swift and sweeping, was to be
her life pattern. The marriage from which she issued was at
her birth already teetering. Her mother, Gertrude Franklin, a
pampered, Southern-bred San Francisco belle, had been pressed
over tearful protestation into marrying Thomas Horn, a prosperous Connecticut-born tobacco merchant, whom she considered a pushy Yankee. With marriage, scorn ripened into hatred.
"They quarreled incessantly," Gertrude Atherton wrote in her
autobiography *Adventures of a Novelist;* "he took to drink, and
as my mother was in hysterics most of the time while I was
on the way, it is a wonder I was not born an idiot." The stormy
couple fastened their affections on their offspring, a blue-eyed,
golden-haired child who looked deceptively angelic. They had
quickly spoiled her into a tiny package of wilfulness, who got
her way, even to prancing on the table during a dinner party
and kicking over the teacups. The Horn's domestic scandal
climaxed when young Mrs. Horn became the first woman in
San Francisco society to file for divorce.

Care of Gertrude was assumed by her equally doting maternal grandparents, while her mother returned to being a belle,
although a sullied one. The new arrangement did nothing to
diminish the child's egocentricity, but it did give it a new direction. Her grandfather, Stephen Franklin, who was the great-
grandnephew of Benjamin Franklin, was a highly cultivated
man. He had come to San Francisco in the 1850s hoping to
recoup the fortune he had lost in New Orleans. He never succeeded, but he did become a formative influence in the new
city as a newspaper editor and later as a minor official of the
Bank of California; and he acquired one of the finest private

libraries in the city. Instead of playing horse with his spirited granddaughter, he read aloud to her, implanting an early interest in books. But the grandmother's efforts to cultivate the domestic virtues in the child were a total failure. Although tied to a chair for her sewing lesson, little Gertrude resolutely refused to make stitches. She was forever running away, returning with wild imaginary tales. If unable to find a listener, she would stand before a mirror and tell them to herself. It was feared she was a born liar.

In time her mother settled on a new husband, a stockbroker with the similar name of Uhlhorn, but who claimed her adoration as completely as Mr. Horn had claimed her aversion. Gertrude and her mother were settled in a fine townhouse and spent their days buying new dresses and bonnets. But this time Gertrude despised the man of the house, and before long the feeling was mutual. After she deliberately hurtled down the bannisters toward him, almost knocking him down, her mother placed her in a local boarding school. Things did not go smoothly, however, and Gertrude was withdrawn. Settled in another school, she was expelled the second day for disturbing class.

But soon there was no more money for boarding schools and the fine house had to be vacated. Mr. Uhlhorn had failed in business. Next, seeking a new stake, he gambled away his wife's jewels. By this time there were two little Uhlhorns, Gertrude's half-sisters Aleece and Daisy. Of that period, Gertrude remembered "moving into small and smaller lodgings in unfashionable streets, eating at restaurants, Mr. Uhlhorn glowering, my mother often weeping, the children squalling."

Then, Mr. Uhlhorn's fortunes brightened somewhat, and the family moved into a fashionable boardinghouse, and after that into a modest dwelling. But now there were recurrent quarrels because of Mrs. Uhlhorn's jealousy of her husband's suspiciously late hours. Gertrude later wrote: "I grew up with the idea that the marital condition was a succession of bickerings." But worse was to come. One night her stepfather terrified her mother by trying to commit suicide with chloroform. He was revived, but only to be rushed by her grandfather aboard a ship bound for South America. Mr. Uhlhorn had forged the name of his employer for a large sum, and his victim had agreed not to prosecute on condition that he depart the country. But there was no keeping the scandal out of the newspapers. Gertrude's mother fell into a prolonged semi-coma, such was her grief for the feckless man she still loved and would never see again.

By age 14, Gertrude had already announced she was "going to be an authoress." The notion was planted by a schoolteacher who singled out her high-wrought compositions to read before the class. Stephen Franklin, again breadwinner for his daughter's brood, was delighted at Gertrude's ambition and took a firm step to mould it. He insisted, to her distress, that she nightly read to him for two hours from the learned books in his library. Frowning and mumbling resentfully, she turned the pages of such tomes as Hume's *History of England* and Thier's *History of the French Revolution.* Later, she stated, "I was educated against my will into a taste for serious reading, and I have never ceased to be grateful." But her compositions more often drew her grandfather's criticism than his praise, and when she proudly showed him a poem she had essayed, he tersely advised, "Confine yourself hereafter to prose."

Her grandfather sacrificed to send her to a succession of schools for young ladies, where she exasperated the headmistresses by ignoring rules, refusing to exercise (a lifelong aversion), and by voraciously reading adult novels. At length in her seventeenth year, he sent her to Lexington, Kentucky, to attend Sayre Institute under the watchful eye of a highly religious aunt who lived nearby.

Kentucky bestirred the romantic in Gertrude and she discovered beaux. They swiftly drove out of her head all authoress ambitions, replacing them with a determination to be a belle like her mother. Although as skinny as a hollyhock she had a head of yellow curls and a piquant air. Under the nose of her shocked but helpless aunt, she flirted, she danced, she sipped mint julep and proclaimed herself an agnostic. When she got herself engaged to two young men at once, her aunt wrote West that she was sending Gertrude home. Kissing her niece goodbye at the train, she told her sadly: "You have your points, Gertrude, and I can't help liking you, but I am free to say that I was never so glad to see the last of anyone in my life. I think you are headed straight for the devil, but I shall pray for you."

Which dismayed Gertrude not at all. She was anxious to test her coquetry in the ballrooms of San Francisco. Giddy with expectation, she had visions of her grandfather's bank associates joining to "bring her out." She would be launched into the glittering social whirl, a toasted belle. Perhaps her grandfather's long-time friend the bank's president, William C. Ralston, would honor her with a ball at his famous Belmont estate.

She was asleep in her Pullman berth somewhere in the high Sierra when a newsboy burst into the train shouting: "Failure of the Bank of California and suicide of William C. Ralston!" She returned to an atmosphere of gloom and straitened circumstances. Home was now the modest family ranch in the country forty miles south of San Francisco.

Just when her life had promised infinite possibilities, all hope seemed gone. Stuck in the country! Even her mother, still beautiful at 38, was down to one suitor, and an unlikely one at that. He was George Atherton, the slight, handsome 24-year-old son of the master of the neighboring estate, the proud Faxon Dean Atherton. The elder Atherton was a New Englander who had made a fortune in Chile, married into a prominent Spanish-Chilean family, and later moved his family to California, acquiring a large tract that is now the town of Atherton. The staunchly Catholic, fiercely moral Athertons considered themselves the most exclusive family in California, and they were violently opposed to their son's infatuation with a Protestant divorcee fourteen years his senior.

Gertrude learned, to her amazement, that George nonetheless was determined to marry her mother and she him, that is, as soon as he could find a job, which he seemed in no hurry to do. Gertrude sniffed her disapproval, but her mother urged her to "treat George decently." So she haughtily tolerated his presence, while fretting at the time on her hands, and wondering what was going on in the city, and where she would ever find a beau. The ranch offered no diversion whatever — or

almost. There *was* George. And several months after her return
to California, she and George rode into nearby San Jose one
morning to meet her grandfather's train, and on the way they
got themselves secretly married by a Catholic priest.

Years later, Gertrude Atherton laughed off that rash, love-
less (on her part) marriage as "one of the most important inci-
dents of my school life." Yet, quite probably, her marriage more
than any other event of her life made her a novelist. What enclosed and stifled her during the next several years generated
such a fury of frustration that she seized upon her childhood
pastime as a frantic act of self-preservation.

At 18, the wild, high-soaring starling found herself in a
coop with her wings clipped. Discovering her marriage, her
grandfather erupted with a terrifying rage, while her mother
collapsed into one of her semi-comas. Gertrude's usual mend-all
smiles and dimples were futile. Her grandfather firmly ordered
her from his house for "acting disgracefully toward your
mother" and advised her to stay out of his presence. As for the
Athertons, they stoically accepted her as an irreversible fact
and the lesser of two evils, but subsumed her to the very bottom of the vast family hierarchy.

Her 200-pound Spanish mother-in-law, who larded tyranny
with kindness, undertook at once to have Gertrude converted
to Catholicism and to tone down her spirits. "*What* you do
next?" the bride was regularly admonished. "*Never* you grow
up?" Yet, the slightest flicker of mental activity on her part
drew a subtle reminder that intellect was out of place among
the female sex. Her whole duty, she was made to understand,
was to be a helpmeet to George. Yet, her lord and master
scarcely inspired such singular dedication. He idled away his
days and spent all of the allowance his family meted out for
them upon himself. Gertrude, who even in lean times had
enjoyed an allowance from her grandfather, now found herself
a penniless heiress. If she needed an item of clothing one of
her patronizing sisters-in-law accompanied her to the city and
selected it. Cut off from her own family, she lacked courage to
counter these assaults upon her dignity. She crouched on the
veranda thinking her daggers, when not patting yawns.

After Gertrude showed promise of becoming a proper Atherton by producing a baby boy and naming it after George, Atherton senior set George up in the brokerage business in San Francisco. He also built the couple a house in a dense wood on a corner of the estate. Gertrude won over her mother-in-law by letting her assume direction of little George's upbringing. This was no sacrifice for Gertrude, for children bored her; she confessed to preferring puppies to babies.

George commuted daily to the city with an important-looking portfolio, but his enterprise was short-lived. He then launched another business, but it was of even shorter duration. He declared he'd had his fill of city offices, so the family assigned him the task of reclaiming their 45,000-acre ranch at Milpitas from the squatters who had overrun it. Keeping house in a crude three-room adobe, Gertrude lived in terror lest the ousted squatters fulfill their threat to "kill every Atherton on the place." But George's management quickly proved inept and the family shifted them to another holding, which he soon bungled as well. He worked for a time as a stagecoach driver, but got fired after overturning a load of passengers.

By this time, Mr. Atherton had died, leaving his estate indivisible until the youngest child had reached majority, which was several years away. But George persuaded his mother to advance him his share of the inheritance for the purpose of financing an ambitious vineyard near Oroville. There was now a daughter named Muriel. Gertrude unhappily found herself tied down with two infants in a dilapidated house in a desolate rural spot. She wearily endured extremes of heat and cold, bad water, bedbugs and runaway servants until that undertaking too went under and they were back at their house in the woods subsisting on a strict family allowance.

For the first time, she took serious stock of her life. For five years she had lived by George's decrees, and where had it gotten her? She was as trapped as ever. Indeed, the trap was even more grueling. George, his possibilities exhausted, hung around the house, mopish and irritable. Always hotly jealous, he was even more so now that her figure had filled out seductively. He accused her of harboring secret thoughts, and well he might. She was thinking hard how she might gain her independence and was wondering if it might be through writing for pay. But she well knew that the Athertons, indeed all of San Francisco society, had the utmost contempt for women who "exhibited themselves in print." She would have to write anonymously.

Telling George she was scribbling for her own amusement, she began writing with furious concentration. First, she wrote brief articles and essays, which found acceptance in a new San Francisco weekly *The Argonaut;* her earliest publications were without pay, but soon they were earning $5 to $10 each. After this warm-up, she scouted for an idea for a novel and discovered it in a newspaper item George had lingered over at the breakfast table.

It concerned the auctioning off of a trunk full of wedding finery and souvenirs of a once beautiful San Francisco socialite named Nellie Gordon, who had died several years before. Gertrude remembered her mother and her friends gossiping in hushed tones about the Gordon family scandal, and she had heard more from the Athertons, whose estate adjoined the Gordon's summer place. Nellie's mother had been an alcoholic, and jealous of her husband's love for their only child, she planted in her daughter her own vice; the girl struggled against it, but after a tragic love affair, she yielded and let her life go to the ruin her mother had prepared.

Altering only the names, Gertrude wrote it down as truthfully as knowledge permitted, filling in the rest with her lively imagination. She let out all the stops in the passionate love scenes. For fillip she wove into the background almost every socially prominent San Franciscan, including the Athertons and the impeccable Mrs. Hall McAllister, sister of New York social arbiter Ward McAllister.

The Argonaut bought it at once for $150 and ran it under a pseudonym with the lilting title of *The Randolphs of Redwoods*. It ran for six installments, from the first raising a furore such as San Francisco had never experienced over the printed word. How very wicked, all agreed, to revive a scandal decent people wanted to forget. Everybody who had ever written for publication was accused of perpetrating the abomination — except the author herself. The large cast of supporting characters trembled from week to week to see what astonishing things they would be made to say and do next. George guessed the truth and was in terror lest his wife's authorship leak out.

Of course, it did, and the Athertons turned on their erring daughter in unison and accused her of callously betraying and disgracing them. Ladies in Spain did not write, Mrs. Atherton intoned. Gertrude was made to understand that there was something gravely wrong with a young mother who would write such things. As punishment the Athertons banished her from San Francisco society for an entire season. When she reentered it, half of San Francisco wouldn't speak to her; some never did again.

Naturally, she began another novel, and George's blackest rages, his most vehement pounding on the locked door of her writing room did not stay her pen. This time she undertook a historical novel, piling up a 300,000-word pistache of history in which figured Napoleon III, Garibaldi, and King Vittorio Emanuele. The heroine was a brilliant American woman who, widowed at an early age, went abroad and influenced the course of European politics. The Eastern publisher to whom she submitted it returned it at once. At first she was surprised and angry, but upon rereading her manuscript she saw it lacked conviction. She decided to hide it in the attic and rewrite it when she had become better versed on Continental intrigue. By then she had reconciled with her mother and grandfather, and she began pouring through history books in his library and that of another elderly gentleman who lived nearby. But while she was fortifying herself to revamp her brainchild the rats ate it.

She let the rats have the last word and attacked a new subject that had piqued her interest: reincarnation. She couldn't resist another foreign setting. The story moved from Wales to Paris and concerned a pair of lovers named Harold and Weir, who discovered themselves to be the reincarnation of their grandparents, who had been illicit lovers. This knowledge for highly intricate reasons led to renunciation and suicide. She titled it with a line of Hamlet's, *What Dreams May Come*.

Publisher after publisher flatly rejected it. Her spirits sank lower and lower, and she told intimates she was convinced her narrow existence would stifle her career. Enveloped by woods, how was she ever to "see life?" Around this time little George died of diptheria. Suddenly, Gertrude had had all she could endure of the Atherton estate. Later she would recall: "I hated it as I have never hated any place since. I hated everyone in it — George most of all." She issued an ultimatum: If George did not move her into town, she would leave him. Seeing she meant precisely that, he took a modest flat in San Francisco, where she lost no time forming a small salon to discuss writing and books. While keeping her novel on its rounds of publishers, she wrote short pieces for the newspapers and *The Overland Monthly*. But she longed to travel, and every time she saw a friend off on a train she grew sick with envy.

Instead, it was for George that travel opportunity suddenly opened. The family was visited by a nephew of Mrs. Atherton, an officer in the Chilean navy, whose ship called at San Francisco while on a training cruise. George, still at loose ends, decided to join the cruise and return to Chile to butter up a godfather who might remember him in his will. He had been gone two months when, without warning, his body was returned to San Francisco in a most startling way — embalmed in a barrel of rum! All was a fearful mystery until a delayed letter shed explanation on what it called "the remnants." George had died aboard ship from a dose of morphine taken to relieve a kidney stone. In that day ship captains catered to sailor superstition against shipping with a corpse, so the navy officers had disguised it by doubling it into a cask of rum and shipping it home under a cargo of coconuts. The letter stated that since the rum had come out of the navymen's rations "causing them to grumble," it would be well if she would "make it up to them."

Had she written such a sequel into one of her novels, the critics would have thought farfetched too mild a word. "Lurid and farcical!" they'd have cried. But those were the circumstances that provided the turning point to Gertrude Atherton's life by severing her hated marriage bond — the bond that had begun scarcely less remarkably a decade before.

Her remaining bonds to San Francisco were severed more conventionally. Far from falling into one of her mother's semi-comas, Gertrude coolly maneuvered a swift escape. She sweetly called on Mrs. Atherton and assured her that while ladies in Spain did not write, they did elsewhere and received handsome remuneration. She would be able to support herself by writing if only she could situate herself in New York where opportunity waited. A modest monthly allowance would make it possible. Mrs. Atherton shuddered at the thought of a woman of her family alone in such a place. But harboring a scheme of her own, she was receptive to bargaining. While adjuring Gertrude not to emulate "that orreeble George Eliot — living with a man who no is her husband," she agreed to provide an allowance if Gertrude would give her little Muriel, who so resembled George, and for whom she would provide in her will as for her own children. Gertrude, who had no intention of taking Muriel anyhow, tried not to accept too eagerly.

Next, she appealed to her grandfather, arguing that the talent he had nurtured in her would be wasted on San Francisco. A little sadly, he borrowed a thousand dollars from the local theological seminary and gave it to her, urging her to keep her writing on a "high moral tone." The members of her literary salon gathered on the train platform to see her off, when accompanied by her long-time maid and a mound of valises she departed East to pursue her dream.

And of course it eluded her most vexingly in New York. She was shocked by the stark aspect of New York of the 1880s — row upon row of indistinguishable brownstone houses and drab commercial buildings. Its grim-faced citizens, always madly on the trot, swept by without giving her a glance. Whenever she came upon a pair of them paused for a moment, they were always talking about money.

Hopefully, she sought out the bohemian quarter she had read so much about and found its stars to be stringy-haired women with dirty necks reading mediocre prose in fetid air. The distasteful creatures even tried to patronize her. She tilted her nose and clicked out. She longed to mingle with the city's higher literati, but she had been stunned to discover that belonging to San Francisco society cut no ice in New York.

Even more infuriating than personal slights was the cavalier disposal of her talents. She had brought along her much-rejected novel on reincarnation and suicide, and soon after arriving she began making the rounds of those publishers whose rejections had been the least insulting. Wearing a fetching widow's rouche on her hat and flashing her most dazzling smile, she asked each in turn to reconsider. Unhesitatingly, all refused.

At length, she discovered a small, new publisher who was not put off by her theme, her highly-charged verbs and unblushing expressiveness. Publication day brought telegrams of congratulation from San Francisco and columns of abusive criticisms in New York. The sum of the strictures was that this irresponsible young Western woman had invaded polite society and committed an unspeakable nuisance; the sooner she retreated to her native wilds the better. One review was so vitriolic that a friend of the family wanted to go down and horsewhip the writer. But she stayed him, averring that the only revenge worth having was success. She vowed she would force the critics to an about-face with another novel already under way.

It was *Hermia Suydam.* Determinedly scribbling in her tiny flat, Gertrude put much of herself into Hermia. Instead of thirsting for fame, however, homely Hermia pines to be beautiful; left on the bench while her prettier sisters and cousins waltzed into matrimony, she becomes a spectator of life. When she suddenly inherits a million dollars she seeks out a skilled doctor to recast her features. Men flock to her flower face, but having observed matrimony's dullness and tyrannies, she shuns marriage and quite without shame takes a handsome lover.

Another new and inexperienced publisher delivered *Hermia Suydam* to the world. Then came the deluge! The invective heaped upon it made the swipes at the first book look like a warm-up. Indeed, it was seriously reported in the press that the author's previous publisher had refused her second "after it had been branded as the most immoral novel ever written in the English language by a consultation of eight learned doctors of letters." Actually, the first publisher had been unable

to undertake it, being on his way out of business due to the
disaster of her first title. Among the terms Hermia's exploits
inspired were "crude abnormality," "lurid sensationalism," and
"gross obscenity." Not only had she undone God's handiwork,
but she had flaunted hallowed tradition that held spinsters
were supposed to wither away over their crochet and pot plants
instead of blooming in illicit love.

But there was more to it than moral indignation. In those
days nearly all literary critics were men, and between the lines
was detectable an annoyance at the author's worldly attitudes — a far cry from the syrupy sentimentality being spooned
out by the run of women writers. It wasn't Hermia's daring that
irked them so much as Gertrude's. She smacked of the "clever
woman," who was still very much *persona non grata* on the
American scene.

That her break might come in Europe occurred to her upon
opening a social invitation. A family connection, then living in
Paris, wrote suggesting she come over for a lengthy visit. Dally-
ing with the idea, she saw a trip abroad as an opportunity to
investigate publishing possibilities in England. She had heard
of a London publisher who reprinted American novels in paper-
back. She shipped him her much-maligned pair, hoping their
notoriety had not preceded them, then boarded a ship for Le
Havre. At thirty, her dream, although battered, was still pulsing.

A few weeks after arriving in Paris, she got a letter from
the London publisher saying her books were on the press and
enclosing a handsome check. Surely an omen! Buoyant with
hope, she crossed the Channel and entered London to a fanfare
of good reviews. Even the distinguished critic William Sharp
writing in the influential *Spectator* liked her Hermia. The English delighted in her headstrong heroines who rushed in pell-
mell where the proper spurned to tread. What American critics
had called abnormal and farfetched, the English termed "true
realism." American realism, they meant, of course; situated an
ocean away it posed no threat to their orderly existence. But
the English also admired her terse, vigorous style, which defied
the formal American writing tradition laid down by the New
England school.

William Sharp took her in tow and introduced her about London as "the coming American writer," and to her surprise she found herself launched socially as well as professionally. It seemed that if one were a foreigner, at whatever level one first strode upon the London social scene established one's rank; admission to one aristocratic drawing room automatically parted the doors of others. But she was not merely accepted, she was popular for her originality and for her habit of freely speaking her mind, both being assets at a dinner party, while offering little risk — any excesses might be written off as American.

Gertrude was immediately enamoured of the land of her Franklin ancestors, although she did not then guess that during the next decade it would hold her longer than any other place. Finding a waiting market for her stories and articles, she sent to Paris for her trunk and settled down to work. While in Paris she had started a new novel that was sure to please her new fans, who seemed to consider California the height of exoticism. It had as its setting the Milpitas ranch where she and George had battled squatters and concerned the tempestuous love affair of an untamed, spirited beauty from a Spanish squatter family and an American millionaire rancher. The millionaire already had a wife, but this hindrance was removed by having her trampled in a cattle stampede. This slight novel was published with the title *Los Cerritos.*

While pleased with her London reception, not for a moment could she forget New York. It was as though she had been invited to the ball, but only after the beau of her choice had spurned her. New York had yet to be won, and she continued to dangle lures in the form of her choicest short stories. Hoping her London credentials might have conferred a new sheen, she took especial pains to have *Los Cerritos* published in New York. The result was no better: she was partly ignored, partly panned, with the added criticism that she had depicted her countrymen unfavorably abroad.

Following a lengthy visit to California, she looked in on New York and found it palpitating over a murder trial that involved a poisoning. Reasoning that a novel built around such a situation would have a built-in appeal for New York readers, she settled down to researching the book she would call *Patience Sparhawk and Her Times.* She attended New York courts, studied prosecution methods, and mastered poisoning technique. All of her heroines had been of an independent cast, but the character of Patience almost classically symbolized the revolt of woman against the tyranny of man in his self-made world. She poured into it much of her own matrimonial experience, including George, who filled the role of the tyrant, oozing Neanderthal dominance from every pore and blustering toward his just deserts, extermination by poison.

Not one American publisher would touch the book. So she returned to England, where she succeeded in placing it with the leading London publisher, John Lane. Its publication drew such superlatives as "brilliant," "scintillating," "singularly interesting," and "altogether a novel to admire." A leading feminist praised it for "the impetus it has given the spirit of independence of women," and the eminent literary dictator of the Presbyterians, the Reverend Robertson Nicoll, called its author "the first of our women novelists." Thus encouraged, the publisher distributed the book in the United States, where it received not a single favorable review, but did find a market that would accelerate and continue for two decades. In time American critics would characterize it as a pioneer book that played a large part in loosening the shackles of women both in life and literature.

But that was still to come. At the time, scanning her disastrous New York reviews, Gertrude thought the critics, vexed at having their opinions contradicted in London, would never judge her fairly. But what if she published anonymously?

The notion of conspiracy exhilarated her. She crossed the Atlantic and established herself in the Adirondacks, then a favored resort of fashionable New Yorkers. In the vast rambling frame hotels she mingled gayly with the glittering hedonistic throng, eyes and ears alert for foibles and excesses. Taming down her realism, she wrote a satiric novel in the form of letters from an English noblewoman to an English friend reporting on the astonishing social and literary types one encountered there among the scrub pines. Her portrayals of the romping celebrities were highly irreverent and some, including two popular novelists, were easily recognized. She baited the trap with her liveliest style and most polished wit.

And her quarry rose with zest. The book was universally praised. "There is the dignity of birth and breeding in every line," declared one reviewer, presenting a dramatic contrast to previous charges of obscenity. "The first novel of a brilliant and witty woman from whom we shall expect great things," said another. But most critics believed it the work of an established writer and speculated who the brilliant, witty, talented author might be. Could it be, one critic wondered, Oscar Wilde? Meanwhile, the book was snapped up like the season's first violets in the flower stalls. At the height of the furore Gertrude Atherton stepped forward and blandly confessed.

Any doubts that she had arrived on the American literary scene were dispelled by *The Conqueror*. That was her 1902 biography of Alexander Hamilton, which she wrote in memory of her late grandfather, whose favorite historical figure Hamilton had been. She did a masterful research job, gathering new material from Hamilton descendants, even traveling to the West Indies to research his youth. For writing it, she invented a new literary form — ever since a staple on the book market — the fictionalized biography, which incorporates the narrative techniques of the novel. She made another departure with this book: for the first (and only) time she gave center stage to a man. But as in all her books, sex came in for detailed attention; she documented Hamilton's illegitimate birth and delved into his extramarital affairs with a succession of prominent New York women. The book's reviews were mixed, but its sales were sensational: it sold well over a million copies.

Her friends thought that with success secure in her pocket she might settle down to a home and husband. Now in her mid-40s, but looking years younger, she remained vividly attractive. When she wasn't writing, there was always some handsome man dancing attention upon her, while others coveted his privilege. It was an arrangement she did nothing to discourage with her flirtatious air, her high makeup, and seductive wardrobe — she especially liked to show off her alabaster shoulders. Her stunning blond hair with its dramatic sweep over her forehead was carefully styled to minimize her rather long nose. Of all men she found Englishmen the most appealing, confessing that after their company she found it hard "to readapt to American men" who she said "lacked the subtlety, the suave polish . . . of the men one meets in London society."

And she moved amidst the most fashionable and intellectual of them, frequenting the same drawing rooms as George Bernard Shaw, then the brilliant theater critic, Aubrey Beardsley, Henry James, Richard Le Gallienne, and the young Winston Churchill. For lovers she tended to prefer non-literary figures, and it was said she acquired a new one for writing each book; he served as a stimulus to creativity, and when the book was done she discarded him, often quite precipitously. But unlike George Sand, with whom she was sometimes compared, she did not seek to manipulate her lovers, any more than she permitted them to manipulate her.

Only rarely did she permit emotion to sway her. After settling in England, one New York beau had persistently courted her by mail, pleading for her to return and marry him. She found herself romantically crossing the ocean, anticipating his kisses — only to discover at their reunion that he "didn't interest me in the least." She quickly exited on the pretext of being needed in California. As a widow, flight was her usual method of severance, replacing the means she had used as a young married matron, which had been to warn an unwanted admirer that George was considering challenging him to a duel.

On another occasion while on a visit to San Francisco, she inspired a throbbing infatuation in a married man and discovered she reciprocated his ardor. There were clandestine meetings and long agonizings over what was to be done about their implacable love. But one day she packed her suitcase and hied to a resort hotel on the ocean near Fort Ross. She had thought to nurse her broken heart, but unlike her heroine Weir in *What Dreams May Come*, she didn't feel the least suicidal. Indeed, she realized she was hugely enjoying her own melodrama. She later recalled: "I had never felt tragic before and might never have the opportunity again. I could enjoy it even

more off in the wilderness by myself and spilling it into a book."
She holed up in the hotel, and while the wintry wind howled
mournfully about the eaves, she wrote *The Doomswoman*, a
romantic novel of Spanish Era California.

And there was her brief romance with Ambrose Bierce. It
began when she wrote the popular California author compli-
menting his writings. Their correspondence grew more intimate, and during one of her trips West they arranged a tryst
in a small California town. But the handsome pair had scarcely
met when they broke into a stormy session precipitated by
their criticisms of each other's work. As the visit ended, when
he was walking her to an evening train, he apologized and
suddenly grew amorous, without noting the inappropriate spot
he had chosen to clasp her in his arms. As she gleefully related
it, "I threw back my head — well out of his reach — and laughed
gayly. 'The great Bierce!' I cried. 'Master of style! The god on
Olympus at whose feet pilgrims come to worship — trying to
kiss a woman by a pigsty!' The train steamed in at the moment.
He rushed me to it and almost flung me on board."

Her New York triumphs inclined her toward neither hearth
nor husband. Instead, her orbit widened. Now that she might
safely leave her New York and London interests in care of
agents she was free to indulge her travel whims. They carried
her, trailing trunks of gowns and crates of books, to Denmark,
to Germany, to France, to Belgium, to Hungary, to Switzerland,
to Italy. She followed a practice of writing each book in a different country; after completing her research and assembling
source books, she boarded a train or an ocean liner for the place
she had been wanting to see and there set up her studio. Of
Continental men, she found she preferred the Viennese.

On alternate years she made a trip back to San Francisco.
Her pretty, dark-haired daughter Muriel, a devout Catholic,
attended a succession of convent schools. Following the death
of her grandfather, Gertrude had assumed the support of her
mother and her half-sisters, both of whom made unfortunate
first marriages and obtained divorces.

During her California visits she nearly always collected
material for a book. In this way she turned out a series of books

that gradually wove themselves into a panorama, depicting all periods of the state's history from early Spanish days into modern times. These included *Rezanov, The Splendid Idle Forties, The Doomswoman, A Daughter of the Vine* (a rewrite of *The Randolphs of Redwoods*), *The Californians, Transplanted, California: An Intimate History, The Horn of Life,* and *The House of Lee.* Once she returned East by way of Montana and took notes for the mining town novel *Perch of the Devil.* Chancing to be at home at the time of the 1906 earthquake, she made use of it as a background in two novels, *Ancestors* and *Sisters-in-law.*

On these visits to San Francisco she invariably created a stir with her stunning Paris wardrobe and sparkling Continental gossip. Her most frequent San Francisco escort was the rich, social bachelor James D. Phelan, who alternated as San Francisco mayor and United States Senator. At a luncheon for Senator Phelan at the St. Francis Hotel she caused a minor sensation by lighting a cigarette in an atmosphere hitherto polluted only by men.

She sampled the offerings of Europe's culture capitals with a hummingbird's restlessness but with a honeybee's industry. She was now turning out at least one book a year. At length, she found one European city sufficiently to her taste to make it her headquarters for several years. This was Munich, which appealed to her severally for its art and intellectual ferment, its stately beauty, its bracing air, and its proximity to her other favored zones of stimulation. Also the inveterate aristocrat in her was drawn to its proud, highly-strataed society. She took an apartment in the Kaulbach Strasse and furnished it with handsome Gothic furniture. Soon, as in London, she was frequenting the best drawing rooms, and for a time she was an ornament in regal circles. But when the Prince of Bavaria offered her, through his equerry, a dubious station in his court, she not only irreverently declined, but mirthfully recounted the overture about town. She was unceremoniously dropped from the Court Circular.

At last she quelled speculation by stating unequivocally in a press interview that she had no intention of marrying again.

"I prize liberty and freedom too much," she asserted "to sacrifice either to any man." In later life she commented on her decision not to remarry. "I was never tempted much . . . once or twice a little bit, but not much." She amplified, "I doubt if I have ever been really in love." She confided to intimates that she was truly happy only when writing. Upon completing a book, if a new idea did not present itself promptly she grew panicky, almost to the point of desperation. Once when suffering a writing block, she traveled to a French religious shrine to pray for an inspiration. When her French landlady asked if she had come to pray for a husband, Gertrude scoffed, "A husband! What is a husband compared to a book?"

Even her interest in male companionship diminishd over the years. She said she had discovered she wrote better without "that particular form of stimulation." The fact of the matter was that she felt superior to any man with whom she had come in close contact, with the possible exception of Alexander Hamilton, whom she came to idolize while researching his biography. Perhaps she regretted that their centuries did not coincide. She lamented to intimates that no matter how attractive a man might seem initially, he always turned out to harbor "some childish absurdity." Short on maternal feeling, she had no patience whatever with childish absurdities.

That she had come to view womankind as being generally superior to men was apparent in her writings. Her favorite theme as a mature writer was the greatness of women. Of course, none of her early heroines had been clinging vines; most had been astonishingly resilient women who coolly endured all manner of sudden catastrophe, from doomed fiancés to depleted coffers. But with the years her female protagonists progressed in character to paragons of nobility, brilliance and accomplishment. Around these dazzling suns, wan male satellites revolved in their uncertain orbits, most crippled by some fatal flaw.

Although the native habitats of these remarkable women range over two continents and they reach in time from before Christ to present day, all of them resemble the author in their independence, industry and honesty; each to one degree or another was an extension of Gertrude Atherton's personality. She seems to have posed to herself the questions: What if I were culturally deprived, or sexually frigid, or growing old, or saddled with an alcoholic lover, or were accused of murder? What would I do about it? She answers through the decisions and actions of her cool beauties (all were beauties, that is, except Hermia and she gains it through surgery).

Endowed with indomitable spirit, there is no obstacle they cannot surmount, no storm they cannot weather. In *Horn of Life,* when a socialite businessman loses the family fortune it is his level-headed daughter Lynn who puts things together again. The San Francisco matron of *Sleeping Fires* rescues a handsome journalist from the alcoholic hell into which he has emersed himself. In *Perch of the Devil,* Ida Compton, a gumchewing Montana hoyden, makes herself refined and wins back her husband from a cultured siren. Elegant Melton Abbey in *The Sophisticates* triumphs over the false accusation of murder and rescues her town from both cultural stagnation and financial debacle. The well-bred women of *The House of Lee* roll up their sleeves and rescue the family estate from the clutches of the Depression. Atherton heroines are quick to recognize scientific discoveries and are not afraid to tap them. In *Black Oxen* the fascinating Countess Zattiany attains an astonishing rejuvenation via the then fashionable Steinach treatment of hormone stimulation (which therapy the author herself underwent in the course of researching the book). And in the Freudian novel *The Crystal Cup* Gita obtains medical correction of her frigidity which had caused her to inflict upon an admirer "an abraided shin, a scratch across his cheek, and a loosened front tooth which sent him cursing out of her presence."

Collective accomplishments by groups of women also inspired Atherton books. In *The White Morning* she depicted the sacrificing German women of the 19th century German revolution; and in *The Living Present* her subject was the French women who braved World War I trenches to minister to the wounded. The English suffragette movement was celebrated in *Julia France and Her Times,* whose heroine, burdened by a lunatic husband attained fame as a militant leader.

Her series of novels set in ancient times were demonstrations that women have always possessed the potential for greatness. She mined Fifth Century Greek history in *The Jealous Gods* to show Tig to be every bit the equal of her husband Alcibiades; and in *The Immortal Marriage* she depicts Aspasia not only as the brilliant partner of Pericles but elevates her from the position of courtesan, to which history has assigned her, to that of morganic wife. The surpassing excellencies of her fictional Roman heroine Pomponia in *The Golden Peacock* moved the New York *Times* reviewer to complain: "The extraordinarily beautiful, extra-ordinarily intelligent, extra-ordinarily strong-willed and completely self-satisfied Pomponia is too domineering, too much the superwoman . . ."

But the author's legions of women readers did not think Pomponia too much the superwoman. For them Pomponia held credulity; they could readily identify with her, having graduated up to Pomponia via a long procession of assertive Atherton heroines. Each had spurned to be relegated to her assigned supporting role, claiming the right to think and act for herself, to participate, if she wished, in business, politics, in intellectual affairs. In short, each refused to recognize the traditional dominion of the male. If there had been a certain validity to the charge that Mrs. Atherton's early heroines were atypically aggressive and emancipated they were to become less and less atypical as her books multiplied and their readership grew.

And they did phenomenally. Since her first book tottered uncertainly off the press in 1888, she had been turning out titles non-stop at the rate of at least one a year. Many of them were runaway best sellers. Before she was through she would pile up 56 books in all. Besides her books she ground out a steady stream of articles and stories for newspapers and magazines, and most of these too waved the banner of sexual equality. The impact of her feminist message was not approached by any other fiction writer, and she was the most read woman writer of her times. Later on, the critics would differ on her position as a novelist (their verdicts ranging from mediocre to first-rate), but they would agree in according her a major role in changing women. By creating alluring models, instead of by exhortation, she subtly released her readers from their Victorian fetters and moulded them into the modern woman.

How did the author confer plausibility upon her audacious superwomen, then nearly as remote from everyday reality as science fiction heroines are today? How did she persuade submerged housewives and hemmed-in spinsters and thwarted professional women to believe in her Hermias and Gitas to the extent of emulating them and breaking their own bonds? Partly through the power and intensity of her writing. Her readers' doubts bounced against her grand authority and were absorbed by it. Every woman might fulfill herself, she bountifully promised. Every woman can!

Another reason women trustingly fell in step behind Atherton heroines was their seeming contemporaneity. Gertrude Atherton was a veritable antenna for detecting up-to-the-minute topicality — fashions, fads, ideas, phobias, current problems. Not only could she divine what was the very latest, but very often she anticipated it. An Atherton heroine wore the very latest cloche hat, danced the latest dance steps, sipped the latest cocktail, and spoke the latest swear words and Freudian lingo. Thus it followed that if the girl in the cloche hat decided not to bear children, or to drive an ambulance at the war front, or to go into business, or to propose to the man of her choice (the one who gave her her head), then she must be acting contemporarily. Even Pomponia had her imitators, for despite her buskins and drapery she was essentially a flapper.

But no less a beacon was the author herself — a shining example of a woman who was her *own* woman. She was legendary both for her hard-fought battle for literary recognition and for her prodigious output. Even in 1917 a literary critic, marveling at how she weathered controversy and at her undiminished productivity, called her "one of the indestructible comets." Yet, her career was not yet at its midway point; more than thirty full years remained ahead. Her whirlpool of energy spilled over into public affairs. During World War I she did relief work on the battlefront for which she received the decoration of the French Légion d'Honneur. She plunged exuberantly into American political campaigns, making scores of impassioned speeches on behalf of presidential candidates Woodrow Wilson and Al Smith. She worked tirelessly for Women's suffrage, serving as a California officer of the movement. She was a public figure on two continents. The literary critic Henry James Forman wrote following her death: "I still recall the searching scrutiny with which every woman looked at her in any house or gathering she entered. She was the talk of the nation's women."

Her perennial youth was likewise the focus of wonder. She looked fully 20 years younger than she was, and with time's passage her friends could detect no slackening of her pace. At 77, she underwent a second series of glandular treatments, but since that therapy is now generally discredited, the benefit to her probably was merely psychological. The only perceptible alteration in her life style was a diminution of travel and a gradual settling down in San Francisco.

There she shared with her widowed daughter Muriel and a bachelor grandson a handsome mansion in the fashionable Pacific Heights district. In an imposing drawing room she reopened her literary salon, interrupted more than a half century before, although with a new membership, predominently the city's younger literati, whom she had come to prefer to her own age group. She presided over it with elegance, wit and consummate assurance. With the outbreak of World War II, she and several other writers operated a club for sailors. Literary figures who visited San Francisco called on her to pay their respects, and the national press, all controversy long forgotten, habitually referred to her, to her disgust, as "the dowager of American letters."

Of course, it never crossed her mind to retire. The books of her final years returned to her theme of depicting California through its various historic periods. She kept in the thick of contemporary life with her plain-spoken articles and letters-to-the-editor. When in her mid-eighties, she eagerly accepted an assignment from a San Francisco newspaper to write a series of articles on lower-level night life. She breezed through the portals of emporiums of doubtful character, interviewing bartenders, bar girls, bouncers and frowsy habitues, whom she chronicled in colorful detail and San Francisco followed with an avidity that recalled the sensation of *The Randolphs of Redwoods.*

On her ninetieth birthday, immaculately coiffed, brightly rouged on cheeks and lips, and wearing a stunning new gown of blue velvet, she presided with sharp-eyed gaiety at an afternoon reception in her honor. San Francisco's then Mayor Roger Lapham was there to present her a gold medal. After accepting with pleasure, she flirtatiously requested an "official kiss" and received two, on cheek and forehead. She had recently completed her fifty-sixth book, *My San Francisco, a Wayward Biography,* a witty, highly-personal description of contemporary San Francisco. Already, she had begun another, a historical novel set against a background of California quicksilver mining. That morning, exactly as she had done for years, she had risen at 6:30 o'clock, brewed a cup of coffee on a hotplate and sat down to turn out her habitual 1,000 words a day before lunch. Her fifty-seventh book was not quite complete when, seven months later, on June 14, 1948, she died in a Palo Alto hospital from the effects of a paralytic stroke.

Women's lot concerned her until the end. Her last publication was a letter to the editor of the San Francisco *News* nominating Eleanor Roosevelt for president. "It is high time a woman was President of the United States," she insisted. However, an obsessive worry of her last years was not that women would lose their fight for equal rights, but that they would muff it. Although she saw women as still being "far from the center" of power, she was convinced they were striding to victory (this was before the onset of feminist apathy in the 1950s). Indeed, she believed they had already reached "the outermost suburbs of sex equality," and she was proud of her part in getting them there. But she worried that women, smoldering after centuries of abuse, would not stop short of revengeful domination over men — thereby sowing the seeds of reaction and a return to inequality. In her writings and public statements she insisted that human happiness required freedom for both men and women. As a warning, she pointed to the example of an early Egyptian society in which women pressed their drive for independence to the point of subjugating males. Husbands were shunted to a domestic role of cooking, sewing, and child-watching; women returned to their professions on the third day after childbirth and the father went to bed with the baby to keep it warm. But during the fifth century, B. C., those abused, resentful spouses, egged on by travelers from patriarchal societies, rebelled, threw off tyrannical female rule and regained the upper hand.

Gertrude Atherton early knew the pain of sexist repression, knew the cost of strength required to escape it (strength some women do not have to spend), knew its scars — the scars that made her wary of emotional commitment and relegated her, despite her splendid professional triumphs and her surpassing benefit to women, to largely an observer role in human relations. She knew the full cost of the destructive battle of the sexes and urged that it end at last with true sexual equality.

"The time will come when the efforts of the most energetic and determined will be realized," she predicted; "and it will be for them to hold the scales even — permanently even — to achieve a happiness that has eluded both men and women since the world began."

Gertrude Atherton midway in her seventy-year-long career as a novelist. (—Bancroft Library)

Sarah Winnemucca in the tribal costume she wore for her speaking appearances in the East. (— *Nevada State Historical Society*)

Sarah Winnemucca

Sagebrush Princess with a Cause

LUCKILY FOR THE FIRST white trappers who ventured into the Great Nevada Basin the Paiute tribe had preserved a myth their chief deemed most important. The world started, it said, with a beautiful forest where dwelled contentedly two boys and two girls — two dark and two white. One day they quarreled bitterly. The angry dark couple strode off in one direction, the angry white couple in the other. The white couple vanished, but one day, promised the myth, they would return. Chief Truckee said the pale hairy men who had been sighted in his territory were the Paiutes' "long-lost white brothers." Joyfully he sought to welcome them, but the trappers fled in haste, put off by the sight of the old chief's jagged front teeth, which he had shattered when chewing a bone. Happily, another pair of trappers let him approach their campfire. There were smiles and handshakes all around, and the trappers presented Truckee the gift of a tin plate, which so delighted him that thereafter he wore it upon his head. Later, his joy overflowed when John Fremont took him on as guide. After he returned home, ever so often the old chief would don the portion of an Army uniform he owned and would sing feelingly "The Star Spangled Banner."

The Princess Sarah Winnemucca, daughter of Chief Winnemucca and herself a chief later in life, most of all was old Truckee's granddaughter. His admiration for white people was the most formative influence in her life. Sarah walked with shining faith toward the white world, and she did not meet personal rebuff there, for she was strikingly prepossessing with her old-gold skin, oval symmetrical face, luminous eyes, and graceful, lively manner. She attended a white school, gave herself a white name, adopted white clothes and customs and took two white husbands.

But in her heart Sarah remained a Paiute. Though she but slowly relinquished her faith that white men meant to do right by Indians, relinquish it she did in the face of mounting injustices toward her people. Unhesitatingly, she trained on those injustices a well of indignation, a keen intelligence, surpassing courage, and when it served her, a scorching temper. Sarah carried her protests to the highest authorities she could locate and when public officials failed to act, she courted public opinion, declaiming eloquently from lecture platforms in stunning Indian costumes. When the opportunity came she did not hesitate to turn authoress. Her candid book *Life Among the Paiutes: Their Wrongs and Claims* tossed up a storm in the nation's capital. Sarah made an imprint upon history and upon her times and left her tribe a tradition of peaceable contention that serves them to this day.

Sarah's birth date is not known for certain. She herself estimated it to have been in 1844, the year Fremont encountered the tribe. But that guess was made in middle age and vanity may have entered into her calculation. She was christened Somit-tone, the Paiute word for shell flower. More appropriately, her name might have been drawn from that other source of names for Paiute girl babies, colorful rocks. There was a touch of flint about Sarah.

She was but a toddler and her sister still in her cradle board when Chief Truckee returned from his travels with Fremont. The old chief was brimming over with talk about how wonderful white people were — how clever, how well-equipped. And how much they knew! Little Sarah was one of his most attentive listeners. She was thrilled by his plan to move the Paiutes to California so they might live near their white brothers. Some Paiutes, however, were not so sure, among them Sarah's father, Chief Truckee's son-in-law. During the chief's absence they had had some glimpses of whites that were far from reassuring. Watching from heights and thickets they had covertly observed the passage of emigrant trains, and while they admired the "houses that moved," they were apprehensive of the "big sticks" the white men carried. Neighboring tribes said those sticks could make thunder and lightning and could kill an Indian. Even more frightening were the rumors that one group of white people had been trapped in deep snow in the mountains and after running out of food they had eaten one another. Paiute mothers coaxed exemplary behavior from their offspring by threatening to feed them to the white people.

Sarah was relieved to hear her grandfather pooh-pooh the dreadful story. The Paiutes and their white brothers would be friends, he promised; moreover, hunting was better on the other side. No Paiute could lightly spurn that. The tribe was then encamped at grassy Humboldt Sink, where the Humboldt River mysteriously sunk into the ground, the place the Paiutes returned to periodically. But mostly they kept on the move, combing the Basin's alkaline wastes for edibles. Fowl and game were rarities, large game almost nonexistent; fish was available only during the spawning season. Their usual menu was pine nut mush, pieced out with roots and seeds, even insects. Mush was boiled up in a crudely-woven basket by dumping hot stones into it. All the roving and sifting for seeds left the Paiutes no time for cultural pursuits; they had no pretty pots, colorful baskets, or elaborate dances. So preoccupied were Paiutes with their stomachs they even eschewed warfare. In the hierarchy of tribes, the Paiutes were relegated to the role of poor relations — except by the impoverished Washoes, who were a notch below them.

Sarah listened anxiously to the arguments. Some Paiutes felt they had nothing to lose by giving California a try, while others were reluctant to live near white people and their dangerous sticks. But the old chief percolated optimism until thirty families agreed to accompany him. He insisted on taking his daughter, Sarah's mother, and her four children, even though Sarah's father refused to go. Upon departing, Truckee appointed Winnemucca chief of the tribal majority who remained in Nevada.

Sarah found the journey to California in the spring of 1847 almost too thrilling to endure. It afforded her first look at white people, who frightened her at first. With their pale eyes and beards they reminded her of owls, and she associated them with the scary hoots she heard at night. The Paiutes' progress was assisted by a letter of introduction provided by Fremont. When handed to white people encountered along the trail, it had a magical effect; scowls promptly changed to smiles and gifts. Sarah ate her first slice of bread, melted a lump of sugar on her tongue, and sipped carefully from a white cup.

Chief Truckee led his awed procession past the new American settlements at Sacramento and Stockton, on to a large cattle ranch on the San Joaquin River. There the Paiutes were accorded a plot to establish a camp. Paiute men were given jobs herding cattle in the foothills beyond the ranch, while some of the women found domestic work.

Chubby, pretty Sarah cautiously explored the fringes of the mysterious white world, attracting smiles and indulgence. A white woman who recently had lost a daughter Sarah's age visited their tent and gave her child's clothing to Sarah's mother. Sarah thought the clothes magnificent, but as soon as the donor was out of sight her mother made a bonfire of them. Every Paiute knew possessions of the dead must be buried with them, else burned. That was disappointing. But Sarah was appeased by the treat that followed — a peek inside the rancher's big stone house. Especially enchanting was the staircase leading to the upper floor and the glistening dining table with chairs upholstered in red. She thought the chairs "the most beautiful things I had ever seen," and she couldn't resist hoisting her small rump onto one of them, against her mother's express instructions. She now understood her grandfather's admiration for white people: there was no end to their marvels.

The Paiute men generally were more content in California than the women. Their small wages seemed bountiful and their fears of rifles subsided. But the women lived in a constant state of apprehension. They worried their men might be ambushed in the hills, and they worried white men might steal their daughters. They complained and sobbed and wouldn't resign themselves. So when spring came and snow had melted in the Sierra passes, Chief Truckee led his people back home.

They returned to find the Paiutes greatly agitated. Recently a strange sickness had spread through the tribe, and some had died. Historians have identified it as cholera, transmitted by flies from a wagon train, but the nervous Paiutes believed whites had poisoned the river. The old chief called for calm and reason. Why would the whites spoil their own water supply? Something else had brought the evil. But he did wonder why the whites had set fire to the tribe's food pits, their store of nuts and dried berries. Why would they do that to their peaceful brothers? The truth was that by the time the emigrants reached Paiute territory they were slightly crazed by weariness and unable to differentiate between fractious and peaceable Indians.

That summer, traffic on the emigrant trail multiplied astonishingly. Fond as she was of white people, Sarah found the noisy, dust-raising throng terrifying. Of course, the California Gold Rush had gotten under way, and the wagon trains were swelled by throngs of swaggering adventurers bound for the diggings on the Sierra's western slopes. The gold-fevered men were too impatient to be friendly to passing Indians; they were more inclined to take pot shots at them. Chief Truckee prudently withdrew his people into the mountains.

Meanwhile, another white invasion was taking place. Mormon farmers were spilling over from Utah, claiming tillable farmland, and more often than not what they fenced in was a favorite Paiute seed and root gathering area. But being highly vulnerable, the Mormons took pains to be friendly with the Indians, and the Paiutes, feeling uncertain and insecure, responded gratefully. Some Paiute men found work on Mormon farms and at so-called Mormon Station (later Genoa), a Mormon trading post that catered to Overland travelers.

Old Truckee could think of nothing better for his granddaughters than an opportunity to learn white ways. The chief became friendly with Major William Ormsby, a tall, amiable Virginian who managed a stage line at Mormon Station, and before long Sarah and her sister Elma were thrilled to find themselves part of the Ormsby household playing with the Ormsby children. The little Indian girls, used to a tent made of

grass and limbs and to wearing dresses woven of leaves, were
delighted to live in a warm frame house, wear long dresses of
printed callico, and learn to speak and write and sing in English. They discarded their Indian given names and chose
English ones. The chief's granddaughters were affectionately
accepted as part of the bustling settlement. Years later Sarah
could remember the names of the settlement's twenty-eight
householders; and recalled that the Mormen men each had
three or four wives, while most of the non-Mormons had none
at all.

But in later years, if in a dark mood, Sarah might brood
upon another memory of her Mormon years. The settlement
had been outraged when a white storekeeper and his companion were found dead on a mountain trail, their bodies
pierced with Washoe arrows. The Mormons had their Paiute
workers deliver an ultimatum to the Washoes to surrender the
killers or risk war. At length the woebegone Washoes delivered
three young men, but the youths vehemently pleaded innocent,
insisting they had been sent only because the tribe feared being
demolished. Sarah overheard the Washoes' pitiful plea, believed
them, and told Mrs. Ormsby the men were telling the truth.
In desperation the young Washoes broke from their captors
and were shot down in flight. Not long after, two white men
confessed to the slaying and to setting arrows in the wounds
to shift the blame. Sarah and Elma were visiting their parents
when the mistake was learned. They did not return to the
settlement.

Precocious Sarah was the apple of her grandfather's eye
during his dotage. Chief Truckee never tired of listening to
her chatter in English and sing Mormon songs. But soon he
fell ill — some said of a lung ailment, others said of a tarantula
bite — and the signal fires were lit on the mountain tops, summoning all Paiutes to come pay their last respects. As the old
chief lay dying with all his family grouped sorrowfully around
him, he sent to the settlement for a Mormon friend named
Snyder. Sarah and Elma listened intently as their grandfather
told Snyder that his California rancher friend had promised
to arrange for his granddaughters' education. He asked Snyder

to take them to California. After that, he appointed Sarah's father main chief of the Paiutes, counseling him, "Do your duty as I have done — to your people and to your white brothers." Then his eyes closed and they thought he was dead, but he opened them again and asked to be buried with Fremont's letter of passage laid upon his breast, and to the regret of future historians that is exactly what was done with that intriguing document.

This time it was no owl-fearing child who crossed the Sierra, but a composed young girl on her way to boarding school. As she and Elma jostled westward in a stagecoach with Mr. Snyder, they passed the white people's latest wonder, the Pony Express, the rider crouched low over his horse, his saddle hung with letter pouches. In Sacramento, their grandfather's friend, Mr. Scott, was waiting to escort them on the next leg of their journey, a thrilling steamboat trip downriver to San Francisco. A day of sightseeing in that astonishing place included a visit to Chinatown. Like any white child Sarah stared increduously at the pig-tailed, trousered women hobbling on tiny feet. Had anybody told her they shared a common ancestry, she wouldn't have believed it.

At the sleepy country town of San Jose, south of San Francisco, Mr. Scott left the little girls in the care of nuns at St. Mary's Sister of Charity School. The black-habited nuns conducted their convent school in a dilapidated thick-walled adobe structure that was part of Mission San Jose. The mission had been built in 1797 by Indian labor, and once 1800 Christianized Indians had lived and worked there under the padres. But in 1860, the two little Paiutes were the only Indians among the convent students, most of them children from well-to-do white families.

Sarah and Elma were enrolled and began their classes. That much is known, but the length of their stay and the level of their education remains obscure. In her book Sarah claimed that they were turned out after only three weeks because "wealthy parents" objected to their children going to school with Indians. But earlier she had told a Nevada newspaper reporter that she had remained in the convent school three years, while on another occasion she regaled an interviewer with details of attending a "select school at San Jose," where she had especially enjoyed her instruction in fine needlework. The three-year version was probably the true one, for Sarah sometimes exaggerated when it suited her. Certainly, her formal education was not extensive. While she spoke correct English, she pronounced somewhat hesitantly, and her spelling was often atrocious.

Whether Sarah returned home in the early or middle 1860s, she found her tribe in trouble. Now it was a silver rush that buffeted them. Forces generated by an ore bonanza flowing from a hill near Virginia City had shunted Paiutes onto a reservation, or relegated them to grim camps on the fringe of the ore fields. They were poverty-stricken, angry and so unruly Chief Winnemucca could no longer control them. Sarah was shocked. What had come over her people?

A most humiliating collapse of their independence and status. As more and more of their food-gathering places were overrun by whites, they had been reduced to begging menial jobs or handouts at the settlements. Many Paiute women worked as domestics, and male employers often seduced them into concubinage. Paiute men had meekly suffered the loss of land and edibles, but they did not peacefully surrender their women. They paid back with raids on white men's provisions and cattle. White men took down their guns. Indian-white clashes finally culminated in a battle near Pyramid Lake in which both sides lost scores of men, including popular Major Ormsby. The upshot was that the Paiutes were herded onto a hastily-created reservation at Pyramid Lake. But as their corral lacked a means of livelihood and since they were not actually fenced in, the Paiutes began trickling back to the setttlements.

Sarah was then around twenty and as eager as any recent student to apply wisdom learned in school. She joined her father, Chief Winnemucca, where he was camped near Virginia City, worriedly trying to keep the Paiutes out of trouble. The stocky chief wore a four-inch bone through his nose that made him look ferocious, but actually he was mild and peaceable. He was also inept. His nephew Numaga, not he, had commanded the Paiutes during the scrimmage at Pyramid Lake. The sad truth, apparent even to his loving daughter, was that the Paiutes in their time of greatest crisis had a chief lacking in both brilliance and leadership.

Sarah confidently stepped into the vacuum. Unlike her sister Elma, who scorned Indian ways and had remained in California to live with a white family, Sarah, for all her fascination with whites, was a prideful Paiute. She wasn't above sharing a bowl of pine nut mush with the humblest Paiute family, and she enjoyed squatting on the ground for a session of Paiute gambling, a noisy game played with sticks. Nonetheless, in her earnest view, the Paiutes were now in the wrong: they were behaving disgracefully with their stealing and raiding. She set about persuading them to act decently. The Paiutes listened respectfully to Sarah but they argued that the whites had acted worse than they. Sarah wasn't persuaded. They must learn to work for a living as white people did, she urgently counseled; then everything would turn out all right. To set an example, she applied herself to the needlework skills the nuns had taught her and peddled her handiwork door to door in the white settlements.

While exhorting the Paiutes to behave themselves, Sarah appealed also to the whites. Silver had swiftly elevated Nevada to statehood with a new capital at Carson City. Sarah, accompanied by her father and brother Natchez, traveled to Carson City to ask the governor to help smooth relations between whites and Indians, and to eject the white squatters who had carved off portions of the reservation almost as soon as it was created. Sarah, dressed in her convent best, her father and brother wearing secondhand Army officer uniforms with epaulets, were courteously received by Governor Nye, the same who was immortalized by Bret Harte in "The Heathen Chinee." Governor Nye assured them of his sympathy and promised aid. Sarah came away much impressed with the handsome governor.

Some time later the trio undertook another mission, making the long trip to San Francisco to call on General Irvin McDowell of the United States Army. At his formidable headquarters at the Presidio, they reported the Paiutes' problems and appealed to him to refrain from sending troops against them, as had been done after the fighting at Pyramid Lake. The general was respectful and amiable, but entirely noncommittal. The general's indifference came on top of indications that Governor Nye had forgotten *his* commitments. The Winnemuccas were in a somber mood during their journey home.

Sarah's dream that the Indians would find salvation by emulating whites soon was punctured further. A cavalry unit, summoned by whites to hunt down cattle thieves, came upon an Indian camp on a small lake and fired upon it indiscriminately, killing eighteen persons. It was a fishing party, mostly elderly Paiutes, women and children, and among the dead was Sarah's youngest brother. Not long after, her Uncle John, who had cleared bottom land on the Truckee River, was killed by a white man who wanted his land.

Sarah was grieved and she was shocked. To get away from white people, she left the settlement and went to live with the reservation Paiutes, whom Chief Winnemucca had left in charge of Natchez. But a white agent, appointed by the Indian Bureau, was the real power there. Theoretically, tribal government was to be left intact, with the agent on hand to see to the Indians' well-being, but with the Indian Bureau two thousand miles away, the agent knew he had a free hand to exploit them. That he would do so was foregone, for it was common knowledge that agentships were obtained through bribery.

Sarah was astonished to find "their" agent operating a humming, diversified business. He was selling reservation timber to a sawmill, had leased grazing rights to white cattlemen and operated a retail store stocked with provisions the government had shipped for free distribution. He purchased the Paiutes' fish and game for a pittance and sold them to whites, holding his suppliers in thralldom by keeping them in debt. Natchez, but hazily versed in Indian rights, was not certain where the agent had transgressed. Sarah was better informed, and she voiced loud complaint. When the agent ignored her, she threatened to report him, even though she didn't know to whom.

When the agent began selling gunpowder, which Indians were forbidden to use, Sarah predicted trouble. It wasn't long in coming. One day a Paiute wandered off the reservation with some gunpowder and was halted by soldiers who searched him and seized the contraband. When the Indian resisted search, he was shot dead. Paiute anger exploded over what looked to them like a trap; a government man had sold gunpowder to an Indian; a government man had then killed the Indian for possessing it.

Sarah and Natchez learned of a plot to kill the agent, and they knew that much as they despised him, they would have to save his life. His death would spark war. Surreptitiously, they called on him and warned him. Then they rushed to halt the plotters at a ford, and made them listen to reason. But they had scarcely caught their breath when word came that two white men had been shot by brothers of the dead Paiute. This was just the opening for which some whites had been waiting. An excited delegation, including the Indian agent, rode upstate to Fort McDermitt to ask the military to ride down and trounce the Indians for once and all.

At Pyramid Lake, worried Sarah and Natchez could only await the outcome. As it happened, the fort commander had heard of their earnest mediations and decided to have a talk with them before making a decision. He sent one of his cavalrymen to summon them to the fort. Sarah dipped a stick in fish blood and scratched out a reply that they would come. She recalled of their anxious ride across the barren plains: "We went like the wind, never stopping til we got there."

On that day Sarah found her career. During her audience with the fort commander, not as an interpreter for her father, but as a Paiute leader in her own right, there in a building dedicated to armed battle, she discovered her own kind of fight. And she put Natchez quite in the shade, where he would remain. A trim, compact figure in a dark waistcoat and a long flared skirt, her black hair sleek on her shoulders, she sat poised before her interrogator and her adversaries and gave an impassioned account of the trouble and the abuses which provoked it. And before she was through she had turned the issue quite around — from a white grievance into an Indian grievance. The convinced commander promised to send provisions to the hungry Paiutes, and further to send troops to shield them from attack.

Irony was ever present in government Indian policy with its parsimonious handouts to a people who until recently had been lords of the land — presents of blankets in exchange for their winter campsites, the gift of a reservation that was really a corral. Sarah's success at Fort McDermitt spawned further irony. After the delivery of three wagonloads of provisions to the Paiutes had quelled their fear of the military, Sarah and Natchez pressed further. They negotiated an agreement whereby the Paiutes might leave the reservation and their gouging agent and occupy a campsite adjoining Fort McDermitt. The fort which had been constructed to protect white settlers from the Indians now offered the Indians refuge from the whites.

Sarah's hopes soared again. Things were looking up for the Paiutes, who now occupied neat rows of tents on the fringe of the military base. And such marvelous tents — canvas ones allotted by the commander. Daily at dawn, rations were distributed to each family head. Sarah assisted in the busy sunrise ritual, it being part of the duties of her first paying job, that of camp interpreter. She won the $65-a-month position on her merits, being conversant in English, Spanish and three Indian dialects.

With the commander's approval, Sarah and Natchez made trips to contact scattered bands of Paiutes and invite them to the fort. Singing the praises of the canvas tents and the daily rations, they were eminently successful; even Chief Winnemucca rode into camp with his retinue. The fort's Paiute population swelled to 900. The Army had decided that feeding the Indians would cost less money and trouble than constantly dealing with Indian-White skirmishes. Occasional work assignments were handed out — cattle-herding and woodcutting for the men, domestic tasks for the women.

Life passed smoothly, yet not entirely to the satisfaction of the chief. He disapproved of the way the soldiers flirted with young Paiute women. The chief was firm set against interracial romance, but he was powerless to halt it, even in his own family. When they moved to the fort, Natchez asked the commander to order his soldiers not to talk to his sister. For her part Sarah affected a cold, impersonal air to discourage male familiarity. Soon she was forgetting to wear it. She found herself strongly attracted to the friendly young soldiers with their flashing smiles and their talk of places she had read about in school. For their part, they were fascinated with the comely princess, and she had her pick of the officers. After her duties she rode out with one, then another, across the plains or along the shady river bank.

During her second year at the fort, Sarah showed a marked preference in riding companions. She had fallen in love with Lt. Edward Bartlett, a handsome young cavalry officer from New York state. His gaiety and impulsive ways delighted her, and she probably was impressed by his claimed relationship to General John Schofield, commander of the Division of the Pacific. The lieutenant was equally taken with Sarah. But to Sarah's family, she couldn't have made a worse choice. They well remembered Bartlett from a brief stint of duty at the reservation, where one night he got drunk and rode about shouting wildly and firing a pistol until forcibly subdued. Sarah remained deaf to her father's admonitions, and early in 1871 when Bartlett received a transfer to Salt Lake City she eloped with him. A new Nevada law which prohibited marriage between those of different race delayed their wedding until they reached Utah.

The couple had lived together only a few weeks when one day Natchez appeared unannounced at Sarah's door and told her their father had ordered her to come home. She went without protest; she had already found her husband out. After returning to Nevada she spoke bitterly to a newspaper reporter of the man she had decided to divorce: "He was nothing but a drunkard. He kept continually sending to me for money after my return home, and I supplied him as long as I could; but what makes me now so bitter against him is the fact that he finally sold all my jewelry. I never want to see him again."

But Sarah was never one to look backward. Having ventilated her resentment, she picked up the former threads of her life. Returning to the fort, she worked for a time as a hospital matron, but soon she was spending most of her time mediating disputes between the soldiers and Paiutes. The sympathetic commander had been transferred, and his replacement was a young officer who looked upon the Indian camp as a nuisance. When some angry Paiutes decided to return to Pyramid Lake, Sarah chose to accompany them. Not long after, the other Paiutes followed: the fort had cut off their rations.

Sarah saw now that the fort experience had only been a side trip that postponed real solution. Clearly, handouts were not to be relied on; moreover, they bred shiftlessness. She returned to her former conviction that the Indians would have to acquire the white habit of earning. And their best chance to earn, she thought, lay in farming. Of course, they would first have to learn how. Back at the fort she had once written a letter to the Commissioner of Indian Affairs in Washington asking the government to provide farming instruction for the Indians. Now she repeated the plea, further urging that the Paiutes be assigned individual farm plots.

Optimistically, she set out to enlist the help of the new agent, a Mr. Bateman; she considered it promising that he was an ordained Baptist minister. The government, plagued with complaints of crooked Indian agents was putting churchmen in charge of the Indians. But "Brother" Bateman turned a deaf ear to Sarah's project. While he was anxious to teach the Bible to the Paiutes, he had no interest in teaching them to farm. Sarah discovered he had leased the reservation's bottom land to white farmers and had renewed the cattlemen's grazing leases. She hastily departed for Virginia City to air complaints to the public and the press. Mr. Bateman retaliated by accusing Natchez of threatening him and had him thrown into jail. Sarah got Natchez released, and they both returned to the reservation without any illusions about their protector.

Still visualizing the reservation as an Eden of tilled fields, Sarah sought to persuade the Paiutes to attempt farming on their own. But they were scarcely more enthusiastic than their agent. They were full of excuses: they lacked tools; the agent might seize the crops for himself; they had heard of a tribe that had broken soil with sticks and planted expensive seed only to have a grasshopper scourge devour it.

Undaunted, Sarah persuaded Natchez to accompany her to San Francisco, where she wangled an appointment with the formidable General Schofield at the Presidio. To Sarah's plea that he help agriculturize the Paiutes, the general intoned that such matters were quite outside his jurisdiction. He suggested that they see their United States Senator John Percival Jones. They traveled to Gold Hill, Nevada, and succeeded in obtaining the politician's ear. Senator Jones, whose absorbing interest was national silver policy, listened courteously, expressed sympathy for the Paiutes, and with an air of largess contributed $20 toward their relief.

All Sarah reaped from her efforts to introduce farming at Pyramid Lake was a harvest of slander. The Reverend Bateman, having cultivated press channels of his own, had it published that she not only was a troublemaker, but was an imposter who falsely claimed to be a chief's daughter, when in fact she was a member of the lowly Digger tribe, and furthermore had had seven failed ventures into matrimony.

Sarah had discovered the peril of crossing the establishment. Nearing thirty, she was weary. She was exasperated with selfish white society and exasperated with her own people who seemed resigned to giving up. At loose ends she wandered north to visit her father, who was brooding at an Oregon hideaway. At this juncture, she might have chosen the most handsome of her father's braves and settled down to motherhood. But a job offer intervened. Sam Parish, the agent at Malheur Indian Reservation in Oregon learned of her arrival and sent a courier to offer her a job as interpreter. For Sarah the job lacked appeal, but her father, impressed with the salary, urged her to accept and promised to accompany her to Malheur with his band.

To Sarah's surprise, Sam Parish turned out to be what had seemed a contradiction in terms: a good Indian agent. Not only did he give his charges the provisions the government sent, but he agreed to try out Sarah's plan of assigning farm plots. When the land had been parceled out, he undertook to teach the Indians to farm. He hired the Paiutes at paid wages to build a dam, dig an irrigation ditch, and erect fences. Under

Sarah's determined prodding, the Paiutes set about becoming farmers with wonder and some zeal. Meanwhile, the agent's wife, assisted by Sarah, opened a school for the children, which so excited the squaws that they sat outside the windows to listen and to join in the singing.

The only threatening cloud was Oytes, the Paiute medicine man whose status had swelled on discontent. He was jealous of Parish and petulantly threw obstacles in his path. Sour Oytes not only discouraged the other Paiutes from working but forced them to give him their pay under threat of conjuring up a dreadful epidemic. Sarah could get nowhere with the man, but Sam Parish knew exactly what to do. Before the tribe he told Oytes, with Sarah translating, "I have $300. If you will let me shoot at you and my bolt won't go through your body the money is yours. You say bolts cannot kill you." Paling, Oytes said in a quavering voice, "Oh, my good father, don't kill me . . . I will do everything you say." Thereafter Oytes kept to his sand and potions.

When trouble came, it was not of Oytes' conjuring. It was rather the replacement of Parish with another agent. The stated reason was that the new agent was a practicing Christian, whereas Parish was not. The Indian's distress at losing their honest agent was matched by their alarm at the new appointee, a Mr. Rhinehart, who as operator of a store at Canyon City had cheated them and illegally sold them whiskey.

Sarah was furious. She got off a spate of protesting letters to government offcials. But there was no stopping the arrival of the dreaded Rhinehart, who swiftly made it clear the reservation belonged, not to Indians, but to the government, whose power he embodied. He also laid claim to the crops, permitting the farmers to keep but a portion. Under new policy the Indians would farm for him, wages to be paid in government provisions. Rhinehart moved in a flock of relatives who outfitted themselves from the government warehouse. Avid poker players all, they encouraged the Indians to gamble with them and soon were raking in all they owned.

In no time Sarah and Rhinehart were at loggerheads. She determinedly sought his removal by reporting him to every official she knew of. Rhinehart found out and treated her with contempt. One day as she delivered to him a vehement tribal complaint, Rhinehart shouted that if the Paiutes didn't like the way he ran things they could depart, and as for Sarah she could consider herself fired. Sarah stayed three weeks longer just to annoy him.

The Paiutes' exposure to the "practicing Christian" led to the greatest disaster yet for the beleaguered tribe and the most dramatic experience of Sarah's life — involvement in the fierce Bannock War of 1878. With Sarah gone, the Paiutes and their bewildered chief fell in thrall to Oytes who recklessly led them to a barren site down river. There, hungry and confused, they fell prey to the rampaging Bannock Indians who had embarked on a fierce last effort to route the white usurper. With the collusion of Oytes, the Bannocks seized the Paiutes' weapons and forced them to accompany them to their tribal stronghold.

Of these events Sarah knew nothing. While they were happening, she was rumbling across Idaho in a buckboard wagon bound, she supposed, for Washington, D. C., to demand Rhinehart's dismissal. In her pocket was $29.25 that her tribe had collected to finance her journey, and jostling with her were three white passengers. One was a widower, who soon would propose. But Sarah's sole interest in the trio was the $50 taxi fare she would collect upon depositing them in Silver City, Idaho, which amount together with the proceeds of the sale of her team and wagon was counted on to buy her an eastbound ticket on the Union Pacific.

The Bannock war dawned for Sarah when, jolting behind her team, she was halted by United States troops who suspected she might be hauling ammunition. She indignantly resisted their search. But when she learned of the Bannock's rampages and of their abduction of the Paiutes, she unhesitatingly sided with the whites. Sending her traveling companions on their way, she offered her services to the Army.

Her reputation being known, they were snapped up at once. Army scouts had reported the Bannocks to be massed in the Stein mountains, 223 miles away, across precipitous terrain. Sarah's formidable assignment, just refused by two Paiute men as too dangerous, was to steal into the Bannock camp, locate the Paiutes and persuade them to seize horses and escape with her to Fort Lyon. When Sarah expressed willingness to go alone, the two Paiute men were shamed into accompanying her. The reluctant pair and a letter identifying her as an Army messenger were her only protection, and the latter, far from being an asset had it fallen into Bannock hands, would have meant certain death.

She accomplished her mission in two days. Riding non-stop but for catnaps with her saddle for a pillow and her horse tethered to her wrist, she stole unnoticed in paint and blanket into the camp of the hostiles. She succeeded in slipping the Paiutes out during the suppertime bustle, only to be overtaken midway by the enraged Bannocks, who had been ordered to return with the heads of Sarah and her father. Half of the Paiutes were forced to return, but Sarah and her father were among the several hundred exhausted Paiutes who made it to Fort Lyon. Her daring feat put her into the ranks of American Indian heroines alongside Pocohontas and Sacajawea.

Later it would bring her a $500 reward, but more immediately it gained her another derring-do detail. The western field commander General O. O. Howard, much impressed with Sarah, chose her for his personal interpreter and guide during his campaign to vanquish the Bannocks. As angry as violated hornets after Sarah's raid, the Bannocks had resumed their forays. They led the Army on a grueling six-week chase up rugged peaks, through plunging canyons, over hot alkaline desert.

Sarah, who knew the territory better than any soldier, galloped about carrying dispatches between Army units. At night she read the Indian signal fires on distant mountains. After engagements she ministered to fallen Indians. But her greatest value was as a divining rod for Bannocks. The Army was constantly plagued by rumors that the Bannocks were in ambush and about to attack. General Howard would send for Sarah. She would gaze ahead and listen solemnly for an interval. Then with bold authority she would pinpoint the Bannocks 500 miles away, 200 miles away, or just around the bend. Once the troops were in a panic because scouts reported the Bannocks massed on an adjacent cliff. The officers, focusing their field glasses, confirmed that it was so. Squinting into the distance, Sarah burst out laughing. She saw at once that the Bannocks, to gain time, had employed the Indian trick of arranging rocks to resemble men.

During the last big battle that so routed and scattered the Bannocks that they never rallied again, Sarah proved herself the bravest of the scouts. Showing no fear, she moved constantly about the front lines gathering information, once going forward enough to recognize the detestable Oytes. Her acts of conspicuous daring were much reported by newspaper correspondents who followed the conflict on horseback. Composing their reports in rear-echelon safety, the newsmen had to depend largely on rumor, which accounted for the false report, blazoned in newspaper headlines, that Sarah had been killed. When she miraculously materialized before her grieving family, such was her father's relief and pride in his war heroine daughter that he conferred on her the title of chief, unprecedented for a woman.

For her bravery and for her staunch loyalty to the Americans, Sarah might reasonably have expected a largess of gratitude and consideration. Instead, she was cruelly duped. It was none of General Howard's doing; indeed he strongly opposed the sequel to the Bannock War, but was overruled. Sarah was totally unwary when she was informed that the Indian Bureau had decided to relocate the Paiutes at Malheur Reservation. Would Sarah use her influence to get them to go willingly? Sarah protested that the Paiutes' latest tribulations had started with bad treatment at Malheur. There was a new policy at Malheur, she was told. Much would be done for the Paiutes there; they had nothing to fear.

After Sarah had analyzed her doubts and rejected them, she relayed the proposal to her people. Alarm swept the camp. Those Paiutes who had been trapped with the Bannocks were especially fearful of returning north. Sarah encouraged calm. She said the Army had never lied to her, and it had promised her the Paiutes had nothing to fear. The proposal was debated vehemently. Those who favored it argued, "It's all right — Sarah approves." In the end the tribe split. Half of them volunteered to go to Malheur; the rest fled the fort to take their chances as fugitives.

Accompanying the northward trek, Sarah did not grow suspicious until the Paiutes were detained at Camp Harney. That Southern Oregon base was supposed to have been a brief rest stop. The delay puzzled Sarah, until she discovered with horror that the Paiutes were not being taken to Malheur, but would forcibly be marched to the Yakima Reservation in the Washington Territory. That was the place Indian war prisoners were incarcerated. The Indian Bureau had knuckled to the settlers, who wanted the Paiutes out of their way. The dread word Yakima spread pandemonium among the tribe. Some Paiutes, including women and children, made a wild dash for freedom, only to be dragged back by soldiers. Terrified, the Paiutes turned their wrath upon Sarah, accusing her of selling them out, even as she, anger boiling in her like lye, cursed the Army for double-crossing her.

Sarah's strident protests caused not a ripple in the official plans. Her tribesmen now despised her, yet she chose to share their fate. The trek to Yakima was made in January across wind-swept mountains through deep snow. Scantily clad, many Paiutes died from exposure; small children froze to death; mothers died in childbirth. When they arrived at bleak Yakima, the bedraggled throng was herded into unheated sheds. "Like so many horses or cattle," Sarah recorded bitterly.

Sarah did not go to the wilderness concentration camp to sit placidly in the snow. She quickly made herself a thorn in the side of the Indian agent, a falsely pious man who bade his charges address him as Father Wilbur. Father Wilbur alternated a campaign for souls with schemes for squeezing profit even from destitute prisoners. So constant and furious were Sarah's demands for the Paiutes — for heat, for clothes, for food, for blankets — she regained the confidence of her tribesmen. She even raised their hopes again. A few months after arriving, she received her $500 reward for her raid on the Bannocks. She vowed to use it traveling to seek relief for the prisoners.

But before departing, Sarah found a way to advertise the Paiutes' plight right there at Yakima. Father Wilbur had devoted much planning to a revival to be preached by an eminent bishop and attended by important visitors from the East. That spring, the Paiutes, through necessity, were going very nearly naked, and Father Wilbur took the precaution of asking them not to attend the revival. To Sarah this suggested possibilities. When the visitors arrived they found the tattered Paiutes camped before the agent's house, and daily Sarah marched her nude revue into the revival tent and seated them prominently. She departed Yakima feeling she was off to a good start.

General Howard may have planted the idea of fighting her cause through public lectures. After leaving Yakima, Sarah went to confer with him at Fort Vancouver, and from there she went straight to San Francisco. Sarah was nothing if not versatile. She stepped before an audience and began speaking like a veteran of the lecture circuit. Declaiming dramatically on the duplicity of the Indian Bureau and the rascality of Indian agents, she became the sensation of San Francisco. Everybody had to hear the fascinating Princess Winnemucca of Bannock War fame. Those who heard her went away talking about the shameful treatment of the Paiutes. A physician wrote he found her "nearly beautiful" in her "short dress of black velvet ornamented with three bold bands." He described her as "speaking with zest, expressing herself perfectly in good English, able to translate quite naturally the most intimate feeling of her soul . . . She did it with such passion and conviction, she had such pathetic emotions that many people were moved to tears."

In Washington, D. C., the Indian Bureau was moved to something else. Reports of Sarah's bold indictments so alarmed officials they decided to appease her. A Bureau man presented himself after one of Sarah's lectures and invited her and her family to visit Washington, all expenses paid, to report on tribal conditions. Sarah accepted at once, and took along her father, her brother Natchez, and her Cousin Joe.

The delegation had scarcely reached Washington when Sarah smelled sham. The government guide assigned to them pointedly instructed them not to leave their hotel without him;

they were to go only to places of his designation and speak only to persons of his selection. Sarah was forbidden to make speeches or to grant interviews. The omnipresent guide kept them at a running pace of sightseeing from morning until night. Sarah said later they were forced to inspect everything in Washington but the old men's home — *there* she drew the line.

Controlled steam-letting was part of the scheme, however, and the Paiutes were paraded before several officials, including Secretary of the Interior Carl Schurz. After extracting Sarah's promise not to make speeches in Washington, he surprised her by acceding to everything she asked for. He signed and presented her an executive order that stated the Paiutes would be permitted to leave Yakima and that each adult male was to be allotted 160 acres of land. Verbally, he promised to ship the tribe enough canvas to supply each family a tent. Finally, the Winnemuccas were taken to the White House to meet President Hayes. That even seems to have awed Sarah not at all. As she reported it, "We were shown all over the place before we saw him . . . at last he walked in and shook hands with us. Then he said, 'Did you get all you want for your people?' I said, 'Yes, sir, as far as I know.' 'That is well,' he said and went out again. That is all we saw of him. That was President Hayes." After that, the exhausted Winnemuccas returned West, the chief wearing the new suit the Indian Bureau had bought him, Sarah guarding with her life the signed executive order.

Of their acquisitions the chief's was to prove the more useful. Sarah's surmise had been all too true. When, one by one, she sought to collect on the promises, she learned she had been served a Barmicide feast. The Paiutes who were still at liberty camped around the railroad station at Lovelock, Nevada, to await the shipment of tent canvas that never arrived. Nor were the promised land allotments ever made. Sarah rode horseback all the way to Yakima with President Hayes' executive order, expecting to return triumphant with the freed Paiutes. But Father Wilbur devastated her by refusing to recognize the paper she carried. Since it had not been directed to him, he said, he could not honor it. Sarah now realized she had been made a fool of. She lost her temper completely. When she told

Father Wilbur her opinion of Christians, the quality of their acts and the value of their word, he threatened to put her in prison encased in irons. Prison doubtless would have been more endurable for Sarah than humiliation before her tribe, and the knowledge that she had been lulled with a piece of paper, the way some Indians were appeased with beads.

Sarah's life for the next two or three years is but scantily documented, for she scrupulously shunned white people. She was now convinced she hated and despised them. For a time she taught the children of the Sheepeater Indians, who camped on the fringe of Fort Vancouver. During this shadowy period of her life she reportedly married an Indian. No record exists of this marriage, however, nor did she mention it in her autobiography. But then she gave her two white husbands very minor billing, which was a correct assessment of their impact upon her life. Sarah was first and foremost a leader with a cause, only briefly and incidentally a wife. She bore no children, probably by choice; the Paiutes practiced a highly effective method of birth control, which they never divulged.

Sarah's attraction to white people was too strong to remain long suppressed. In time it was a romance with a white man that overcame her bitterness — overcame it enough for her to marry him. He was Lambert Hopkins, a good-looking, ineffectual civilian employee of the Army, who was several years her junior. She met him while visiting her sister Elma, who had married a well-to-do Montana lumberman. Sarah and Lambert were married in Montana in the spring of 1882 and resided there until the following spring, when they traveled to Massachusetts.

Sarah had been invited to deliver a series of lectures there under the most impeccable auspices. Her sponsors were the high-minded and aristocratic Peabody sisters, Elizabeth and Mary, the latter the wife of the eminent educator Horace Mann. They had addressed themselves to "Indian problems" and having heard of Sarah's campaign, wished to be elucidated at the source. Presenting herself, Sarah impressed them at once as the genuine article, and they made quick to see that Boston — *their* Boston, that is, was exposed to her presence. Beacon

Hill, no less than Nob Hill, was delighted to find an authentic Indian who was attractive, well-mannered and in command of the English language.

An astute observer of human nature, Sarah did not attempt to emulate the Bostonians. She affected for her platform appearances what she divined they would expect of her. Her costume included a modest-length dress of buff-colored deerskin with beaded fringe and red leather leggings. A leather pouch was suspended from her belt, and her black hair fell sleek and unadorned. Her gripping accounts of the Paiutes' misfortunes gave her audiences ample scope for their practiced indignation. Speaking invitations flowed in from other strongholds of altruism in New York, Connecticut and Pennsylvania. Sarah dashed about, while making Boston her headquarters for her latest project — the suggestion of Mrs. Mann — writing an autobiographical account of the Paiutes' troubles.

One highly interested observer of Sarah's Eastern activities was the Indian Bureau. With her book in the works, the Bureau decided she had gone far enough. Another invitation to Washington would scarcely have beguiled her. So the Bureau rashly published in its journal *Council Fire* the charges that Rhinehart once had made in a desperate effort to counteract her indictments of him — the wild concoction that Sarah was a veteran of a Nevada bordello. Marked copies of that issue were mailed freely in the circles where Sarah was making her appeals.

It was a tactical error. Aristocratic Boston would not brook irresponsible slander upon one who had received its coveted accolade. The Bostonians flew to Sarah's defense. So did Sarah's admirers in the West. Three generals, several lower military officers, government officials, and a prominent judge were among those who sent letters refuting the foolish charges and vouching for Sarah's high character and patriotic contributions.

The smear boomeranged. It threw sympathy to Sarah, heightened demand for her lectures, and boosted sales of her book, *Life Among the Paiutes: Their Wrongs and Claims.* Moreover, it spurred Sarah's bold new plan to go over Indian Bureau heads and get Congress to legislate relief for the Paiutes. The Peabody sisters helped her compose and circulate a petition demanding that the Paiutes be settled on land of their own. A Massachusetts Senator agreed to introduce the measure. In the spring of 1884, Sarah and a group of distinguished Easterners appeared before a Congressional committee and spoke for the bill. Later that year it passed Congress.

Sarah, accompanied by her boyish husband, returned to Nevada in the fall of 1884 a full-blown celebrity. With her father dead, she was indubitably the number one Paiute; and she was probably the best known Indian in the country. Indian censure of Sarah had dissipated in pride for her dazzling achievements. Every Indian in Nevada wanted to greet their authoress. Sarah dashed from town to town receiving their homage and promising that their brothers at Yakima soon would be freed and all Paiutes given land. That she cut a swath rather like a present-day movie queen is suggested by this item in the Reese River *Reveille* for September, 1884:

> "During the recent visit of Princess Sarah Winnemucca to Carson City she was always followed about the streets by a squad of Washoe squaws who, however, kept at a respectful distance gazing at her with unmixed admiration. On the evening of her lecture a large number gathered about her hotel waiting to get a last lingering look at her. Just as the Princess emerged through the main entrance of the hotel, rigged out in good toggery, an exclamation of delight ran along the line of Washoe squaws; but the zenith of their pleasure was arrived at when the Princess spoke a few kind words to each. Their usually expressionless faces were lighted up with joy and no one not present at that street audience can form a real idea of the capacity of a Washoe squaw's mouth."

Considering the harshness of 19th century Indian policy — iron repression that would culminate in the 1890 massacre at Wounded Knee — it is not surprising that even Sarah's Congressional triumph was snatched away. She had believed Congress to be the nation's ultimate authority, but it failed her too. Secretary Schurz, smarting under her indictments of his department, had the last say after all. He refused to implement the rebuking legislation, and a new Congress did not force the issue. Of course, as the cruelly disappointed Paiutes saw it, credulous Sarah had been duped again. The Paiutes risked their lives by escaping from Yakima. Some of them, at great odds, wound their way back to Pyramid Lake.

Deeply depressed and obsessed with failure, Sarah went with her husband to live with Natchez, near Lovelock. For a time she taught a few Indian pupils with financial aid from the Peabody sisters. But after a life of daring and action, drilling small children in the alphabet could not truly engage her. And she must have reflected bitterly upon how her own schooling had beguiled her into seeking the unattainable. Her husband, far from being a mainstay, was a burden. He idled away his days, spent her money, stole from Natchez, and in 1887 died of tuberculosis.

Having contracted tuberculosis from her husband, Sarah closed her school in 1889 and went to spend her last days with her sister in Montana. She was now chronically despondent Her old spirit was visible only in the aggressiveness she devoted to the one pastime that could lift her sadness — stud poker. Raking in a pot, her eyes shone with the old fervor.

When she died October 17, 1891, probably age 48, her tribesmen measured her, as she had come to measure herself, by the sum of her failures. It remained for a later generation to recognize her magnificent efforts and to find inspiration in them. At a time when most Indian tribes have dispersed, her present-day descendants still occupy their high reservation around Pyramid Lake. They are quite probably the most peacefully contentious Indians in the world. For decades they have battled in the courts and protested before government agencies to protect their rights and holdings. Most reservations have long since been lost by their tribes, but the Paiutes have actually augmented theirs. In the 1940s, they recovered 2100 acres which white squatters had pinched off during the 1860s. Later they sued for and won an increased flow of water to raise the lake level, which had been lowered by a dam, then won a restocking of their lake with trout, which had disappeared when the lake dropped. Most recently, in 1973, they won a court order to increase the lake's inflow to replace water lost by evaporation. Filing lawsuits has become more of a Paiute tradition than weaving tule baskets.

Their victories have not brought the Paiutes the easy life. Raising cattle — their present occupation — on their grueling preserve presents a formidable challenge. But since the Paiutes during their age-old occupation of their high desert have never known nor expected easy living, they can rejoice in their 20th century recoup. And they know that wherever she is, their lively princess who bequeathed them their tradition of courage without bloodshed is rejoicing too.

Gertrude Stein relaxes at a San Francisco hotel during her
busy last visit to America, in 1935. (— *Bancroft Library*)

Gertrude Stein

A Westerner in Paris

BREAKING HER Paris exile of 31 years, Gertrude Stein in 1934 paid a visit to her native land. The massive, shingle-headed, shirted-and-vested figure accompanied by her tiny, tart companion Alice B. Toklas for six months toured about in a rented Ford speaking to college students and clubwomen, granting interviews, attending her astonishing opera *Four Saints in Three Acts,* and autographing the best seller *The Autobiography of Alice B. Toklas,* which of course she wrote herself. Her procession was spectacularly triumphant. National figures and high society scrambled to meet her; Eleanor Roosevelt invited her to tea at the White House. She was discussed everywhere from factory assembly lines to the floor of Congress. Fame indubitably had arrived, and Gertrude hugely enjoyed being "a lion — a real celebrity," which she had said she would have to be before she would come home again. She returned happily to France the most publicized woman in the world.

Probably no one had ever courted fame so assiduously as Gertrude Stein. She said she had yearned "to be immortal, almost from a baby on," and she had striven for it unwaveringly through probably the most discouraging apprenticeship of anybody who ever made a name in literature. It is popularly believed she jotted down capriciously whatever popped into her head. On the contrary, most of her writing was composed with painful deliberation, and she was serious to the point of desperation. The philosopher William James, under whom she studied at Radcliffe College, once said that the difference between ordinary people and geniuses depends on "the amount of steam

pressure chronically driving the character in the ideal direction." All her life Gertrude Stein was chronically driven, and
the motivations that propelled her were generated in Northern
California, the scene of her most atypical childhood.

Ever analyzing her particular essence, Gertrude was convinced she was as she was because of having had a Western
upbringing, instead of the Eastern one she barely and thank-
fully escaped. Her family were on the verge of settling in New
York City when they decided to move to California. She believed the West had emboldened her to be wholly herself. Her
largest, most ambitious and favorite novel *The Making of
Americans* was devoted to a comparison of the New York and
California branches of the Stein family only faintly disguised.
The cast of characters variously symbolized Easterners, who
were unable to be wholly themselves, and Westerners possessed
of the courage to go their own untethered ways. It was a recurrent theme in her writings.

Lured by the legendary California cornucopia, the Daniel
Stein family moved West in 1880 over the still new transcon-
tinental railroad. Gertrude was then five years old. In his youth
Daniel had emigrated with his brothers to Baltimore where
they prospered together in a clothing store and where he married Amelia Kaiser. In time testy, impatient Daniel shifted his
mercantile operation to Allegheny, Pennsylvania, and it was
there that Gertrude, his fifth and youngest child was born.
Later Europe seemed to becken and he packed his family off
to Vienna. A letter back to Baltimore reported "our little Gertie
is a little Schnatterer. She talks all day and so plainly. She
outdoes them all." But before long Daniel was in New York
with the intention of joining his brother Solomon in banking.
However, Northern California's population surge seemed to
promise better investment opportunity, so the much-traveled
family packed up for still one more move.

After scouting out prospects in San Francisco, Daniel in-
vested in real estate, the San Francisco Stock Exchange, and in
a cable car company, from which he extracted a vice presidency. He delighted his family by settling them across the Bay
in Oakland in a big rambling frame house in a semi-rural dis-

trict on the town's eastern fringe. To the city-bred children it seemed idyllic. A rose-covered fence enclosed rolling lawns and flower beds, and there were tall, singing eucalyptus trees, even a cow and haymow. Gertrude, a sturdy little girl with a large head, there experienced what she was to remember as her "first conscious enthusiastic pleasure . . . a sun setting in a cavern of clouds." She was moved to write a piece about it for her teacher.

But all was not so roseate as Gertrude's sunset. Daniel's family — his passive, conventional wife, three sons and two daughters — never felt really secure. His career followed a roller coaster pattern of soars and dips, especially after he began investing in mining. Luxuries and servants and governesses alternated with lean times. Once Gertrude and her brother Leo, two years her senior, began collecting together books they planned to sell should their father go bankrupt. These intervals of panic indelibly fixed in their minds the importance of success.

Their father's success-seeking included clapping stern regimens upon the Stein household; he was forever decreeing rules of health and conduct and forever changing them. Now it was strict vegetarianism, then a grape diet "cure"; or he would order a specific nutritional formula and require diners to polish off everything on the table. At intervals the children were marched regularly to Sabbath School, then the routine would be abandoned. Focusing on Gertrude, he decided she was to master household tasks. Suddenly he would demand that she demonstrate bed-making or buttonhole-sewing. Of course, she couldn't, for when she wasn't escaping domestic tensions by voracious eating, she was out following her natural tomboy bent, fishing on Lake Merritt, wielding a jig saw, or smoking in the barn. Years later she was to recall of her father: "He had impatient feeling in him that she was not the kind of daughter he had wanted to have . . ." He wanted a demure Victorian young lady and by age twelve Gertrude was a sassy 135-pound squab in wrinkled serge and muddy shoes. Her father's attitude seemed all the more unfair in that to the rest of the family she was the pampered baby sister. Leo bitterly remembered his father as an "exceedingly disputatious" man "with no book learning whatever."

The mother had been a buffer between the irritable father and his resentful offspring, but as her health failed she increasingly kept to her room. Slight, bespectacled Leo had as an escape hatch keeping his thin nose in some abstruse book. Gertrude's uneasiness took the form of worrying about immortality; urgently she read the Bible searching for promise of an after life.

Gertrude was never close to her sister Bertha, and the death of her mother when Gentrude was fourteen made her emotionally dependent upon Leo. Their bond tightened when they discovered what they considered their narrow escape: the fact that their parents had planned on raising five children and had conceived Gertrude and Leo after two preceding infants had died. Gertrude said their replacement status made them "feel funny"; and no doubt it stoked their determination to make a vivid imprint upon the world.

Gertrude and Leo detested their father's dictated formulas, yet were always imposing regimens upon themselves. Deciding to become a literary figure, Gertrude forsook her fishing pole and spent all her free time hunched over a reading table at the Oakland Free Library. Leo was as systematically preparing himself to become a scholar. He was also cultivating his own food fetishes, a preoccupation which lasted for the duration of his life. At one time he took to chewing each mouthful exactly 32 times.

After his wife's death, Daniel Stein burrowed into business affairs. Rarely at home, morose and withdrawn when there, he no longer issued edicts and seemed oblivious as the household routine disintegrated. The older brother Mike was away at Johns Hopkins University, and the other children followed their personal whims to the extent of quitting school. Gertrude and Leo became inseparable, shutting out all others from their urgent discourses and private jokes. They came and went as they pleased, sometimes taking long rambles in the coastal mountains behind Oakland, talking "endlessly about books and people and things." Fancying themselves marooned intellectuals, they longed to be free to investigate the world's culture capitals.

Quite unexpectedly a way opened. As Gertrude wrote later: "Then one morning we could not wake up our father. Leo climbed in by the window and called out to us that he was dead in his bed and he was . . ." Gertrude had just turned sixteen. In letters to Baltimore relatives, Mike expressed his grief at "the loss of dear Pa," but Gertrude and Leo did not conceal their relief and would remain unsentimental about their father for the rest of their lives.

Mike dutifully shouldered the task of unscrambling Daniel Stein's complicated, debt-ridden business affairs. He also assumed guardianship of the family, moving them to a house on San Francisco's Turk Street. Gertrude and Leo, who had exhausted the shelves of the Oakland library, happily discovered the Mercantile and Mechanics Library and the reading room at the Marine Institute. Doting on his precocious youngest brother and sister, Mike indulged their taste for expensive art prints and supplied tickets to the Tivoli Opera and Bush Street Theater.

Better still, after getting the business on a sound footing, Mike succeeded in making a profitable sale of the father's transportation franchise to the railroad magnate Collis P. Huntington. His feat was much admired by San Francisco business heads, who said Huntington might have wangled it for nothing. Most admiring of all were Mike's four charges, for it assured them of incomes for life and freed them to do as they pleased.

The middle brother Simon, considered the "dull one," was quite satisfied to remain in his regular job, gripman on a cable car, but Leo lost no time packing his valises to enter Harvard University. When 22-year-old Bertha decided to go live with her Aunt Fannie in Baltimore, Gertrude, deprived of her alter ego Leo, decided to go to Baltimore too and there sort out her vague ambitions — none of them domestic.

She departed East in 1892 in high spirits, bent on testing her equipment for conquering the world. On her Baltimore relatives she applied her newest formula "winning by being winsome," and she was an immediate hit, putting sober Bertha

quite in the shade. Everybody took to the buxom 18-year-old
with the sparkling, candid gaze and the exploding contralto
laugh who talked non-stop and was curious about everything.

To her delight Gertrude now learned she was a "typical
Westerner," or so the Baltimorians branded her freewheeling
ways. Blithely she shrugged off social formalities, propped her
feet on the furniture, and threw on any old thing to wear,
behavior she probably had cultivated in rebellion against her
father's authoritarianism. One male Baltimore relative recalled
of her: "Gertie? She went flopping around the place — other
girls wore corsets then, but I never liked corsets anyway — big
and floppy, sandaled and not caring a damn." Ever after Gertrude was to visualize herself, and so characterize herself in
her writing, as a daring, freedom-loving, unconventional representative of the honest West.

Being winsome for adoring middle-aged relatives soon
palled. She missed Leo. Visiting him at Cambridge, she found
women studying at Radcliffe College (then called Harvard
Annex) under the same instructors who taught the men. Soon
she was an "Annex girl," living in a boardinghouse a stone's
throw from Harvard Yard and Leo's bolstering presence. For
her composition course she turned out long themes in which
she exploded vehemently into her subjects. A recurring topic
was to contrast New Englanders and Californians, the cold and
rigid against the warm and easy-going, the effete wastrel with
the hardworking pioneer. Cambridge too branded her Western, and again the tag was affectionate. She was considered "an
original" and "great fun." Years later former Annex girls would
delight in remembering her as a big, bouncy girl "swinging
down the corridor full of life and sanity and humour."

Gertrude and Leo communed on long walks about snowy
Cambridge and trolleyed to museums and concerts in Boston.
But in one respect she was disappointed: nobody complimented
her writing. Not only did her themes come back scratched up
with grammar and punctuation corrections, but laden with
criticisms of trite phraseology and cluttered thought. She was
humiliated. Years later she recalled of this letdown: "Like
almost everyone else I wanted to be a writer, but nobody en-

couraged me much." Her Cambridge writing was painfully serious. While there she began and abandoned a novel about adolescent struggle.

Admission to a restricted psychology seminar conducted by Professor William James repaired her ego. She became one of his stars and participated in an important study to determine the "bottom nature" of a group of subjects. She co-authored an article reporting the conclusion that people reveal their basic character through repetitions of speech and mannerism; a scientific journal later printed the study. Gertrude was thrilled to be considered a James protege and, always responsive to praise, she listened interestedly when he told her she had a scientific bent. After taking another James course, she decided to follow his advice to obtain a medical degree as a basis for becoming a clinical psychologist.

There followed a distressful Baltimore period during which she sought to settle down to medical study at Johns Hopkins. Sharing a house with Leo, then undertaking a second degree in biology, she also plunged into biology with brisk application. Doubts descended quickly. The factual courses she found boring, the practical application distasteful, especially obstetrics. Her efforts at injecting originality and humor into the antiseptic atmosphere met withering disapproval. With dismay she learned that Professor James expected her to intern in an insane asylum. Clearly she had gotten onto a wrong track; yet the lodestar of success kept her plodding on.

She found distraction in a circle of bright, arty young friends for whom she and Leo held open house. They highhandedly exhorted their friends to follow their example, to shake off constraints and paddle their own canoes. Then Leo bogged down in biology — he detested lab work — and departed on a world tour. Gertrude felt uneasy without him and became anxious about her health. She decided on a physical fitness regimen and undertook to learn to box. A professional gave her instructions in her living room, and the house rang with shouts of "Give me one on the jaw . . . now one on the kidney!"

Leo's defection from biology probably contributed to the abandonment of Gertrude's medical career. Her grades dropped when he left. Yet at the beginning of her final year she was still at an impasse. She couldn't bring herself to leave school, but neither could she conquer her boredom. Her friends' exhortations to "Remember the cause of women" failed to rouse her, nor did Leo's letters urging her to win her degree. "If you had my superior talent for loafing it might do," he wrote, "but you haven't so it won't."

The dilemma resolved itself when she failed her final examinations. Given another chance with an assignment to make a model of an embryo human brain, she flaunted indifference by constructing the model with the spinal cord twisted ludicrously under the embryo's head. Her professor, grimly unamused, swept the travesty into a wastebasket, and Gertrude was relieved of her boredom officially. At which she shrugged and packed her valises to spend the summer touring Spain with Leo.

Back in Baltimore at summer's end she seems to have considered emulating her friend Florence Sabin and making medical research her career. She undertook a study of brain tracts and settled down to work. But the project palled quickly and she began talking of joining Leo again.

In the spring of 1902 she set up housekeeping with Leo in a Bloomsbury flat in London and began a schedule of reading an exhaustive list of novels at the British Museum. Daily she trekked there in heat or rain and planted herself in the reading room. She broke routine only to accompany Leo to Surrey to visit the art historian Bernard Berenson, with whom Leo had become friendly in Italy. There they met Mrs. Berenson's brother-in-law Bertrand Russell, who Leo described in a letter as "a young mathematician of genius." Berenson later recalled his concern that Gertrude's monolithic bulk might topple over. Conversely, Gertrude thought him far too thin and persuaded him to go on a diet of milk and eggs.

This cerebral gathering sparked lively debates, the most frequent subject being "Europe versus America." Both Steins were passionately chauvinistic. They conceded that Europe held marvelous stimulations, but for a living place they much preferred America. Leo stated his intention to return there and establish a home for himself and Gertrude, possibly in Connecticut. The arguments started Gertrude meditating about the characteristics of her country and its regional variations, thoughts that were to provide the genesis of her later novel about Americans.

Of course, she and Leo did not settle in Connecticut, or anywhere in the United States. As the world knows they became enthusiastic residents of the Paris Left Bank, immersed themselves expertly in French art movements, and conducted a famous Saturday evening salon. But not before Gertrude had once again traveled back across the Atlantic for a listless sojourn in New York City. Meanwhile, Leo's planned return to the United States kept getting postponed. Having decided to become a painter, he wandered to Paris to sketch statues at the Louvre. Enrollment in an art class created need for a place to paint, which led to the lease of a small *pavillon* with detached *atelier* and an invitation to Gertrude to come share it.

At 27 rue de Fleurus, an address destined to figure in both art and literary history, Gertrude unpacked her trunk in the fall of 1903. Now 29, she had fully decided to become a writer, but she was not resigned to becoming an expatriate. She had come over with the understanding she would spend part of each year in America. Her later recollection of her arrival and the beginning of her writing career was hardly dramatic. "I joined him and I sat down in there and pretty soon I was writing . . ." "In there" was the *atelier*. Changeable Leo had not used it for painting after all. Lined with their books and the Japanese prints Leo had been collecting, the room with its potbellied stove made a pleasant writing studio for Gertrude. Without delay she began spending most of her waking hours there scratching away in French school notebooks in her big loose scrawl. Sometimes she worked until dawn.

In less than two months she had completed her first novel. Primarily a psychological study, it echoed the Eastern-Western theme of her college compositions. The heroine was a Western college girl, much like herself, who she depicted as warm and above-board, while the antagonist was a cold dissembling Easterner. Its style was conventional without the slightest hint of what soon would boil up from the school notebooks. Making no effort to market that work (it remained unpublished until after her death), she began forthwith a second novel. Equally conventional and with a college setting, it was abandoned before completion, but later she inserted the material into *The Making of Americans.*

Leo took an interest in Gertrude's writing, reading it, appraising it, encouraging it. An admirer of Flaubert, he urged her to read the novels of the French master of characterization. It was at Leo's suggestion that she undertook to translate Flaubert's late work *Three Tales,* stories of working class life, as a means of analyzing his techniques. Gertrude's indifferent French produced no translation of worth, but the exercise inspired her to write a realistic trilogy of her own, portraits of three Baltimore servants, two German women and a mulatto girl, which she called *Three Lives.*

Meanwhile, she was absorbing other influences. She and Leo had discovered *L'Art Moderne,* which was in an astonishing state of ferment. Young artists had tossed tradition into the Seine and were brazenly experimenting. Impressionism, the last iconoclastic art movement, was fading out and something even more scandalous, the luridly-colored *fauvism,* was having its brief run. Leo, now interested in collecting, had begun buying paintings, some for the price of a tube of paint.

Gertrude, who always caught Leo's enthusiasms, accompanied him to the rather seedy art galleries where these innovators exhibited. The art world soon became aware of the conspicuous pair. They were hardly to be missed. Brown as tobacco from walking tours in Italy, they dressed in a determinedly eccentric manner in loose-fitting clothes of brown corduroy and bulky sandals that pointed upward like the prows of gondolas. Gertrude now weighed more than 200 pounds. Tall, thin, long-faced Leo, already bald, affected glittering gold-rimmed spectacles and a reddish pointed beard. They wore an air of consummate self-assurance and were rumored to be peculiar millionaires.

When they entertained friends in the atelier, Leo called attention to their growing art collection. As he stood before the paintings — unframed works by Monet, Renoir, Cézanne and Matisse — discoursing passionately on their techniques, his most attentive listener was Gertrude. She had shared in the art purchases, but she had admired the painters more for their bravura than for their effects. As she came to understand the paintings, she began to compare painting technique with writing technique. These innovators painted their subjects with bold strokes and colors, deemphasizing background and detail. They sought to capture the essence of their subjects rather than outer reality. Why couldn't she do with words what the artists were doing with paint? Heretofore she had adhered to accepted writing patterns — it had never occurred to her to throw over the traces in literature.

Now borrowing suggestions from canvas, especially from Cézanne, she boldly began to flout the rules. In writing the story of the mulatto maid, she omitted to endow her with a past, or a specific setting, or even definite physical features. Instead she probed her inner being as she moved around in her unchanging, trapped situation. In this story grammar is still conventional, but Gertrude was on her irreversible road to Steinese and soon would take another giant step with techniques suggested by another painter.

One day at Sagot's gallery, Gertrude tried to keep Leo from paying $30 for a painting of a child. She thought the child's feet "look like a monkey's." Leo bought it anyhow — their first Picasso, the now famous "Young Girl with Basket of Flowers." The next time they dropped by Sagot's, Picasso was there, and the gallery owner introduced the painter to his new patrons. Picasso, then 24, was immediately intrigued with Gertrude's face. He delighted her by inviting her to pose for a portrait.

During her many sittings on a broken chair at Picasso's disheveled studio she came to know Picasso intimately — the beginning of a lifelong friendship. Moreover, she learned what modern art was all about straight from the ringleader of the art revolutionaries. The stocky, black-eyed, lively little painter, then progressing from his blue and rose period and about to lead the pack into cubism, declared that "the present, nothing but the present" was the artist's concern. The function of art, he insisted, was to express feeling about the *now* of existence. In his painting Picasso did not undertake to tell a story nor prove a point nor do anything but convey his feeling about a moment in time.

Gertrude experimented with ways of capturing the immediate present with words, but found she could not pin it down with conventional narration. So she invented a method based on the findings of her college study of bottom nature: that people reveal themselves by repeating themselves, over and over in minute variations. Instead of writing a plotted novel, she would closely observe a set of characters in a continuous present that would fill a novel as though it were an unwinding canvas.

Since her Radcliffe days she had been making notes for a novel about her family and its connections which would probe the meaning of "this being an American," especially a Western American. Now she began it, incorporating her new technique into psychological studies of the Steins, who she called the Herslands. Oakland became Gossols. She later remembered the "long tormenting process" of conveying all she wanted to tell about her characters. The following is but a portion of her passage describing her father's food preoccupations:

> Mr. Hersland always liked to think about what was good for him in eating, he liked to think about what was good for every one around him in their eating, he liked to buy all kinds of eating, he liked all kinds of thinking about eating, eating was living to him, eating was beginning to him, beginning was all living in him, always he was interested in changing in having new ideas new ways of eating, eating was living for him, ways of eating were ways of beginning for him . . .

At times the task of shaping prose to fit both scientific theory and art technique seemed beyond her powers. Making it all the more grueling was the discouragement she was getting. Leo refused to take this latest work seriously. His blunt opinion was that her new style was "abominable." He urged her to abandon it. More tactfully, her friends told her they preferred her earlier work.

Leo's defection was the more disturbing. Hitherto, whatever her project, he had dispensed help and encouragement. An intimate said Leo had always acted as Gertrude's "dictionary and encyclopedia, supplying on demand" whatever she required. All her life Gertrude found criticism distressing and Leo knew it. But he was in no mood to dissemble, having recently received from Matisse a shattering critique of his painting. The siblings' long-simmering rivalry over which of them was the family genius had come to a boil. In time the heat of their separate bids for fame would dissipate every residue of their former deep affection.

Gertrude's spirits were at a nadir when Alice Toklas arrived and supplied a badly-needed cheering section. She was a San Francisco friend of the Michael Steins, who were then living in Paris. When Alice came to Paris with a friend Harriet Levy, she looked up the Steins and at their flat she met Gertrude. Alice was 31, bookish and an amateur pianist; and she was yearning, having spent the previous decade in unrelieved boredom as housekeeper for her widowed father and grandfather. A modest legacy from her grandfather's gold mine at Mokelumne Hill had financed her trip. She astonished everyone by the swiftness with which she entwined her life with Gertrude's.

In due time Harriet Levy returned to San Francisco, and Alice moved into 27 rue de Fleurus. Alice's cousin, Annette Rosenshine, the later sculptress then studying art in Paris, recalled: "Alice stepped into Gertrude's life when Leo failed to give Gertrude his support in her literary ambition. Alice sorely needed this outlet for her thirst for fame. In the past friendships with both Harriet Levy and me had shown her need to pull strings, but we, her San Francisco puppets, had been too inconsequential." Alice, the frustrated impresario, had found the perfect diva.

In later life Alice often said that she had known three geniuses "for whom a bell rang" upon meeting them: Pablo Picasso, Alfred North Whitehead, and Gertrude Stein. With her private bell still ringing in her ears, Alice delved into reading Gertrude's huge, handwritten novel-in-progress. She found it, so she claimed in her memoirs, "more exciting than

anything else had ever been." Alice was far from the bland
pudding she at first appeared. Although she was quiet and
daintily polite, her small deep-set grey eyes missed nothing,
and she formed decided opinions on everything and expressed
them with an acid wit. She could make Gertrude roar with
laughter. Gertrude was delighted that Alice had what she considered the "California quality"— independence. Discovering
Gertrude's taste for Western cooking, Alice turned out such
delectables as corn bread and lemon pies.

Soon the sprightly little figure was two-finger pecking at
an ancient Blickensdoerfer typewriter transcribing Gertrude's
near illegible script. Alice also undertook to correct the proofs
of *Three Lives*, which Gertrude, finding no publisher, was having printed herself. Who can say whether Gertrude sans Alice
would have reversed course and returned to a more lucid
style? But there is no doubt that Alice's enthusiasm for the
literary experimentation reinforced Gertrude's faith in it. There
were no more paralyzing doubts during the three years more it
took to complete the mammoth work which would run to
nearly a thousand printed pages.

In 1908, it was finished, and while Alice launched the huge
manuscript into the oceanic mail routes in quest of a publisher,
Gertrude girded for a new stylistic adventure. By then the
ever-restless Picasso was deep into cubism, an attempt to give
painting a third dimension by painting his subjects from several
perspectives at once. Leo had taken himself off to Italy; his
influence on Gertrude was over. "The disaggregation of Gertrude and myself," he wrote a friend, had freed them "to suck
gleefully our respective oranges." Picasso had become the most
important man in Gertrude's life. She felt they had quite similar natures, and Picasso was inclined to agree. He told her she
was equally as unhappy as he was. She couldn't resist following his latest artistic suggestion.

Zestfully she began "doing portraits." In these pieces dis-
connected passages discribing different facets of the subject
were spliced one against the other in a prose style that retained
the rhythm and some of the repetition of her other work. She
cubistically portrayed Alice, then Picasso, of the latter stating

in part: "This one was one having always something being coming out of him, something having completely a real meaning. This one was one who was working and he was one needing this thing needing to be working . . ."

When Picasso turned to painting cubist still lifes, Gertrude tried her hand at that too, using similar subjects: "A Caraffe," "A Box," "A Seltzer Bottle," "Sausages." Nor did she hesitate to follow her leader into collage. Picasso covered his canvases with snippets of cloth and newspaper, metro tickets and other handy items. Gertrude's equivalent of collage was to break up her sentences into disjointed verbal snippets set down without logical arrangement. Sometimes she coined new words such as *wellies, splats, condies, leet il* and *meal one aires,* which stood out rather as did Picasso's metro tickets and curls of string.

With Picasso beckoning before and Alice cheering behind she had plunged ever deeper into incomprehensibility. But so exhilarating were her verbal gymnastics she launched them in a new publishing venture. Collecting her portraits, still lifes and collages into a volume with the affectionate title of *Tender Buttons,* she dispatched it to a New York vanity press. The publisher, possibly scheming to disarm criticism with prideful claimer, stated in his announcement brochure in 1914: "The last shackle is struck from context and collation, and each unit of the sentence stands independent and has no commerce with its fellows."

Soon the last shackle was struck from drama as Gertrude turned to playwriting. These plays, her version of abstract landscape painting, are even less like ordinary painting than her novels were like ordinary novels. Bereft of story, they had neither dialogue nor dramatic action of the usual sort. There were occasional snatches of words and song, combined, ritual-like, with dancing and sweeping movements about the stage by a huge fantastically-garbed cast.

Never before had literary effort been so uncommunicative. Yet, Gertrude seemed unaware of the extent of her departure. "It's all *there,*" she would insist when reproached for obscurity. She was, of course, aware she was innovating. But she was surrounded by innovators — radical painters and revolutionary musicians creating atonal music, while her friends Isadora and Raymond Duncan were making ballet yield ground to modern dance. The flamboyant Duncans were from Gertrude's old neighborhood, where Raymond once had made forays on the Stein apple orchard. All these cocksure rebels made Gertrude feel quite in the mainstream with her literary abstractions.

Another reason she could not gauge her communicability was her isolation from readers. Her two books and the few magazine pieces thus far in print had mainly been read in America and England. She was far from oblivious of readers, however. Indeed, she was anxious to multiply them. She wrote her friend the American critic Carl Van Vechten: "I've got ten years' work and I want to dispose of some of it . . . waiting for publication gets on my nerves." She could still speak plainly when she wanted to. Alice still kept the bulky family novel on its rounds of the publishing houses. *Three Lives* had been favorably reviewed in the United States, and Gertrude and Alice were in London to sign a contract for a commercial English edition when World War I erupted. They were cut off from France for several weeks, but as soon as the German advance on Paris had been halted they hurried home. Of course, the shipping blockade soon severed contact with the United States.

Legend has it that Gertrude's famous postwar salon was composed of those who came to pay her homage as a literary figure. It was more nearly true that she became a literary figure *because* of those who came. The war, which she had ridden out in France, had brought her increased association with Americans. For a time she drove an ambulance and had close contacts with doughboys. With peacetime had begun the arrival of American expatriates escaping puritanism and prohibition. Most settled in Montparnasse and played at starving in a garret, using a sidewalk cafe as their living room. New arrivals quickly heard of Gertrude Stein and sought out somebody to take them round. Few had read her writing; what they wanted was to see her much-discussed collection of modern art.

Gertrude was glowing with patriotism and warmly welcomed Americans. In the atelier, now handsomely furnished with Renaissance furniture and English chintz, Gertrude stood before the paintings, explaining them as Leo once had. Leo now lived in Florence, Italy, with his wife Nina, a former Paris street singer and artists' model. He had carried off some of the Renoirs and Matisses, but had left the Picassos, which he didn't like. Alice, wearing a black ostrich plume or a velvet bow atop her bangs, daintily dispensed *eau-de-vie* and poured tea from an elaborate silver service. The tone of the salon was slightly formal. Gertrude never cared for the gritty variety of bohemianism.

Her salon was now dominated by writers, all young and soaring on the success of a first novel or book of poems, or merely on rosy expectations. A woman friend brought Sherwood Anderson, who sent Hemingway, who brought F. Scott Fitzgerald and Zelda. Jo Davidson, the sculptor, came and later brought the journalist Lincoln Steffens. After a look at the paintings, there was scintillating book talk, and everybody listened fascinated as Gertrude pronounced her bold opinions. After they left, a few of them read her writings.

Hemingway did. He made an immediate hit with Gertrude by asking to read her big unpublished novel. Soon he was incorporating certain of its techniques into his short stories. He placed a piece in *The Little Review* that he said was written under the influence of Gertrude Stein and a bottle of Beaune. Other salon habitues, including Anderson, likewise discovered the uses of Stein techniques.

But the Saturday night exchanges were *quid pro quo:* Gertrude benefited too. While she spurned writing pointers, she was eager for publishing help. After her long wait in the literary wings, she was impatient to move into the limelight, and her guests happily aglow with brandy were eager to escort her there. She still wrote cubist portraits, and some of her regulars encouraged her to compose their likenesses, which they undertook to get published. Her portrait of Jo Davidson was printed in *Vanity Fair,* and *The Reviewer* ran one of Carl Van Vechten, who persuaded the editor to also print one of Gertrude's stories. Sherwood Anderson not only wrote her up as a writer of influence for *The New Republic,* but he composed a complimentary introduction to her new private publishing venture, a collection called *Geography and Plays*.

It was Hemingway who most assisted the transformation of Gertrude Stein from unknown to celebrity by the feat of arranging publication of *The Making of Americans*. In 1925, he coaxed a doubtful Ford Madox Ford into printing the 17-year-old novel in his Paris-headquartered *Transatlantic Review*, of which Hemingway was an assistant editor. Although the journal went defunct before the family saga was well into its first generation, the interest it created spurred another obliging young American to pick up the ball. Publisher Robert McAlmon brought out a small edition of the book in Paris. He also included one of Gertrude's pieces in an anthology of new writers. Janet Flanner, *The New Yorker*'s Paris Correspondent, wrote in 1926: "No American writer is taken more seriously than Miss Stein by the Paris modernists."

The accolades mounted. After sipping tea at the atelier, the redoubtable Edith Sitwell returned to England and got Gertrude an invitation to speak at Oxford and Cambridge Universities. The excitement over her lectures inspired Hogarth Press of London to publish them together with some short pieces. Then, the young composer Virgil Thompson invited her to collaborate on an opera. By the late 1920s, all of the literary magazines were clamoring for something, and the American publisher Harcourt, Brace had contracted to bring out an abridged edition of *The Making of Americans*.

Paris with its large American colony — roughly 30,000, many participating in the arts — was then for all practical purposes the capital of the American literary world. And Gertrude was the acknowledged queen of the expatriates. Her comings and goings were closely monitored by the international press, which also helped itself to Stein quotations and misquotations apropos of anything and everything.

Naturally, Gertrude was exhilarated by all this. But something was lacking: readers. Very few people from the general public had read her books. She was shrewd enough to know she was a literary cult. It was thrilling to hear that *Three Lives* was selling at $12 on the collectors' market, but knowing its rarity had inflated the price, she would have preferred a cheap edition for the man on the street. And it was a mixed pleasure to be quoted by journalists who obviously hadn't read a word she had written.

She wondered if her roadblock was distribution. In 1930, she decided to set up her own publishing house to bring out inexpensive editions of her writings. To finance it she sold her 1905 Picasso "Woman with a Fan" to Marie Harriman, wife of the future governor of New York, for a price that neatly set her up in business. She christened the venture Plain Editions Press and made Alice director. Delighted with her title, Alice assumed her new duties with the same composure with which she served as Gertrude's editor-manager-hostess. Unfortunately, the bookbinder gave the first book too tight a spine which prevented it from staying shut and stunted sales. Undaunted, Alice shepherded other works through Plain Editions, but disappointment hung over the enterprise.

In the fall of 1932, Gertrude, aged 58, had another inspiration. Their friends had often urged Alice to write her memoirs, but she could never get around to beginning. The weather was fine and they were prolonging their stay at their country place at Belley near Lyon. Gertrude jocularly told Alice she would write her memoirs for her. With her usual egotism she made herself the main character and put in lots of gossipy anecdotes about the habitues of her Paris salon. What's more she wrote it in a perfectly lucid style that mimicked Alice's conversation, which was terse, tart and wickedly witty. An expert at catching speech rhythms, Gertrude brought off a near perfect imitation of Alice, unmasking herself as author only in the final paragraph. The book was written in six weeks.

No one was more astonished than Gertrude when the book she tossed off as a lark became an immediate best seller. It was snapped up by a public eager for a voyeur's peek at the colorful eccentric and at Paris' fascinating art and literary circles. Reviews were glowing. The checks rolled in. Then came realization of her dream of being accepted by *Atlantic Monthly;* it ran a serialized version of the book. When the *Saturday Evening Post* publicized one of her pieces she was indubitably lifted out of literary cult into "apple pie." And the American press discovered that a tabloid photograph of Gertrude Stein in shirt and vest was as eye-catching as Sally Rand in flesh-colored gauze.

The dazzling fountainhead of success they had courted so long gave Gertrude and Alice the greatest thrills of their lives. Gertrude rushed out and bought a new eight-cylinder Ford and for her poodle Basket had "the most expensive coat made to order by Hermes." Alice had the atelier redecorated and hired an accomplished cook.

Wonderful as it was, for Gertrude it was also most confusing. When her popularity prompted an invitation to make an American lecture tour "to take the tribute due you," she hardly knew whether to accept for hardly knowing what she was expected to say. Who was really wanted over there: literary innovator or anecdote teller?

She couldn't resist going, though. Suddenly, she passionately wanted to see America again. Thirty years had passed since her last visit; that resolve to return yearly had somehow gotten mislaid. As it turned out she needn't have worried. It scarcely mattered what she said, for what was really wanted was a look at her in the flesh.

Shrewdly realizing she had become a public figure and that the public did not take her seriously, she confined herself mostly to being amusing. She presented herself in billed cap, a bunchy tweed suit, woolly stockings, round-toed oxfords and a broad grin. Her standard lecture was titled "what is english [sic] literature that is to say what do I know about it that is to say what is it." It was two parts foolishness and one part wisdom, and after its delivery she gave zestful answers to sensible questions and as-good-as-sent retorts to impertinent ones. To the Chicago professor who inquired, "What is a rose," she informed him, "My dear man, if you don't know I can't help you." She laughed a lot and most of the time was in great good humor. But at a Hollywood party when a film mogul asked enviously how she succeeded in getting so much publicity, she shot back it was because discerning readers saw merit in her work. Her answer revealed he had struck a nerve.

Following a Pasadena lecture, she and Alice departed north in a drive-yourself-car to see Yosemite and to look for Alice's birthplace in the San Joaquin Valley near Stockton. After that they veered coastward and cruised through "acres of orchards and artichokes." At the elegant Del Monte Hotel in Monterey they took a respite in preparation for exposing their emotions to their old girlhood haunts in the San Francisco Bay Area. Gertrude counted on her visit home to restore her confused identity.

In San Francisco a flower-bedecked suite at the Mark Hopkins Hotel atop Nob Hill greeted their return. Alas, the scene from the windows presented a view wholly unfamiliar. Cultural luminaries came to escort Gertrude to City Hall where the mayor pinned a corsage of roses on her tweed suit and presented her a key to the city. To a Baltimore relative she penned: "The newspapers are full of the Oakland girl who made good in a big way." Gertrude Atherton, San Francisco's literary lioness, honored Gertrude with the biggest and most elaborate literary cocktail party in the city's history. But there were no familiar faces.

Between lectures at several Bay Area colleges and before San Francisco and Oakland clubwomen, she searched for her childhood in the places she had known. She found her old Swett School still standing in Oakland, and out in her former neighborhood in the Fruitvale district she could recognize a few houses. But the old Stein house was gone. "The big house and big garden and the eucalyptus trees and the rose hedge naturally were not any longer existing." Only the contour of the hill was familiar. It frightened her and made her think of Leo, once her comforter, Leo who, since their separation decades before she had seen but once and from a distance, Leo who had spent years in psychoanalysis and had written one inconsequential book. She looked for a place in the country where she and Leo had ridden their tandem bicycle, but it had been swallowed by the city. Of Oakland, she declared, "There is no there there," meaning she said later, correcting other interpretations, that she couldn't find her youth there. Going home had made her sad.

For long after she speculated worriedly on why so little of her California past came back to her. Later she wrote of the fruitless quest: "You can go back to where they are and they can be less real to you than they were three thousand, six thousand miles away."

The most publicized women in the world returned to Paris still uneasy, still uncertain how to serve her huge new public. The *Atlantic Monthly* had congratulated her upon becoming lucid — upon "piercing the smokescreen with which (she had) always so mischieviously surrounded herself." Her publisher, Random House, was pressing her not for a serious work but for a sequel to the autobiography, an account of her American tour. Her serious works still sold slowly. Random House had brought out a collection of her cubist portraits, but they quickly showed up on remainder tables. Alternately, she took pleasure in her fame, then felt uneasy about it. For months she could write nothing.

Finally, she was at work again, writing lucidly about her American trip, putting the banal on a par with the significant, and giving her writing occasional touches of her style innovations. The work was quickly published in 1937 as *Everybody's Autobiography*. Then she wrote an intimate, entertaining book about Picasso, followed by *Paris France,* a valentine to Paris and Frenchmen, both urban and rural. These amiable books were confined to the personal, the nearby and the trivial, and all were commercially successful, although not in league with her first hit. Her daring now mostly took the form of astonishing statements. Then she wrote a charming children's book about a little girl who climbs a mountain carrying a garden chair, not stopping to rest until she reaches the summit. Finally, she reaches it and sits in her chair and sings. Gertrude had reached a summit of a sort and she was singing, but not exactly the song she had planned.

Then, in the late 1930s she abruptly changed course and burrowed deep into esoterica again. This was her novel *Ida.* Its enigmatic heroine had something of Gertrude in her, but she had more of Wallace Warfield Simpson, with whom Gertrude was fascinated. Random House published *Ida* with Bennett Cerf's introduction stating he was publishing it even though he "rarely has the faintest idea what Miss Stein is talking about." It sold poorly.

In those pre-war years Gertrude and Alice were at their most stylish and social. They moved into an elegant apartment at 5 rue de Christine in a building where Queen Christina of Sweden once had lived. They went out often, celebrities among celebrities. Gertrude's arrival was awaited at every art opening, where wearing chunky Renaissance pendants over a brocade vest, she stole the show as she scratched her clipped head in concentration and gesticulated with an ornate walking cane. Still collecting art and artists, she searched for a new genius to match Picasso, but her new discoveries consistently failed to ripen.

Always politically naive, she underestimated Hitler. In her view he was a romantic posturer who would stop short of bloodshed. As Europe's tensions mounted, she entertained a succession of anxious American visitors — Thornton Wilder, Bennett Cerf, the Henry Luces. She shrugged off their warnings. "Europe is not big enough for a war any more," she insisted.

France's war declaration in September, 1939, caught her by surprise while vacationing in the country. She and Alice believed it would end quickly and ignored official advice to flee to Switzerland. Quickly the Germans occupied the district and administered it from Vichy.

There Gertrude and Alice made themselves as inconspicuous as possible and cultivated resourcefulness and friendship with their rural neighbors. And there, in 1945, looking rather bedraggled after four years of uneasy seclusion but little deprivation, they were noisily discovered by American reporters traveling with the American army of liberation. They were taken for a jeep ride, and Gertrude was swept off to a radio station, where she broadcast her joy at being free again. "I can tell everybody that none of you know what this native land business is until you have been cut off from that same native land completely for years. This native land business gets you all right."

Her energies, so long dammed, sprang forth like a thawed waterfall. Back in Paris, where she rejoiced to find her art collection intact, she swept into a whirl of activity. She looked up old friends, helped revive the culture scene, inspected new art, and reopened her salon, enlivening it with American uniforms. She reactivated her career by sending her publisher the manuscript of the journal she had kept during the occupation. Rushed into print as *Wars I Have Seen,* it enjoyed both a popular and critical success.

Life Magazine arranged for her to make a speaking and reporting tour of American bases in Germany, during which she fell in love with GIs. Afterwards, she dashed off the entertaining book about GI talk and thought, *Brewsie and Willie.* In it she predicted soldiers were returning to an America in which industry increasingly would try to make automatons of them, while government would attempt to stifle thought. Her book was a plea for Americans to protect their freedom.

While filling a speaking engagement in Brussels in November, 1945, she suffered a severe attack of indigestion. Her Paris doctor advised her to see a stomach specialist, but she would not. During the following spring she was somewhat irritable. In July, while on a motor trip to Luceau she became ill, and a doctor advised a frightened Alice: "Your friend will have to be cared for by a specialist, and at once." Against her will, Gertrude was carried to the American hospital at Neuilly, where an examining doctor decided her condition was so grave that surgery would be useless. Refusing to accept the verdict, Gertrude called in another surgeon and stated: "I order you to operate." She remained brave and hopeful as she was wheeled into the operating room, but there surgery established she had inoperative cancer, and early that same evening she died. She was 72.

A year and two days later, Leo died in Florence of the same disease. Alice remained in Paris after Gertrude's death and lived 21 years longer. Gertrude's will directed that income from her books go to Alice during her lifetime, afterward reverting to the Stein heirs. Alice faithfully continued to serve Gertrude's reputation, cooperating with biographers and assisting Yale University in preparing manuscripts for publication. She also wrote three books of her own, two cookbooks and her memoirs *What Is Remembered,* which in style much resembled the earlier autobiography. She died in Paris in 1967, age 89, and was buried in a Paris cemetery beside Gertrude.

How fares the literary reputation of Gertrude Stein, now nearly three decades after her death? It can be said at this writing — as it could not have been said as recently as five years ago — that her place in literature appears secure.

She often said she was ahead of her time and predicted that after her death she would be fully understood and appreciated. Accordingly, she willed to Yale University her unpublished manuscripts with a financial provision for their publication. In 1951, Yale University Press began publishing in succession eight volumes of her serious writings, including her first novel. None of these books created any more reader excitement than her earlier serious works had done. As before, scholars, intellectuals and students read them, but the general public did not, and with no new popular work to revive interest, her readership declined. She was back in cult again.

Then, in the early 1970s came a sudden, surprising upturn of demand for her books. Two happenings probably assisted this revival. One was the publicity attending the acquisition of her art collection by the Museum of Modern Art in New York. Installed with much fanfare were some 200 of her paintings, sculptures, drawings and prints, which her heirs had sold for several million dollars. The other spur was the women's liberation movement, which had boosted the readership of women authors in general, and which applauded Gertrude for her emancipated life style. But whatever the stimuli, all at once her works were snapped up in the book stores. Soon publishers were rushing to reprint her works. Interested reviews and popular articles followed.

Simultaneously, something quite unexpected happened. Her works became popular for reading aloud. It was discovered anew that her work appealed more to the sense of hearing and to the subconscious than to the surface level of intelligence. Her writings were heard frequently on radio and television.

Actors gave them public readings. People read her works aloud to each other in private living rooms. Everybody said how much better her writing communicated when heard. As one theater reviewer stated: "Even passages which seem to be hopelessly belabored come out surprisingly patient, illustrating that Stein was willing to take the greatest pains in attempting, not to confuse, but to illustrate a point." Which was exactly what Gertrude always insisted she did. A reporter who once asked about her difficult style was told: "I cannot afford to be clear because if I was I would risk destroying my own thought. Most people destroy their thought before they create it. That is why I often repeat a word again and again — because I am fighting to hold the thought." Some present-day thinkers believe we have moved into an era when sound predominates strongly over print. If so, Gertrude's writings orally presented may come into their full bloom of meaning.

But regardless of whether her vogue swells or dies, Gertrude Stein's impact upon literature will be felt for decades to come through the writers she influenced, directly or indirectly. Especially through Hemingway, who liberally utilized her techniques. But where she had applied her theories rigidly like a scientist, he adapted them to his artistic purposes. He modified, bent and diluted her uses of rhythm and repetition, her methods of character analysis, her use of the simple declarative statement and of a simple, adjective-sparce vocabulary. In short, he took what would further his goal of communicating experience directly to the reader, rejecting the rest. A whole school of writers, in turn, emulated Hemingway. Today apprentice writers and literature students study these effects unaware they came from Gertrude Stein.

Surviving also is the essence of her personality. Even during the years of her literary decline she herself was well remembered. References to her abounded in journalism, in fiction, in theater, in casual conversation, as they still do. For a half century she has been a point of reference, a symbol. This side of her, the personal magnetism that she called her winsomeness, she always regarded as Western. Several years before her death, she wrote: "After all anybody is as their land and air is. Anybody is as the sky is low or high, the air heavy or clean and anybody is as there is wind or no wind there. It is that which made them . . ." No matter how prolonged or distant her exile, she always remembered she came from the land of the high sky and the brisk wind off the broad Pacific.

Probably the most salient feature of her character and her writing was her daring — her defiance, her robustness, her freshness, her raw courage, all qualities often regarded as Western. Even though she held an essentially tragic view of life she faced life always valiantly and with hope, never losing conviction that one must make the very best of life one can. She was by bottom nature an existentialist.

Just as she selected her painters for their bold defections, the public embraced her for daring to live and write as she chose, for being as different and eccentric as she pleased. No doubt many of those who first praised her writings were in part defending her right to experiment and make unprecedented departures in literature. No other writer has ever been so daring. Her very name suggests high individualism, and while it may provoke a smile, the smile is affectionate and pleasurable, for its wearer has been reminded that he, if he chooses, can be as daring and free as Gertrude Stein.

Jeannette Rankin in 1911 when a social worker and organizer for woman's suffrage. (— *Montana Historical Society*)

Jeannette Rankin

Woman of Commitment

WHAT MAKES A REFORMER?

For Carry Nation, her husband's death by alcoholism soon after their only child was born changed her from a mild matron into an avenging fury who, Bible in one hand, hatchet in the other, set out to destroy the nation's saloons. The forty-year crusade of Dorothea Dix to obtain humane treatment for the mentally ill began when, as headmistress of a Boston finishing school, she was asked to conduct Sunday School for women prisoners and found insane women locked in unheated cells.

Jeannette Rankin, the most dedicated reformer the West has yet produced, got the nudge in childhood. The experience of growing up in the gun-ruled territory of Montana moulded the convictions that powered her lifelong effort to persuade people to get along together and let each claim his just share of the public good. A half century ahead of her time, she was a giant in the fight for women's rights, world peace and electoral reform. In 1916 she won election to Congress, thereby becoming the first woman in the United States to sit in a national legislative assembly.

Among reformers she stands out too for endurance. Beginning her career in the opening decade of this century, she continued to wave her banners through her active eighties, right up to her death in 1973, three weeks before her ninety-third birthday. If she did not sell all of her reforms to the American public, the remaining ones are no longer branded crackpot or utopian, but have been endorsed by many of the country's top leaders and thinkers.

The Rankin reform package, which had its origins in Montana's wild oats, also owed something to the birth order of the Rankin children. Jeannette, born June 11, 1880, was the first of seven offspring of John Rankin, a Missoula rancher and lumberman of Scotch extraction, who had come down from Canada seeking gold. As the lone Rankin boy came exactly in the middle of the stair-step series, Jeannette became her father's companion and assistant. As an adult she would recall that her father "encouraged me to exercise my judgement, always flattered me. We always discussed everything." At table he had her sit close to his "good ear." The diminutive child galloped alongside him about the ranch and sawmill, her narrow slanting grey eyes scrutinizing everything. At the rough and ready logging camps, she would pitch in and cook meals for the lumberjacks. She even learned to take the responsible post of sawyer, operating dangerous equipment. She didn't talk much, but her ears were always perked for what grown-ups were saying.

And much of it was bloodcurdling. What she heard about the violent goings-on, past and present, out on the plains and in the roistering mining camps had a lasting effect on her. There were chilling tales of the Montana gold rush, a brutal era during which the territorial governor barely escaped assassination and his successor died mysteriously. She heard stories of how the harrowed decimated Indians made their last desperate stands against the remorseless military. Chief Joseph of the Nez Percés was her favorite hero. After soldiers massacred squaws and children in their tents, he had sought to lead the remnant of his tribe to Canada, only to be ambushed in the Bear's Paw Mountains. Scarcely less distressing were the current events of Montana. Fearful battles raged in the mining camps of Butte and Helena for the spoils of the rich copper veins. Rival mine crews looted and fought each other with picks and dynamite, while their masters bribed judges and politicians to gain possession of disputed claims. Why, Jeannette wondered, didn't people settle their differences peaceably?

Solemn Jeannette was also the mainstay of her burdened mother. Straight-laced Olive Pickering had met and married the disappointed gold-seeker-turned-carpenter after journey-

ing out from New Hampshire to become the second schoolteacher in the district. As babies followed in close succession,
little Jeannette dutifully watched over her younger siblings.
She read Bible stories aloud to them (even though the Rankins
were not churchgoers), and her eyes sometimes brimmed with
tears at the climactic passages. Her precocious awareness of
society's imperfections conferred an air of maturity. "Nothing
daunted or baffled her," her sister Edna McKinnon recalls.
Jeannette comforted and protected and bossed them. She even
made clothes for them on an old treadle sewing machine — the
practical sort she thought they should have.

Jeannette's unruffability extended even to the ranch animals.
High in Rankin family lore was Jeannette's cool rescue of old
Shep, the family dog, whose errant wanderings pinioned him
in a steel trap. Summoned to the scene of distress, she saw at
once that the only solution was to amputate the captured foot,
which she promptly and efficiently did herself. Later, she
fashioned a little leather paw and attached it to the stump with
a firm strap, permitting Shep to resume ambulating as a quad-
ruped. On another day she was an angel of mercy to her
father's favorite horse. When the creature tore its shoulder on a
barbed wire fence, Mr. Rankin sent for Jeannette who came on
the run with needle and thread. Neatly sutured together again,
the horse quickly recovered.

Expanding into building contracting, John Rankin became
prosperous constructing stores and residences for growing Missoula. In the early 1900s he built his family a ten-room house in
town, and the family afterward spent their winters there,
returning to the ranch in summer. A pretentious mansarded
and cupolaed house, it had two Missoula rarities, hot-air heat
and a bathroom with a tin tub and hot water. At first the envy
of Helena, the house later raised eyebrows. The Rankins never
got around to furnishing it commensurate with its fine facade,
for by the time the house was completed the older children
were nearing college age, and instead of investing in Empire
sofas and golden oak bureaus, the earnest Rankins gave education top priority in the family budget. Jeannette later recalled:
"They'd say the Rankins never could afford anything in the

house, but we could always afford a railroad ticket to go East —
always sent off to school."

Eastern schooling didn't beckon at first. Jeannette stayed
at home in Missoula and attended the new University of Montana. When in high school she once prodded herself in her
diary: "Go! Go! Go!" Yet, in college she found that none of the
career choices really interested her. At length, she settled on an
education major, then had doubts. She talked of going into
nurses' training, but her father convinced her she was too inde-
pendent-minded for that profession. Not long after proudly
watching his favorite daughter graduate in 1902, John Rankin
died unexpectedly of Rocky Mountain spotted fever.

That fall Jeannette took a teaching position in a rural school
near Missoula, continuing to live at home. The attractive new
teacher was medium-tall and slender with intelligent eyes in
an alert oval face. Her mouth was thin but it broke easily into
a sincere smile, and she was always well-dressed in clothes
she made herself. But instead of looking forward to weekend
dances and box suppers where the schoolteachers sized up
marital prospects, Jeannette preferred staying home with her
family.

She hovered solicitously over all of them, but her fondest
smiles were for Wellington, then attending high school. Wellington was a bright large-framed, square-jawed boy with an
outgoing disposition. She was far from having Wellington all to
herself, for all the Rankins doted on him, but she and Wellington had a special rapport in their agreement on how much in
the world needed changing. As a school debater he was indig-
nant at the sullied state of Montana politics and the high-
handed ways of the copper kings. He had decided to become a
lawyer and upset their applecarts. Jeannette was dipping into
muckraking literature and reading about settlement houses,
especially about Jane Addams' work in the Chicago slums.

One family member remembers Jeannette as "always looking for things to do." Being useful was a necessity. For years
she had been indispensable at home, but now with the younger
children growing up and hired help plentiful, her thoughts
turned elsewhere. Her reading had convinced her that society

was plagued by cruel inequities, and she yearned to help right matters. She learned of a settlement house project in San Francisco, and one day she boarded a train to go there and offer her services as a volunteer. After four months at the bustling Telegraph Hill Neighborhood House, she knew she wanted to train for social work.

In 1908, at age 28, she went to New York City and enrolled at the New York School of Philanthropy. Wellington was already studying law at Harvard University. At the school that was the forerunner of Columbia University's School of Social Work she found kindred minds, but she found something more in the astonishing city. Exploring the sooty working-class districts she found them teeming with wretched humanity. Social injustice was even more flagrant than she had imagined. The maimed miners in Butte were blood brothers of the exploited newsboys, pale tenement dwellers, squinting seamstresses, weary shop girls. Everywhere she saw need for government regulation. But if the tainted legislature back in Helena exemplified law-making, how were the regulations to be enacted?

Quite by chance Jeannette discovered a promise of remedy. Social work students spent part of their day assisting seasoned professionals, and one day Jeannette's superior sent her out to obtain literature on woman suffrage. She had scarcely been aware of the suffrage movement, but as she glanced through the pamphlets she became fascinated. Postponing delivery, she sat up most of the night reading. She recalled of her initiation: "I had thought the only reason women didn't have the vote was because they hadn't asked for it." With indignation she read that men opposed votes for women on the grounds that women were incapable of helping run the government. Did men think *they* were making a grand success of it? The government corruption she and Wellington had deplored was *male* corruption. New York's stifling tenements existed because of *male* irresponsibility. Women voters would never be so callous. She returned for more suffrage literature.

For all the glaring need, social work positions were few in those laissez-faire days. Upon completing her course, in 1909, Jeannette returned home jobless. While composing mail applications, she cast a captious eye over Missoula. Upon inspecting its jail, she found it badly run; also she discovered the town lacked a public bath. The town fathers were rather astonished by her complaints, while the sheriff insisted she was "cooking it all up." Nonetheless, she did bestir some improvement at the jail before a job came through from Seattle.

Working in a Seattle orphan asylum, Jeannette was shocked to find her charges living in near poor-farm austerity. Few children were adopted in those days, and it was felt that coddling would ill prepare the waifs for their bleek futures. Jeannette found it useless to complain, for no standards existed. Again it struck her forcibly that there would never be proper welfare regulations until women effected them through the ballot.

Suffrage hopes were reviving just then in the state of Washington. Voting on a woman suffrage amendment had been set for the fall of 1910. Western women had led the nation in persuading men to let them vote; women in Wyoming, Idaho, Utah and Colorado had been marking ballots for years. But resistance had hardened, and since 1896 every suffrage referendum in the country had lost. The National American Woman Suffrage Association was looking to Washington to break the deadlock.

Jeannette was elated. She ordered a quantity of suffrage posters and walked about posting them conspicuously. Her baker let her place one in his window, and later he told her a woman had inquired who was blanketing the town with posters. Expecting to be congratulated, Jeannette looked up the woman, who turned out to be the leader of the Seattle suffragettes. The fight was not being waged as frontally as Jeannette had supposed. Under the direction of the astute Oregon suffrage leader Abigail Scott Duniway, the campaign was proceeding surreptitiously to avoid alerting the liquor interests. The liquor men feared women voters would push prohibition, and if they thought suffrage had a chance they would arouse male fear of closed saloons.

So Jeannette volunteered for undercover work. Suffrage strength grew without parades and with few open meetings, but with plenty of appeals to individuals and groups in private parlors. When the work moved to the countryside, Jeannette was sent to line up the little town of Ballard. Arriving there, she found Ballardians reluctant to even accept a leaflet. She had to search two days for a meeting place, then only eight people came. She returned to Seattle feeling defeated — only to be complimented on her success. She had been tested in a stronghold of "antis." Her campaign role expanded swiftly and she shared in the triumph of election night when a telephone call from Seattle wakened their national leader Mrs. Carrie Chapman Catt in her New York bed with word that Washington had carried suffrage by nearly two to one.

That victory was still ringing in her ears when Jeannette went home for Christmas and such a surprise awaited. A Montana legislator had announced he would introduce a bill for a suffrage referendum. Jeannette hastened to Helena to thank the enlightened man, only to hear upon arriving that he had made the statement when inebriated — as a joke! Undaunted, she called on the astonished legislator and argued tactfully that since he had announced his intention it was his duty to follow through. In turn, he astonished *her* by agreeing, on condition that she come and address the legislature on why it ought to hold a referendum. Jeannette, who had never made a speech before, with astonishment found herself accepting.

On the awesome day she arrived at the capitol wearing a stunning suit of her own styling and armed with a speech jointly tailored by herself and Wellington. She was escorted into an assembly hall so packed it overflowed into corridors and anterooms. On the speakers' platform blazed bouquets of flowers purchased by assessing legislators fifty cents apiece. After an equally flowery introduction, she smiled out from under her Gibson Girl pompadour and told her audience that she had been born in Montana. When that drew wild applause, she moved confidently to her first point: "Taxation without representation is tyranny." At last she finished, blushingly acknowledged applause, and supposed her ordeal was over. To her horror, the session lapsed into banter as grinning legislators speculated roguishly on the consequences of letting women into voting booths. One wag proposed that the franchise be limited to cases where husband and wife bore children alternately. Jeannette's hopes scraped bottom, but in the end a majority of the legislators voted for the referendum. The tally was short of the two-thirds required for passage, but it promised that victory was not far away.

Jeannette Rankin had found her path. Her brilliant work in Washington and Michigan was not lost on her suffrage superiors, and when she was offered a job as a paid worker in New York, she didn't hesitate. She had already perceived that social work, while necessary, only patched up social ills. She wanted to uproot them, and she believed voting women would commit themselves to that task.

In New York she drew the exacting assignment of campaigning on the streets. She and her colleagues would wait on a corner until some amiable-looking individual or couple appeared, then ask them, "Will you please stand for a few minutes?" They would then direct their speil to their captive, hoping desperately their oratory would magnetize others. When and if a group formed, a petition would be passed.

Jeannette was thrown into association with a group of brilliant young women, several of whom would become well known. Among them were Elizabeth Irwin, founder of the famous progressive school The Little Red Schoolhouse; Florence Kelley, pioneer in factory reform legislation and head of the National Consumers League; and Katharine Anthony, who would write popular biographies and remain a lifelong friend of Jeannette. In after hours they gathered in a tiny Greenwich Village apartment and discussed the millennium for women they believed was just around the bend.

In the fall of 1911, California suffragettes borrowed Jeannette to help direct their campaign for a suffrage amendment. The liquor forces tipped heavy coffers for vote-buying, but the women won the day. Mrs. Catt then sent Jeannette on suffrage business to Ohio and Wisconsin, and afterward appointed her a national field secretary, a job that required much travel. Jeannette bloomed in confidence and attractiveness. January, 1913 found her lobbying in the New York legislature in Albany. She succeeded in getting a suffrage amendment introduced, but it failed passage. Among those she failed to convince was a young state senator, Franklin D. Roosevelt, who told Jeannette woman suffrage was all right for the West, but it probably wouldn't work in the East.

All the while she was scheming how to pick up her threads in Montana. In 1912, she returned with a well-laid plot to move her home state into the suffrage column. Wellington helped her perfect it, and phase one went off without a hitch. She made a swift barnstorming tour of the state to recharge the existing suffrage organizations, and gained the women's assistance in persuading labor to endorse the franchise. Then, they coaxed the promising gubernatorial candidate Sam Stewart to include suffrage in his reform platform. The suffragettes helped Stewart win, and not long after his inauguration he got the legislature to approve a suffrage referendum for the following year. With these solid accomplishments behind her, Jeannette returned to the field.

Early in 1914, she came back and went into action. Her campaign strategy revealed her genius for organization. From her Butte headquarters she cast out a network of county organizations that closely resembled political party structure. Imbued recruits canvassed the farm vote on horseback, sitting down in ranch kitchens and talking over the farmyard fences. Jeannette set out on a 9,000-mile speaking tour, radiating energy, friendliness and style. In Lewiston she wore a stunning gold velvet costume, and the local editor said she looked like "a young panther ready to spring." She was in her element, doing what she passionately believed in and basking in the admiration of her family.

Her resourcefulness was tested when a Montana bank collapsed, taking the campaign treasury with it. Swiftly she repeated her fund drive. Even more disturbing were the "antis," a delegation of Eastern women opposed to suffrage. The stylish group enlisted some of Helena and Butte's richest "bonanzarines." Helena society was said to "consist of the twelve women who could afford to lose the most at bridge." The suffragettes succeeded in wooing away part of the bridge set, and to publicize their catch they seated them decorously in open cars and drove them up and down Last Chance Gulch, Helena's famous main street, horns tooting, banners flying.

But the biggest dent in the antis' front was self-inflicted. As in California, the liquor forces were fighting suffrage and the Eastern women were embarrassed to be allied with them. At a secret meeting the women asked the liquor men to work more covertly. News of the meeting leaked out, linking the two groups closer in the public mind. The suffragettes cried "Gumshoe methods!" The episode sullied the antis' image of propriety and may have nudged the suffragettes to their squeek-in victory. But victory it was, and Montana became the eleventh state to grant women full suffrage.

By now she was a star in the suffrage firmament. Mrs. Catt kept her on the run to Pennsylvania, to New Hampshire, to Washington, D. C. Late in 1914, she helped maneuver the long dormant national suffrage amendment out of a Congressional committee and onto the floor. The bill didn't pass, but the vote was encouraging.

In 1915, she was secretly carrying a political bee in her bonnet. Her Montana victory had set her dreaming of running for office. While lobbying in Washington it occurred to her the constitutional amendment would have easier going if a woman were sitting on the floor of Congress. Quietly she began boning up on the legislative process and on reform legislation. That summer she made a vacation trip to New Zealand to study the much-lauded reforms of that country where women had been voting for two decades.

In the fall she returned home with her mind made up: she would run for Congress as a Republican, the party of her father. Wellington, by then practicing law in Helena, applauded her plan. So did Mrs. Catt, who felt women could not be better symbolized in the political arena than by her capable field secretary. That the Montana suffragists would approve, Jeannette had taken for granted. But they did not. Awed and astonished, they felt she was shooting too high. Why not try instead for the state legislature? The Republicans were even less elated. They advised Wellington to "keep Jeannette from making a fool of herself." While disappointed, Jeannette was only momentarily unsettled, for Wellington's enthusiasm had grown. "Run," he insisted. "I'll pay for your campaign, and I'll elect you!"

In mid-July, 1916, Jeannette rose at a dinner in a Butte grill and announced she would seek the Republican nomination for Congress. Wellington, large and handsome, flanked her, beaming pride and pleasure — her campaign manager. Montana at that time elected its two Congressmen at large, and she would have to stump the whole State. But that held an advantage: state-wide she was better known than any of the seven men in the race. Moreover, she had a ready-made organization. By then the suffragettes had decided her campaign was a brilliant idea and were eager to participate.

A skilled and seasoned speaker, she set out on the campaign trail with the applomb of a Chautauqua orator on a sold-out tour. Admirers flocked to hear her again. She spoke on street corners, from the rear of open cars. She greeted men as they emerged from mine shafts and socialized in dance halls. For men who had voted for her referendum, it seemed no great step to consider voting for *her*. A political reporter for the New York *Evening Post* noted that "her finesse in rough-and-ready places was as expert as in any Washington drawing room." She was equal to any question, any situation. Wellington suffered when she was heckled, but she shrugged it off like confetti. She promised to work for child welfare, worker protection, prohibition, a more democratic government, and of course for the suffrage amendment. Another Rankin theme, little noticed then but much remembered later, was her appeal to women to use their votes to abolish war. Although World War I had erupted in Europe, President Wilson had vowed to keep America out. The American public was unaware of his deepening involvement.

She swept the primaries with a vote triple that of her nearest opponent. And in November, despite a Democratic landslide, she won — the first woman to be elected to national office. It catapulted her to world fame.

From a book on that era, *Washington Wife* by Ellen Maury Slayden, comes this account of the 36-year-old Congresswom-

an's debut in the House of Representatives on April 2, 1917:
"The chief interest of the morning . . . was the new Congresswoman . . . escorted by an elderly colleague, looking like a
mature bride rather than a strong-minded female . . . before
she could sit down she was surrounded by men shaking hands
with her. I rejoiced to see that she met each one with a big-
mouthed, frank smile and shook hands cordially and unaf-
fectedly. It would have been sickening if she had smirked or
giggled or been coquettish; worse still if she had been masculine and hail-fellowish. She was just a sensible young woman
going about her business."

The war outlook had darkened since her election. Now
Europe's guns seemed alarmingly close. American fear of German submarine warfare, which had grown steadily since the
sinking of the British liner *Lusitania,* had just about sunk American neutrality. Insiders said Wilson had called this special
session to say he could no longer keep the country out of the
conflict.

So it happened that on her very first day in Congress, the
first Congresswoman heard a solemn President ask the House
and Senate to declare war. During the frenzied four-day debate
that followed, the world tensely awaited their decision. In
Washington there was little doubt Wilson would get his way,
but there was much speculation on how the new "representative of womanhood" would vote. Her anti-war statements were
widely quoted in the press, but it was reported she hadn't made
up her mind.

Many clustered round to help her make it up. Grave-faced
pacifists wearing white arm bands urged her to vote against
war. But most pressure was from the other side. Suffragettes,
who considered her *their* Congresswoman, urged her to vote
in favor. Her vote wouldn't stop war, they argued, but it might
stop suffrage. Mrs. Catt, advised of her resistance, came to add
persuasion. From Montana came Wellington to insist that the
Central Powers must be stopped; he himself was preparing to
enlist in the Tank Corps. This news proved a final, crushing
blow to her spirits, and her staff thereupon reported Miss Rankin to be nearly distraught.

The House finally voted on April 7 at a weary three o'clock in the morning. The Senate already had passed the war bill, overwhelmingly. From the start of the House roll call, the "ayes" were greatly in the majority, with but a scattering of "noes." The Gallery was overflowing, and as the roll call droned toward the letter "R," many eyes focused on the much-publicized "lady from Montana." The clerk called "Miss Rankin." No answer. But members were permitted to pass the first roll call, and the clerk resumed the call, finished, then began recalling the tardies.

The crowded chamber fell abruptly silent as the slender, blue-clad figure rose somewhat unsteadily and grasped the seat ahead. Violating House tradition against uttering more than "aye" or "no," she stated, "I want to stand by my country but I cannot vote for war. I vote no." Accounts vary on whether she thereupon burst into tears or radiated serenity, but one thing is certain: she had voted her conscience, a conscience molded by those Indian massacres and copper wars of her Montana childhood.

She expected denouncement and she got it. Editorial writers had a field day. The bold suffragette who had taken potshots at male error was pinned like a butterfly in a display case, called everything from a traitor to a sentimental fool. The unkindest cut was the New York *Times'* citation of her vote as proof of "feminine incapacity for straight reasoning." Mrs. Catt said she "forgave" Miss Rankin her "error," but most suffragettes were scornful. And the word from her constituents back in Montana was overwhelmingly negative. Her party made it plain she could not expect to be renominated.

However, she still had her term. And her colleagues remained friendly, regarding her without censure. They were grateful she did not buttonhole them about suffrage, or invade their jolly sanctum, the House Cloakroom. She worked hard and she worked long, keeping busy three secretaries and a volunteer, her sister Harriet. The latter, a pretty young widow with two small daughters, had joined her in Washington along with their widowed mother, and they all shared a vast rambling apartment on California Street that was more or less an extension of her House office. There was even a spare bedroom to accommodate visiting female constituents. Everybody pitched in, visitors and all, to make the first Congresswoman an unmitigated success.

And by the gauge of accomplishment she was. One of the steadiest attendants on the House floor, she stuck it out through the dullest debates, her pen flashing over her note pad. Moreover, she often seized the initiative. Despite a mountain of war legislation she managed to wedge in reform bills. She introduced bills to grant women citizenship independent of their husbands, and to provide instruction in the hygiene of maternity and infancy, arguing wryly, "The government has always offered instruction in the hygiene of pigs." Both bills passed in later sessions. She sponsored legislation to provide equal pay for men and women in war jobs and in the Civil Service and introduced a bill which didn't pass to provide allowances for the dependents of American soldiers. With the aid of private investigation she paid for herself, she collected evidence of employment abuses in the primarily woman-staffed Bureau of Engraving. When Bureau officials dragged their feet, she got action by threatening a Congressional investigation.

And near the end of her term she guided to victory in the House the woman's suffrage amendment bill. History books tell us women were "given the vote in grateful recognition of women's work in World War I." The tired suffragettes knew they were never *given* anything. Victory came as the wages of decades of dogged groundwork, capped finally by a crescendo of brilliant coordinated effort. The National Woman Suffrage Association had continued to bombard the states with hard-fought referendums, while their Washington team worked ceaselessly to nurture favor in Congress. Since 1912, they had sought to coax Wilson out of the anti-suffrage stance he had assumed while governor of New Jersey. In January, 1917, the militant Woman's Party launched a non-stop-until-victory regimen of picketing the White House and persisted despite physical abuse and mass arrests. "DEMOCRACY SHOULD BEGIN AT HOME," blazed their banners past which Wilson drove out in the afternoon with his elegant new wife.

Early in 1918, Miss Rankin decided suffrage had sufficient favor in Congress to risk placing it on the agenda. On the afternoon of January 19 with the galleries packed with suffragettes she opened debate on the suffrage amendment to which President Wilson finally had given his blessing. Surely, the gentlemen could see, she said, that women were determined to vote and wouldn't stop trying until they succeeded. Look at how women were working in foundries, in high explosives, in blast furnaces, in the fields. How, by any order of logic, could they be held incompetent to govern themselves? "And how can we afford to allow (the world) to doubt for a single instant the sincerity of our protestations of democracy?"

The vote was a cliff-hanger. Four supporters had raised themselves from sick beds to come. Congressman Barnhard of Indiana was borne in on a stretcher during the last roll call. The clerk's count, made amidst near bedlam noise and confusion, revealed a tally of 270 to 136 — precisely the two-thirds majority required to pass a Constitutional amendment.

Jeannette took a break to celebrate with her suffrage sisters, who had long since forgiven her. Joyfully they sang their battle hymn "Old Hundred," confident that total victory would follow (Senate passage was in 1918, full state ratification in 1920). For Jeannette that exhausting, satisfying day wrote an end to one chapter in her life, for she was already anticipating another. That wrenching decision to vote against war had made her know indubitably that for her peace came before anything else; and the horrifying first world war had reinforced that conviction. Despite her dim chances, she felt it her duty to seek a return to office so that she might insist upon a workable peace treaty.

May, 1918, found her in Zurich, Switzerland, delegate to an international woman's convention, and now an ex-Congresswoman. She had lost her bid for reelection. Her Montana political foes had gerrymandered the state into two Congressional districts, making hers predominantly Democrat. So she had tried for the Senate, but the copper interests had used their power to defeat her. Upon vacating her House seat she had traveled to Switzerland to join an assembly of women from the recently warring countries. The women had gathered in mutual alarm at what an assembly of men were doing 500 miles away.

The alarming men were the delegates sitting at the Versailles Peace Conference. It seemed to the women that the men were not plotting a peace but another war. The victors, especially France and England, were set on extracting both monetary and territorial reparations, and Wilson had been unable to counter excessive demands. The women on the lake drew up a declaration protesting the harsh treaty, warning it would sow seeds for another war. Fearing they would not be heeded, they organized the Women's International League for Peace and Freedom (WIL), dedicated to permanently abolishing war. Jane Addams, Jeannette's early heroine, was elected president, while Jeannette was made vice chairman of the executive board.

Thus at age forty after a decade of exciting public life and personal acclaim, she entered the anonymous, unsung ranks of workers for peace. The peace movement was then so new, so small, so outcast, so poor that its converts worked largely unoticed and without salary. Her government experience made her most useful to the League in Washington, D. C., and she was able to maintain an apartment there because she received seventy-five dollars a month from her father's estate and was compensated for lobbying for social welfare legislation for the National Consumers League.

Shunning capital society, she lived quietly with her mother and was quickly forgotten. When anybody mentioned her it was to wonder: "Whatever happened to Jeannette Rankin?" She did not slacken her work pace nor did she affect the humble garb some peace workers did. She was always smartly coiffed and dressed with chic in the pigeonhole office in which she often served as her own secretary. Summer vacations were spent in Montana at Wellington's Avalanche Ranch. Wellington, who had started out specializing in claims against the copper companies, had risen swiftly to become the most successful lawyer in Montana.

During a Christmas vacation in 1924, Jeannette acquired her own hideaway, 64 acres of Georgia farmland ten miles from the state university town of Athens. She built a spartan little house — one large room and sleeping porch — that had neither electricity nor plumbing, but was heated by an ingenious appliance of her own invention that reminded her family of her early expertise at the sawmill. A car radiator connected via pipes to a fireplace and distributed even warmth. Cooking was accomplished on a kerosene stove in an abandoned cotton crib that she had moved behind her house. With a view to future income she planted a grove of pines, 200 pecan trees and a fruit orchard.

Actually, Georgia did not represent an escape from peace-seeking, but a new approach. Her political appeal had always been to grass roots, and she had a theory about Southern grass roots and peace. During the war debate some of the strongest anti-war arguments had come from Southern Congressmen. Since that time in her peace work she had detected a strong aversion to war among Southerners. She attributed it to the region's lingering Civil War wounds and decided the South, particularly the locale of Sherman's firey march, might be fertile ground for a peace movement.

The rancher's daughter effortlessly made friends with the local farmers' wives. They advised her on berrying and jellying and gardening; she talked to them about peace. Soon she had organized their children into recreational clubs, separate ones for boys and girls. While the girls sewed and while the boys tinkered with crystal sets, she told them peace stories. Before long, amidst Athens' polite groves of academe she had a thriving Georgia Peace Society going. It all came about as naturally as peach blossoms in the Georgia spring.

Meanwhile, peace was resisting on other fronts. After 1925, her duties as field secretary for WIL carried her on lecture tours across the country. But her faith in the League had diminished; she deplored its tendency to concentrate on holding congresses and distributing food. She argued for a network of local peace units. She was no longer encouraged by American foreign policy or by the debates in the League of Nations.

In 1928, her hopes fixed upon the French-initiated Kellogg-Briand Pact, which condemned "recourse to war for the solution of international controversies." By then she had parted service with WIL and was lobbying for the Pact under the auspices of the Women's Peace Union. She and her thriving Georgia groups held a statewide conference to encourage public support for the Pact. The Georgia newspapers covered the conference respectfully, and the participants enthusiastically decided to make the peace conference an annual event.

The realm of pacifism is by no means placid. The goal of curbing man's fighting tendencies arouses strong passions and firm "positions," and none was stronger and firmer than Miss Rankin's. A purist, she held that in matters of peace, compromise had never worked, never would. She soon clashed with the wishy-washy Union, transferring her services to the National Council for Prevention of War. This predominantly Quaker organization was closer to her thinking, and she would remain with them nearly a decade for a pittance as remuneration, although she would have her tilts with them too. Under their banner she lobbied and propagandized in turn for the World Court, for a Constitutional Amendment to outlaw war, for disarmament conferences, for neutrality legislation and antiwar profit law.

Early in the thirties she became convinced that a horrible world war was approaching. Although 62 nations had signed the Kellogg-Briand Pact, it had proved no hindrance to the Japanese invasion of Manchuria. The League of Nations was disintegrating. The major powers had embarked on an arms race. She was among the first to see that Hitler threatened world peace, and she charged urgently that American economic policy and diplomacy were encouraging the dangerous man. She lobbied relentlessly against nourishing his regime. Nobody seemed to see the menace in him. Exasperated at the myopia of her countrymen, she journeyed to Geneva at her own expense to try to persuade the League of Nations to use the Treaty of Versailles to curb Hitler. Her suggestion was spurned. She complained angrily that the League people "treated me as if I'd said, 'Let's take off our clothes and roll in the streets.'"

As her fears mounted, her patience grew short. She argued with her employers over lobbying tactics. She caustically criticized other peace groups. She accused the Women's International League of "playing Lady Bountiful," the Fellowship of Reconciliation of "doing nothing but praying." Even Georgia had foundered. Along with latent peace sentiment she had encountered a deep-dyed regional conservatism and suspicion of outsiders. An element had criticized her from the beginning, and as her peace following grew and she used it to prod Georgia Congressmen into less militant stances, her attackers, including the American Legion, grew blatant and enlisted a sector of the press. The "Montana intruder" was painted a dangerous radical who was trying to undermine the manhood and patriotism of Georgia. She filed a libel suit against one virulent newspaper, and eventually won it, but in the meantime it was her intimidated peace following which dissolved into impotency.

Her Georgia problems included the burning of her home. Unhesitatingly, she bought another house (for $300) a few miles away on the outskirts of Watkinsville. Later, she turned over her house to a black farm family and remodeled the nearby share-cropper shanty for herself. She covered its tamped earth floor with Oriental rugs and devised another heating system, this one a mechanism for twisting newspapers into fireplace logs (a rather similar one has since been commercialized).

Her anger at governments for appeasing Hitler grew to near contempt at their about-face after Hitler invaded Poland in 1939. Those European powers which in her view had created him, now rushed headlong to fight him. In Washington she detected an urge to follow. It was 1917 all over again — the government maneuvering toward a war the public and press emphatically opposed. Somewhat shrilly, she began accusing certain politicians of warmongering. Her tactics became blunter. When a new electee arrived in town, she demanded to see him, hoping to implant wisdom before he could be infected. The new Senator Truman was startled by her unequivocal opposition to war, while she was shocked by his frank espousal: "Well, I've always liked war. I feel we made all our advances in civilization from war." One writer compared her persistence with militarists to that of "an elderly lady beating her umbrella over the head of a man beating his horse."

In 1939, as the government geared for a huge navy expansion, it seemed to the tired and anxious pacifist that nobody heard what she was saying. Desperate to amplify her voice, she decided to run for Congress again. Montana had remained her voting place, and her district now was more equitably divided between Republicans and Democrats. Covertly, she began campaigning early with speeches before high school assemblies. In June, 1940, at age 60, she cast her hat in the ring.

Again Wellington encouraged her and funded and managed her campaign. They aroused nostalgic memories. Newspapers broke out with "then and now" photographs of the still handsome pair — he robust and stocky, she elegantly slender. Wellington was now a well-known political figure; he had served as state attorney and as United States district attorney, but had failed in races for governor and the United States Senate. After a brief marriage, which ended in divorce, he had resumed his favorite private role, aiding and protecting his big close-knit family.

Running her usually friendly, fast-moving race she won the nomination against a field of three men. Then, while the Nazis ravaged Western Europe and conviction grew that "We'll be in it soon," Jeannette Rankin insisted, "We don't have to be." She promised frightened women she would work to keep their sons, husbands and sweethearts at home. And again she was elected.

When she claimed her House seat in March, 1941, braced to resist any drift toward war, she found pro-war sentiment burgeoning. American merchant vessels were plying the Atlantic provisioning France and England, and Congress was preparing to arm them. Futilely she cast votes against lend-lease and convoys, and introduced measures to require Congressional or electorate approval of military intervention.

Then, most disturbing of all, came rumors that Roosevelt was weakening to Churchill's entreaties to join the fray. Especially he was weakening to Churchill's pressures to join in an ultimatum to Japan to guarantee the inviolateness of British interests in Asia, else face economic blockade. Miss Rankin recognized, and said so, that a blockade would be a serious, perhaps provoking blow to a country so dependent on imports. But Congress was not invited to consider an ultimatum, and it was rumored Roosevelt had ignored the Neutrality Act and delivered it on his own.

She was on a train en route to Detroit to make an anti-war speech when she heard on a radio that the Japanese had bombed Pearl Harbor. While horrified, she did not consider it an "unprovoked attack." She was convinced that the United States, goaded by England, had with calculation provoked Japan to flail out in desperation. Hastily, she returned to Washington.

When the War Resolution was sped to the highly excited House, the Montana Congresswoman sought unsuccessfully to speak, but was shouted down. When the roll was called she voted against it, stating firmly, "As a woman I cannot go to war, and I refuse to send anybody else." The Senate already had unanimously voted for war, and in the House hers was the lone "no" among 288 "ayes."

Few government figures have been as ostracized as Jeannette Rankin. Outside the House chamber a threatening crowd surrounded her, and police had to escort her to safety. Thereafter, her Congressional colleagues shunned her. The press ignored her. Boos assailed her in public. The abuse continued even after a responsible sector of the press, including *Life* Magazine, reported on the basis of evidence, that the United States had in fact secretly served an ultimatum on Japan and our forces in the Far East had been put on the alert for a retaliatory attack. (Scholarly research since then has reinforced the charges.) The Montana rancher's daughter sometimes compared the provocation to "tickling the hind leg of a mule."

She departed office depressed. The war promised to be a long one, and the peace movement lay in wreckage. Her labors of a quarter of a century seemed for nought. Yet at 62, her energies, physical and mental, were undiminished. A project formed out of her enthusiasm for travel and for India, the home of Gandhi, who had toppled a mighty oppressor via non-violent resistance. Wellington had made her the gift of a ranch that returned a modest income, and as soon as travel was possible again she made the first of seven extended, spartan rambles over India. Enduring all manner of transport and accommodations, she made friends with the natives and got to know them intimately. Her opener with women was to compliment their earrings; children responded to chewing gum and Lincoln pennies. Gandhi was then so burdened, arising daily at 4 a.m., that she decided to postpone a planned interview until her next visit. Soon after her departure, he was assassinated.

She returned again and again, visiting ashrams and villages and city slums, and getting to know Nehru and Indira Gandhi. Always her valises were amply stocked with aspirin for her tic douloureux, the painful neuralgia that gripped her right cheek. Her exposure to raw poverty and suffering in her travels convinced her that only in a peaceful world could human misery be attacked with any prospect of solution.

During those years she applied hard criticism to her failed approach to peace and studiously mapped out a new one. Instead of trying to turn career politicians into peacemakers and reformers, why not revise the election procedure to make it possible for peacemakers and reformers to be elected? The practice of electing but one Congressman per district virtually shut out the more peace-inclined citizens — women, minorities and young adults. Congress was a bastion of older white males, always the gung-ho war starters. Her plan called for large Congressional districts with several Congressmen. Then a voter might vote for both a man *and* a woman, a black *and* a white, an educational expert *and* an economic expert. In short, minorities might be drawn into the democratic process.

The Presidency too might become representative. She had long advocated electing presidents by direct vote, and to that scheme she added a means of making a truly democratic selection. Presented a sizable list of democratic candidates, the voter would list his preferences from first to last. The winner would depend not only on the number of first choices, but also on the general attitude toward him expressed in the other choices.

In the late 1960s, she launched her campaign to sell "Multi-member Congressional Districts" and the "Direct Preferential Vote for President." Working alone, as was her style, she began talking to small groups and mailing out a persuasive leaflet she had composed. When ears perked up at her provocative proposals, she was emboldened to beard the lions in Washington. She buttonholed individual lawmakers and when possible addressed government committees. She was not surprised to find that after an initial flash of interest came fear her plan would puncture party power and disturb their kingpin constituencies. Whenever a state legislature was considering revising its state constitution she showed up to propose that they write multi-districting into their new code. Whenever she gained floor discussion of her proposal she was encouraged, for she knew important change was not wrought overnight.

The general public remained oblivious of her until one day in January, 1968. That morning Americans were astonished to hear on television and their car radios that Jeannette Rankin at 86 had returned to Congress. Not as a Congresswoman this time. She had led several thousand women from all over the country to Washington to demand a halt to the Vietnam War and to present Congress a petition from thousands of other objectors to the then five-year-old conflict.

Interestingly, the project had started in Georgia, the peace garden she believed had died of blight. An Atlanta remnant had kept the faith, and at the time that college campuses were holding teach-ins against the Vietnam War, they asked Miss Rankin to address a small peace group at the home of Nan Pendergrast. That May day in 1967, Miss Rankin told the little group that if "10,000 women had mind enough they could end the war." The gist of her speech went out over the Associated Press and peace-minded women in other cities were inspired to organize "The Jeannette Rankin Brigade" to protest the war; and she was asked to lead it.

So the lady from Montana was back in Washington, again causing consternation. Her plan to lead the women to the foot of the Capitol steps raised fears as to what sort of nuisance they might commit there, so Washington police dusted off a forgotten 1882 law forbidding "assemblages" on the Capitol grounds. Miss Rankin said the prohibition was "undemocratic and probably unconstitutional." When the group's lawyer was unable to persuade a judge to enjoin operation of the statute, she led her following of neatly-dressed, predominantly middle-aged women through uncleared snow to a small park at the rear of the Capitol. Then she led a delegation of sixteen women, including Mrs. Martin Luther King, Jr., into the Capitol building where they delivered their petition and paid prearranged visits with Senate Majority Leader Mike Mansfield and House Speaker John McCormick, both elderly white males. When she told Senator Mansfield she favored bringing the soldiers home from Vietnam, he objected, "But how can we do this?" "The same way we got them there," she told him, "by planes and ships."

One press account referred to Miss Rankin as a "senior hippy," which appellation she shrugged off. "I don't mind — I've been called everything." But she instructed her lawyer to appeal the denial of her suit to enjoin the 1882 statute, and several months later the Supreme Court by a unanimous decision found the law unconstitutional.

She was rather taken by surprise by "women's lib," the new feminist revival that got under way in the late 1960s and which quickly discovered her to be the oldest living suffrage leader. She was delighted with the spunky young women and spoke at their gatherings. But she was a mite impatient that ideas she had advocated sixty years before were considered new. And she chided women for not resisting war enough, for not insisting on their rights enough. "You have to be stubborn — stubborn and ornery," she insisted. "When the men make fun of you, that's when you know you're getting on well." Suffrage had not freed women, she said, because they remained economically fettered to husbands and bosses and were afraid to speak or vote their minds. The new thrust for economic equality was good, she said, but she told the women that to attain true equality they would have to gain election reform and wrench away the older white male grip on government.

She bounded into her nineties, buoyed by extra adrenalin from sheer exhilaration at being more in demand than she had been in decades. Not merely was she a star of the peace and feminist movements, but even more gratifying, her electoral reform ideas were being taken up by political writers and thinkers such as Ralph Nader and John Lindsey. In high vitality she addressed dinners and conferences throughout the country, served on committees, endorsed politicians, granted interviews, answered fan mail. In Georgia between forays she took brisk walks with her dachshound Sam and ate one meal a day, mostly health foods, including yogurt she made herself.

In mid-February of 1972, at age 92, she made a peppery speech in Nashville, Tennessee, to the Southern Women's Conference for Delegate Selection, after which she flew to New York to receive the first Susan B. Anthony award from the National Organization of Women as "the outstanding living feminist." From there it was south to Atlanta to address the Georgia Women's Political Caucus in Atlanta, then back to New York to attend the fourth reunion of the Jeannette Rankin Brigade and to appear on several radio and television shows. To a reporter who asked whether she lived in Montana or Georgia, she replied, "I live in an airplane."

The Vietnam War recently had ended (officially) when this writer visited Jeannette Rankin on a mild spring evening in 1973 at a retirement home near Carmel, California. Purchased with funds from a generous bequest from Wellington, who died in the 1960s, her new home was a well-appointed first-floor studio apartment with a wide panel window that faced the folded mountains enclosing the placid valley. Nearby lived her widowed youngest sister Edna; she, Jeannette and one other sister on Long Island were the last of the John Rankin family.

A glance about the L-shaped studio revealed its owner did not spend her days idly contemplating that view. Lining the walls were shelves of much-handled books, and scattered over the blond utilitarian furniture were place-marked books, current issues of intellectual quarterlies, newspapers (including the New York *Times*), pamphlets, stacks of manuscripts, heaps of mail, file folders, a typewriter, pencils and pens.

Among them Jeannette Rankin sat rigidly upright, a fragile figure in a sand-colored wig and an elegant polka-dot chiffon dress with a wide ruff collar — and almost mute. Some months before the muscles of her throat had begun to deteriorate, the aftermath of surgery to remedy her troublesome "tic." Her voice now nearly gone, she was reduced to forcing gutteral, largely unintelligible sounds from her esophagus, as do people who have had radical throat surgery. Her health, which had seemed invincible, had foundered on something so small as nerve endings.

Had pride led her to face the interview alone, unaided by her part-time secretary? She attempted conversation, but initially I could not translate any of her vocal sounds into words. We were both dismayed. She broke the impasse by frankly expressing her anger that her body was failing her, hindering her work. Pointing to her mouth, she grimaced, conveying how much she hated her condition. Then she shrugged and brightened. Her frailness threw her strong facial features into relief, and with her slanting black-rimmed glasses and white ruff, she rather resembled an eagle.

Thus we arrived at an understanding to work it out as best we could. She answered my questions variously by nods and head shakes, by frowns, by gutteral sounds, by pointing to lines or sections of manuscripts which, under her direction, I ferreted from file drawers. I repeated what I believed she had communicated and received either vigorous nod or vigorous head shake. Thus, circuitously, I arrived at some of the thoughts of the country's most dedicated pacifist in her ninety-second year at the close of her fifth war.

Much on her mind that evening was a revelation about World War I made in a new book by the British journalist Colin Simpson. Simpson had marshaled evidence that the *Lusitania*, the supposedly unarmed British liner whose sinking by Germany had drawn the United States into war, in reality had been heavily armed and carried a large cargo of munitions. Simpson further charged that the United States government learned the ship had been armed but concealed it from the American public. Of course, it substantiated Miss Rankin's long-held contention that Wilson had let England draw the United States into war against the wishes of the electorate. Her eyes flashed indignation as she gazed at the incriminating evidence. "History might have been different, had this been known in time."

But future peace was what mattered now, she emphasized. Did she believe we had learned anything from the long, gruelling Vietnam War that would help us hold the peace? Furious head shake. So long as we maintained a huge military machine, the military and its supporters would find ways to use it. But there was no chance of demilitarizing until the government was made truly democratic.

Was she optimistic that our government *would* change? Her eyes glinted. The new awareness of women, she felt, held high potential. If women would thrust themselves into government — press for office, press for electoral reform — *they* could change government. She wished more women would exhibit the grit of Congresswoman Bella Abzug and Shirley Chisholm and editor Gloria Steinem. Women's maternal instincts told them to oppose war, she said. In her opinion Indira Gandhi and Golda Meir had kept the peace in their tinderbox countries better than their male counterparts.

On that spring evening that was less than two months before her death (in her sleep on May 18), I sensed that Jeannette Rankin's hopes were intact, if tempered. Once she had believed that conquering war would prove no more resistant than winning the franchise. But she had found she had taken on the stickler of all time. Historians tell us that the human inhabitants of this planet have waged war on each other at least 15,000 times since they assumed the vertical position. Patently, the habit lies deep in the psyche.

I gathered that if once she had believed headily with Giraudoux's protagonist *The Madwoman of Chaillot* that "Nothing is ever so wrong in the world that a sensible woman can't set it aright in the course of an afternoon," she had revised her faith roughly thus: "We can break our habit of warring if sensible men and women of all colors and creeds and ages cooperate toward that end in a truly democratic government. And if they work exceedingly hard at it."

Isadora Duncan as photographed in her thirties by Arnold
Genthe. (— *Bancroft Library*)

Isadora Duncan
Immeasurable Gift of Beauty

IN THE HALF CENTURY since her death on the Riviera — that preposterous death that was the collusion of an Italian sports car and a Spanish shawl — many writers have sought to capture the singular essence of Isadora Duncan. Promising "the real Isadora" or "the other Isadora," each biographer clears the blackboard of earlier portraits and proclaims his the true likeness.

In Isadora's case, the irreconcilables of her nature *can't* be jettisoned. Isadora *was* irreconcilable; she *had* no singular essence. Her contradictions confused *her* no less than others — she scorned attempts to classify her. The innovative dancer from San Francisco was both a saint and a sinner, a spartan and a sybarite, an idler and a perfectionist, a teasing courtesan and a loving mother, a revolutionary who spouted Marxian ideology and an aristocrat who reveled in privilege. She spent fortunes on educating proteges and assisting friends. Yet she sponged on well-wishers and left bills unpaid. She was all those things, each of them sincerely. One at a time.

From childhood she preferred illusion to reality. She was a player of roles, a spinner of dreams, and in late life, of nightmares. It was, of course, this protean power that gave her creativity its electrifying surprise and made her one of the great dancers of all time. Just as it was the very intensity of her dreams which excluded all traditional technique and artifice — all but her inner light. "So dreamy-limbed," one poet said of her. And in liberating her art form from its former bondage, she gave it a wholly new direction, opening the way for the free and honest modern dance.

Although this compulsion to escape reached culmination in the famous youngest member of the family, all the Duncans had it. Both her Irish maternal grandfather Thomas Gray and her Philadelphia-born father Joseph Duncan were lured West by the promise of the Gold Rush, and once there they continued to court ever brighter promises. Both leaped in and out of a succession of ordinary jobs, apprenticeships, business ventures, real estate flyers. Both had a flair for innovation: Gray established the first ferry service across San Francisco Bay; Duncan constructed the city's first skyscraper and its first safe-deposit boxes.

Duncan also wrote poetry and mingled with the city's "artistic set," and one night some now forgotten salon hostess introduced him to a dreamy piano teacher, Dora Gray. By then he was into banking, but his sheen didn't blind Dora's staunchly-Catholic parents to the fact of a previous marriage. Infatuated Dora married him anyhow and bore him two sons and two daughters. But by the time Isadora was born, on May 27, 1878, he had disappeared with a price on his head. His flamboyant bid to corner the city's banking business by offering twelve per cent interest instead of the usual seven had broken his bank and brought charges of forgery and felony. He was captured crouched in the closet of a lady friend, but by charming witnesses, judge and jury, he went free after four mistrials. That upheaval together with habitual infidelity, convinced Dora to divorce him. The resilient Duncan reestablished himself in Los Angeles, married again, and made and lost another fortune before dying in a shipwreck.

For Dora and her brood there followed lean years in Oakland, where she moved and tried to make ends meet on the proceeds of piano teaching. They lived in one drab house after another, a jump ahead of the landlord. Dora told her children, "Material things are unimportant. What matters is culture." And that, she assured them, they had. At night she read aloud poetry or from the work of Ingersoll (she had replaced Catholicism with atheism). More often she played the piano and encouraged her children to dance. "Aren't we happy, darlings!" Dora would trill.

The children agreed — so heartily they became bored with school and dropped out. Isadora quit at age ten. Dora let them all follow their impulses, never scolding or disciplining. While she taught lessons at her pupils' homes, her offspring danced, staged theatricals, published their own newspaper, and read in the Oakland Free Library.

Observing Isadora's dancing aptitude and her fondness for it — the child often danced trance-like, forgetting to eat — Dora stinted to pay for ballet lessons. But Isadora, who spurned authority early, chaffed at the disciplines of ballet instruction and refused to continue. The family discovered another talent in the pretty auburn-haired, grey-eyed child. She was skilled at handling creditors. Glib and smiling, she easily persuaded the grocer or the butcher that the Duncans were expecting a sizable check, and meanwhile wouldn't they fill her shopping basket?

The Duncan children's cavortings attracted neighborhood children, and out of it grew Elizabeth's and Isadora's dancing classes, which brought in some cash. Augustin and Raymond helped instruct, although Raymond's interest lay more in recitation, Augustin's in play-acting. Delighted with this fountain of creativity, Dora played piano for the classes and applauded the theatricals. When their father, Joseph Duncan paid a visit and put a down payment on a San Francisco house for them, they were able to shift their activities across the Bay. There they found a higher-paying clientele, the children of San Francisco high society.

By this time the Duncans had made a galvanizing discovery — audiences. After staging entertainments in private homes, the exuberant troop stepped up to commercial theaters in small satellite towns. Their varied bill of dances and playlets expressed the Duncans, but it also reflected a California fad, a back-to-nature craze in decor that had invaded the arts. A Berkeley magazine *Home Chimes* and a book by a Berkeley author *The Simple Home* were preaching the credo of rustic simplicity. The thing in decoration was unfinished walls and floors, hand-hewn furniture and denim curtains. The Duncans costumed themselves in plain loose-fitting garments decorated

only with leaves and sprigs and performed against a backdrop
of plain blue muslin. Their dancing, which they defined as
"natural movements," combined walking, running, skipping,
leaping and arm-waving. The bill was only moderately successful, but there was always applause for the graceful dancing of
the elfin youngest child with the snub nose and soleful eyes.
From the first, Isadora was that type of creator who achieves
rapturous loss of identity in art, one with Flaubert, who once
said, "What a delicious thing writing is — not to be you any
more . . ." To her sister Elizabeth, a plain, sensible girl, dancing was an absorbing occupation, and hers was the impetus for
their growing school, whose routine Isadora found tedious.

In one of their ballroom dancing classes, Isadora discovered
what was to be another powerful motivation — love. The conflict of her art and her loves was to supply the peculiar rhythm
of her life. The object of her pristine passion was a handsome
young pharmacist named Vernon, who was making his entry
into society and wished to be introduced to the intricacies of
the waltz, mazurka and polka, then *de rigueur* on Nob Hill.
Isadora was scarcely in her teens, but with her hair piled atop
her head, she looked older, and she was smitten not with a
schoolgirl crush but with a deep fixation. Between lessons,
when she all but swooned in Vernon's indifferent embrace, she
was in a daze of exaltation. To her diary she confided the "terrible thrill of floating in his arms," but Vernon departed unaware of the flame he had ignited. During the two years it
burned Isadora walked miles to pass his drugstore and to
moon at the light in his boardinghouse window. News of his
marriage to a society girl plunged her into black despair. Ego-
centric by nature, encouraged to believe sensibility all-impor-
tant and lacking a broadening education which might have
protected her, she was utterly vulnerable to personal defeat.
Her reaction was the one that would always attend disappointment — the impulse of flight. She resolved to leave San
Francisco, become a famous dancer, and dedicate her life to
art.

She wangled auditions with managers of traveling theatre
companies. Chewing their cigars, they gazed with bewilder-

ment at her turnings and leapings to Mendelssohn and told her
it had no place in the commercial theater. "It's more for a
church," one suggested. Fuming at his verdict, Isadora called a
family council and in an emotional tirade convinced them she
must go East where *real* impresarios would value her. She was
always able to manipulate her family with the same suasion
she trained on the butcher; her mother especially could deny
her nothing. The Duncans scoured up all available cash together with a few pieces of family jewelry and purchased two
railroad tickets to Chicago for Isadora and her mother. The
other children would follow as soon as Isadora was on the
boards.

Chicago in the summer of 1897 was scarcely more attuned
to her art. The letter of a San Francisco newspaperman introduced the Duncans to Chicago's bohemian set, which applauded Isadora's dancing and toasted her with mugs of beer.
But it could offer nothing more. The indifference of theater
managers to Isadora's act and the readiness of landlords to
eject them for nonpayment brought Dora Duncan to near collapse. Isadora, however, remained confident, buoyed up by her
romance with a middle-aged painter, an emigrant Pole with
flaming red hair and beard, who talked poetically, although
vaguely, of marriage.

For her mother's sake, Isadora accepted a music hall offer
of $20 a week that stipulated she revamp her act into "some-
thing more peppery"— direction she braced to resist. Billed as
"The California Faun," she danced ethereally in rustic garb,
and when the manager insisted that she add the pepper, she
quit in indignation. But soon after, the eminent producer Augustin Daly came to town and she laid seige to his headquarters, at length obtaining an audition that brought an offer of a
small part in a New York revue planned for fall production.

New York proved somewhat more enthusiastic, if parsimonious. Arriving there on borrowed money, she discovered dancers
went unpaid during rehearsal weeks, a stinging blow, as her
family had accompanied her to share her success. Being cast in
a pantomime was another disappointment. She balked at the
rigid pointings and gesticulations until threatened with dis-

missal. Daly next cast her as one of Titania's dancing fairies in his staging of *A Midsummer Night's Dream,* but she refused to follow the motions of the other fairies, and one night seized the spotlight with an impromptu dance that stopped the show. Daly upbraided her for courting applause at an inappropriate juncture of the play and banished her to a dark corner of the stage. Brooding in ignominy, she accompanied the troop to its Chicago booking and a joyous reunion with her semi-fiancé. He wanted to join her in New York, but her family scotched that by making inquiries that unveiled him a married man. Isadora returned to New York disillusioned with both love and the theater. She resigned from Daly's company determined hereafter to keep her art for the concert stage, where she might dance unfettered by any inspiration but her own.

She awaited that opportunity with a confidence both arrogant and innocent. Elizabeth chose to await it more practically: she rented a Carnegie Hall studio and advertised for pupils. Soon they were all teaching again. After classes Dora played far into the night, while Isadora rehearsed for fame. As it turned out, opportunity awaited no farther than the adjoining studio. Its occupant was the brilliant young composer Ethelbert Nevin, and after glimpsing his charming neighbor at her practice, he suggested a joint concert.

Before a select audience in the small Music Room at Carnegie Hall, Nevin played while Isadora danced in front of the plain blue curtains that would become her trademark. The audience was thrilled by her original dancing with its slow undulating movements punctuated by surprising leaps and sudden runs. Present were several pillars of New York society, and as the Newport season was getting under way, the concert opened new vistas. Mrs. Vincent Astor invited her to dance at an afternoon gala on the lawn of her summer villa, an invitation that proved nearly as magical as the wand of a fairy godmother. Isadora became an instant Newport fad, invited everywhere to divert the likes of Fishes, Belmonts and Vanderbilts. It was thrilling to have New York's nabobs shouting bravo, but the checks Isadora was handed scarcely began to meet her expenses.

A strenuous season led to no substantial engagement, and Isadora wondered if success might not be awaiting her in London. When a hotel fire destroyed their studio, her family agreed to accompany her there, if means could be found. Summoning her charms, Isadora paid calls on her stinting Newport patrons sadly confiding their fire losses and her need to get to London. She managed to collect $300, not enough to transport them to London in high style, but it did pay their way, in late 1899, on a cattle boat. All but Augustin, who while playing Romeo in a minor theater company, had impregnated the 16-year-old Juliet; he remained behind in New York, where in time he became a moderately successful actor.

London, delightfully different on the surface, proved almost a repetition of New York. First grueling poverty, then discovery by the artistic set, who launched Isadora on the drawing room circuit. All were delighted by the freshness and ebullience of the little American dancer with the tragic eyes. Famed actresses Ellen Terry and Mrs. Patrick Campbell cooed adulation; even the Prince of Wales, the future Edward VII, paid her a pretty compliment. Alas, London hostesses were even more closefisted than Newport's; they considered a bowl of strawberries ample pay for diverting them. But Isadora acquired a suitor, a middle-aged art gallery director, who presented her in a series of dance concerts in the courtyard of his gallery. Isadora's rose-girdled figure weaving between potted palms and around a playing fountain was said to be "Botticelli like." But on the whole London found her dance too odd to take seriously.

In London, the Duncans spent much time in the British Museum studying Greek attitudes portrayed on urns and the Elgin Marbles. Isadora incorporated Greek poses into her dancing, while Grecian garb prompted abbreviation of her drapery. Raymond changed into Greek sandals and tunic, at least, his singular version of them, and would wear them the rest of his life. He crossed the Channel to pursue his Greek studies at the Louvre, and Mrs. Duncan and Isadora soon joined him, Elizabeth having returned to New York.

In Paris Isadora indubitably arrived. If New York and London mistrusted the novel, Paris welcomed it. Its artists were then scuttling tradition and passionately experimenting. The watchword was simplicity. Eric Satie was stripping music down to basics, and painters were reducing objects to spatial abstractions. After an interval of hungry obscurity, Isadora was discovered by the Paris intellectuals. They hailed her a primitive genius who had rediscovered the dance by refusing to accept artificial positions and gestures. She was said to follow the suggestions of nature, the movements of wind and waves, of birds and moths, which primitive man had followed but civilized man had forgotten. Isadora joyfully responded with a torrent of creativity, improvising spontaneously from within, never dancing the same twice.

There was no keeping this delicious secret from high society. Soon Isadora was executing her winged creations on a little lattice-backed stage in the drawing room of the Countess Greffuhle, the reigning Paris hostess. The Princess de Polignac stole her from the Countess by going one better: opening her spacious painting studio for public concerts, for which the fashionable paid to see the remarkable child dance so breathtakingly in her filmy tunic.

According to her friend Mary Desti, it was at this time that Isadora availed herself of another fetching freedom. One evening when changing into her tunic in the wings and sipping a glass of rye (even then she liked a drop of alcohol before making an entrance), she spilled the liquid into her dancing slippers. The wet shoes adhered to her stockings making it difficult to wriggle them on. When the curtain began to part, she abandoned the effort and stripped off shoes and stockings and tripped onstage barefoot. Everyone exclaimed over the beauty of her high-arched feet, so she decided that in the future she would keep them visible.

She was the sensation of the season. Artists sketched her; poets spun poems to her. She was plied with music hall offers, which she airily spurned. By now, she knew with certainty that the concert stage awaited. It arrived in the form of an offer to tour Central Europe on a bill that included the celebrated Art Nouveau dancer Loie Fuller and the Japanese tragic dancer Sada Yacco. The tour was the springboard for her phenomenal climb to fame. For Isadora, success in the grudging world of the concert stage came with astonishing swiftness.

Sophisticated concert goers in the music capitals of Germany and Austria recognized her genius at once. She was acclaimed as the first original American dancer. Earlier Americans who had tread their boards had interpreted one or another of the European dances, utilizing patterns handed down by tradition or variations dictated by choreographers. The young Californian had brought something wholly her own.

What was it? Isadora, herself, could not have said then. Years later, in her autobiography, she explained she had discovered that the body possesses a natural urge, one lost to civilization's false restrictions, to react to emotional stimuli with spontaneous physical movement. She had learned, she said, to free her body to move in response to the stimuli of music. She accomplished this by "concentrating all my force" on the solar plexus, which she believed to be the "central spring of all movements," thereby causing it to respond to "the rays and vibrations of the music." In her opinion, "the peculiar environment of my childhood and youth had developed this power in me," enabling her to "shut out all outside influences and to live in this force alone."

But Isadora's highly communicative art never needed explaining to an audience. Even the most uninitiated marveled at her ability to sustain movement with unfaltering emotional truth through lengthy musical compositions, later through whole symphonies. She conferred on dance a new dignity and depth. Heretofore, dancing had been considered lightweight, lacking validity except as diversion. Besides, there was the singularity of her personal magnetism, the quality that would defy her many imitators. Herself transfixed in her dream, like a possessed pied piper, she drew others into her ecstasy.

Within weeks she was a solo attraction. The night her troop danced in Vienna, a Hungarian impresario, Alexander Grosz, came backstage and offered her a contract to dance alone at Budapest's Urania Theater. For thirty spring nights in 1902, she danced to a sold-out house. One night, as an encore, her improvised "The Blue Danube" received a standing ovation.

Ordinarily a concert artist, upon entering the portal of success, moves for a time with extreme caution, endeavoring to keep a grip on his passkey. Isadora, having won her key, had an urge to cast it away — for love. In her autobiography, in the dramatic prose she employed to treat matters of the heart, she wrote: "My life has known but two motives — Love and Art — and often Love destroyed Art, and often the imperious call of Art put a tragic end to Love."

In springtime Budapest, scented with lilac and throbbing to gypsy violins, love called Isadora in the form of a black-eyed well-built young actor Oscar Boregi, who later became Hungary's leading actor. He was then playing Romeo, and upon falling in love with Isadora, he gave his theatrical role a new interpretation. Their romance, Isadora's first authentic love affair, affected her even more profoundly. She fled with him to a peasant hut, forgetting her Budapest engagement and her contract to tour the Hungarian provinces. She recorded the "unsurpassing joy of waking at dawn to find my hair tangled in his black scented curls." She had found, she said, "Heaven on earth."

Her manager and her anguished mother at length were able to separate the ardent couple. Having extracted the promise that she might soon rejoin her lover, Isadora sadly began her tour. She suffered agonies of longing. But upon returning to Budapest, she found Boregi in a new mood, preoccupied with his new role of Mark Anthony; soon after he suggested that they part and continue their separate careers. Devastated, she signed a new contract with Grosz and set out bravely to fill her commitments. But in Vienna she suffered a breakdown in health that required weeks of recuperation before she could face an audience again.

Her melancholy lifted, and she kissed the hem of her dancing tunic and vowed never again "to desert art for love." Resuming her tour, she danced gloriously to mounting adulation. In Munich students nightly unharnessed the horse from her carriage and drew her to her hotel. The ardor of the ovations when she danced to the Berlin Philharmonic at Kroll's Opera House were reported around the world. American news-

papers headlined: ISADORA DUNCAN PLEASES BERLIN
WITH HER CLASSIC DANCES and CALIFORNIA GIRL
SUCCEEDS.

Part of her rededication to career was her famous pilgrim-
age to Greece. She had longed to commune at "the very holiest
shrine of art," and now with her Berlin bank account bulging
with the proceeds of her tours, she could afford it. She invited
all of her family, and at Raymond's suggestion they decided to
approach Greece in the proper spirit: by traveling as primi-
tively as possible.

They crossed the Adriatic in a small sailing craft, tacking
to follow the route of Ulysses, and upon landing at Karvasaras,
they knelt and kissed the soil. They proceeded inland on foot
along narrow byroads, carrying olive staves. Upon reaching
Athens, they adopted the peplums and tunics of Ancient Greece
and looped fillets around their heads, attire the modern Greeks
found astonishing. They climbed the steps to the Parthenon
trembling with anticipation. Soon they decided they had
"reached the pinnacle of perfection" and should remain in
Greece forever.

With that in view they resolved to build for their habitation
a temple that should be "characteristic of us." After searching
the surrounding countryside for an appropriate site, they decided on a bald mountain top about four kilometers from the
Acropolis and paid an extortionate price. Raymond designed a
temple rather after the Palace of Agamemnon with two-foot-
thick stone walls. Stone had to be carted up the height at great
expense. While the massive walls inched heavenward, Isadora
danced on the slopes of the Acropolis and organized some
urchins into a Greek chorus to accompany her. By official invitation she performed at the Theatre of Bacchus.

Midway through their ambitious project, the Duncans made
an appalling discovery: there was no water for miles around.
That shock coincided with notification from Isadora's bank that
her account was exhausted. Abruptly their Greek dream died —
of desiccation, you might say — and the Duncans departed "the
holiest shrine" via not the most romantic routes but the most
economic ones.

For Isadora there followed a period of relative calm and sustained productivity. Back on the concert circuit, she was happily reunited with fans in Austria and Germany. Critics sensed a new depth in her work, and she was even more picturesque with her hair bound in ribbons, Grecian style. She expanded her repertoire, dancing to the music of Wagner and Beethoven. Making Berlin her headquarters, she took a flat with her mother and sister and conducted a weekly salon for artists and writers.

Also, at this time she indulged a long-held wish to found a school for young dancers. She envisioned it as a "paradise for children," but she also envisioned a vast ensemble of fragile figures weaving decoratively in the background, while she danced upstage. After leasing a large residence in Berlin, she advertised an offer to adopt girl children and bring them up in beauty and enlightenment. The response was overwhelming; her street was blocked with arriving parents and offspring. After selecting forty little girls, she purchased forty little beds, each with white curtains. Isadora delighted in escorting "my children" on decorative walks through the parks, but relegated most of their care and instruction to her mother and sister.

While she seemed engrossed in her art and her school, there were signs of restlessness, such as her inclination to court scandal. Her tunics grew thinner and skimpier, sometimes provoking low whistles from the audience. When Isadora danced at the Wagner Music Fesival at Bayreuth at the invitation of Cosima Wagner, her see-through costume caused a stir. The Cosima sent her daughter to prevail on Isadora to wear a chemise underneath, but she wouldn't. Moreover, she was seen frequently with Frau Wagner's son-in-law Heinrich Thode, although Isadora insisted their attachment to be purely spiritual. And once when King Ferdinand of Bulgaria entered the Wagner villa everyone rose in his honor except Isadora who remained languidly reclined on a couch. But she seemed so innocent, her friends forgave her anything, without noticing that their forebearance usually goaded Isadora to new excesses.

Into her vague discontent walked Gordon Craig. Handsome, blond and willowy, but withal a fiery, forceful male, Craig was an experimental stage designer and director, as revolutionary in his art as Isadora was in hers. Indeed, their artistic goals were highly similar, he stripping stage design down to basics, she dispensing with the trappings of dance. He was the illigitimate son of the English actress Ellen Terry. When he went backstage after one of Isadora's Berlin concerts, her fascination was instant, and she invited him to supper with her and her mother. After supper the pair went out for a carriage ride and disappeared for more than two weeks, during which Mrs. Duncan frantically besought the police to find her "kidnapped daughter."

They were immured in Craig's strange Berlin studio, a large bare room painted black with artificial rose leaves scattered over the floor. There, in Isadora's words, "I flew into his arms with all the magnetic willingness of a temperament which had for two years lain dormant." In Craig she had found her match. He too was of the ether. She wrote in her autobiography: "He was one of the few people I have ever met who was in a state of exhaltation from morning til night." He was also notoriously noncooperative with the commercial theater and as a result was then, as most of his life, impecunious. During their tryst the couple slept on the floor of his unfurnished studio and subsisted on meals delivered on credit from a delicatessen. Isadora had grown used to comfort. She recalled: "In spite of my mad passion, I was a bit tired of sleeping on a hard floor." Although not at all tired of Gordon Craig, she finally picked herself up and returned to her outraged mother.

Her manager contrived an interruption in the form of a Russian tour which stirred more controversy. The sight of the young dancer had a galvanizing effect upon the Russians. They scarcely knew whether to be more astonished by her near nudity than by her bold departure from their dancing norm, the classical ballet. Everywhere her appearances set off battles between admirers and detractors. Converts applauded furiously to drown out the hisses of die-hard balletomanes. At least one duel was fought over her art. Finally, artists and intellectuals tilted the balance in her favor, and she became the toast of Russia. She even left an imprint on the ballet. Fokine, the

famous dancer-choreographer, was inspired to depart from
fixed positions and incorporate freer movement into his work.
Deeply impressed as well was Sergei Diaghilev, who was to borrow much from her for his Ballet Russe. "She gave an irreparable jolt to the classic ballet of Imperial Russia," said Diaghilev.

But for Isadora, the most memorable event of her tour was
witnessing, in St. Petersburg, the mass funeral procession of the
martyred workers, shot down before the Winter Palace. She
sided passionately with the workers in the tragic confrontation.
Her impoverished childhood and early struggle for recognition
had given her a strong democratic bent. Ever after that Russian
experience she was to view herself as a political revolutionary,
although she scarcely resembled one. In her autobiography, she
recalled: "If I had never seen it, all my life would have been
different. There, before this seemingly endless procession, this
tragedy, I vowed myself and my forces to the service of the
people and the downtrodden." She left Russia in somber mood.

She returned to Berlin and to Craig's arms — and trouble.
As she made no effort to conceal their affair, it became public
knowledge. A group of aristocratic Berlin women had formed a
committee to assist her school; but now, sniffing disapproval,
they announced they were withdrawing. In defiance, Isadora
scheduled a lecture on the dance and discoursed as well on the
right of women to have love affairs, provoking a major scandal
as her tunic ill-concealed her pregnancy. Dora Duncan was
humiliated. When Craig showed no inclination to propose to
her daughter (he already had fathered several illigitimate children), Mrs. Duncan booked passage for New York.

Isadora awaited the birth of her child at a beach cottage on
the Holland coast, where Craig came and went and she walked
the sands and brooded. As with every big turn in her life, she
embroidered upon her predicament. She persuaded herself that
out of libertarian principle she had elected to bear a child out
of wedlock. In reality she felt far from heroic, and attempted
suicide at least once, before bearing in difficult labor her daughter Deirdre.

Afterward, she made a trip with Craig and the baby to
Florence, Italy, where he designed a stage set for Eleanora

Duse. Although still in love, they often quarreled. Craig's perpetual state of excitement was by no means an endless meadow of delights; he was given to fits of anger, especially if interrupted at his work. Engrossed in his ideas, which were to revolutionize the whole trend of the modern theater, he frankly put career first. Isadora also suffered jealousy of the more conventional sort. Many women found Craig irresistible.

Sadly, she faced the fact of their deteriorating relationship. Further her manager and her bank balance importuned her to return to work. To the world a soaring symbol of freedom, she found herself now grounded by the consequences of her impulses. Responsibility tugged at her. There was the care of her infant Deirdre whom she adored. And who if not she was to support her forty adopted charges upon whom the moral ladies of Berlin had shut their purses?

But at age 25 Isadora was nothing if not resilient. Her lover and her patrons had proved faithless, but all was not lost. Resolving to shun creative males hereafter, she focused her ardor on a beautiful young man with mayonnaise curls, a spectacular wardrobe, and no intellectual inclinations whatever. She approached her work with a similar attitude of gaiety and composed a delightful number to Schubert's "Moment Musicale," which celebrated the rapture she found in music. Further, she nourished the hope of persuading some country to support her school. She would take her little pupils on tour and a captivated public would urge their government to back her school.

Her entourage entrained prettily for Russia, the children in identical traveling suits. But Isadora's Russian fans disappointed her. It had been one thing to applaud her concerts and quite another to ask their government to divide its subsidy between their proud Imperial ballet and a dance without tradition. However, the visit afforded Isadora an exciting meeting with Stanislavsky, during which they discovered they used similar techniques. Isadora had been working out basic dance movements to express the primary emotions, while Stanislavsky had been doing the same thing with acting expressions and gestures. They had many exciting discussions.

Crossing Russia off her list, she invaded London. Dancing at the Duke of York Theater, she and her pupils drew applause and the Duchess of Manchester had them dance at her country house before the royal eyes of King Edward and Queen Alexandra. But the English viewed Isadora as a never-never creature who had no business running a school. Certainly, her plans did sound nebulous. When asked what she expected her pupils to do when they went out into the world, she airily replied, "We shan't go out into the world. We shall go to Greece and live under the olive trees by the sea."

The summer of 1908 found her a passenger on a stylish liner crossing the ocean she had viewed from a cattle boat eight years before. She wasn't returning to New York to flaunt her fame, however, but to meet her bills. Her return to Berlin had met a barrage of creditors. The offer of Charles Frohman to arrange an American tour had seemed providential, so she had departed, leaving her children to the care of Elizabeth.

It came near to proving the opposite. Presented as a Broadway attraction during a record heat wave, Isadora was all but ignored. Frohman next attempted a budget tour of small towns that proved equally disastrous. But Walter Damrosch stepped forth with a proposal to present her at the Metropolitan Opera House, dancing to his 80-piece Philharmonic Orchestra. Such was her acclaim, Damrosch afterward took her on a triumphal cross-country tour, marred only by preachers' fulminations against her transparent tunic. Church criticism subsided after President Theodore Roosevelt appeared in a box at her Washington concert, applauded briskly, and afterward stated: "What harm can these ministers find in Isadora's dances? She seems to me as innocent as a child dancing through the garden in the morning sunshine and picking the beautiful flowers of her fantasy." Isadora remembered that tour as "probably the happiest time of my life. . . . There was a marvelous sympathy between Damrosch and me, and to each one of his gestures I instantly felt the answering vibration."

Still lacking was a sponsor for her school. It was a resumption of that quest that brought her Paris Singer, with whom she would have her longest and most conspicuous love affair.

She took twenty of her pupils to Paris and made appearances at the Gaieté-Lyrique, ending each with a post-curtain appeal for her school. One day Singer appeared in her dressing room, preceded by a card borne on a silver tray by a body servant, and the thought flashed in Isadora's mind, "My millionaire!" She had joked to friends that she was looking for a millionaire benefactor, and here he was, handsome in the bargain, a six-foot bronzed creature with golden hair and a small elegant beard. When Singer told her he admired her art and wished to support her school, Isadora dissolved into her newest dream: Singer was a modern Lorenzo de Medici, a genius who would do for dancing what the Florentine prince had done for Renaissance poets and sculptors. She always endowed her lovers with genius.

Actually, Singer was nothing of the sort. The English-educated heir to the Singer Sewing Machine fortune was a millionaire playboy who dabbled in the arts. He was more captivated by Isadora than by her dancing. But he was the soul of generosity, and soon they were lovers, and anticipating Isadora's wishes was his favorite pastime. Her pupils gamboled alternately at his villa on the Riviera, at his English country house, and at the Paris studio he provided. Isadora had the best theaters and orchestras, the best accompanists for practicing and creating new works. Wearing stunning gowns from the house of Paul Poiret, she flashed in and out of smart shops and restaurants. Between engagements Singer cruised her on the Mediterranean in his yacht or hosted parties that would bring contacts with people who could assist her.

The public believed their affair idyllic, especially after Isadora bore Singer a son, a cherubic child named Patrick. But intimates knew the high gales of their relationship. Viewing her life as rent by the conflict of art and love, Isadora never seemed to realize the conflicts in her attitude toward her lovers. Burdened creatures! Not only did they face the impossible task of matching her dream of them, but her complex feelings commingled the affectionate sensuality of her father and the resentment of the male implanted by the bitter, rejected Dora Duncan, who had ordered her offspring to crouch in a closet when their father called. None of the Duncan children found lasting relationships. Both boys had brief marriages; Elizabeth never married, although she bore a stillborn child by a Czech dance instructor.

With her other lovers, Isadora had competed for fame, but with Singer, whose only career was watching his investments, she lacked this focus of contention. She found other ways to compete. She compared their friends, his from society, "women with feathers on their heads," her "more worthy" ones from the art world. She measured her socialist ideas against his capitalist role. She taunted him on these scores before their friends, the while flaunting flirtations, even though her greatest fear was that she would lose him. When sufficiently provoked, Singer had a fearful temper, and she was ever stoking his boiling point; yet, upon reaching it, she rushed in with supplications. Not always successfully. Sometimes Singer fled to his yacht and weighed anchor, and that route probably prolonged their relationship. They were ever parting and making up. Her previous lovers, lacking yachts, had ended their affairs still loving her. Gordon Craig said long after her death, "I loved her, I still do. But she might have ruined me." There was something of the female spider in Isadora; her men sensed danger and drew back.

She and Singer were separated but considering reconciliation at the time of the great tragedy — the sudden death of Isadora's children. A taxi carrying the children and their Scottish nanny swerved off a rain-swept boulevard beside the Seine to avoid striking another car; alighting from the taxi, the driver failed to properly apply the brake, and the car rolled into the current drowning all occupants. Deirdre was six, Patrick nearly three.

Isadora's grief was torrential. To quell it, she added another mode of escape to her kit of anodynes, one to which she would ever after be addicted: the drug of speed. Rapid shifts of places, pursuits and relationships, swift modes of travel. Change always change and numbing acceleration. After the funeral and burial in Paris, she was like a wounded woods creature as she pursued a frantic zigzag course about Europe and Asia Minor, sobbing herself to sleep at night, by day experiencing hallucinations in which she heard and visualized her dead children.

After working briefly among war refugees in Albania, she went to Turkey, where she took up with a melancholy youth scarcely past boyhood. They parted and she went to Switzerland, acquired a car and drove compulsively around the lakes. Then, on sudden impulse, she drove non-stop at high speed to Paris, where she stayed but briefly before racing to the Riviera. Then it was on to Venice, where she hired a gondolier to oar her about all night.

Eleanora Duse, disturbed by reports of Isadora's erratic behavior, sent for her to come to Viareggio. Duse consoled her pain and persuaded her to dance for her. Still pursued by hallucinations, Isadora obliterated them in an affair with a young Italian sculptor. She proceeded to Rome, where Singer succeeded in reaching her via telegraph and persuaded her to return to him in Paris. They had an emotional reunion. In a luxurious apartment overlooking the Place de la Concorde, she received her friends, all eager to cheer her.

Hoping a new school would anchor her, Singer purchased a former hotel in the Paris suburb of Bellevue and had it remodeled under Isadora's direction. The dining room to be used as a studio was draped in blue. Isadora seemed her exuberant self again, endowing her school with a typical dream: it would be to Paris what the Seminary of Dancing Priests had been to first century Rome in the year 100 A.D., when the priests danced at quarterly purification rites to cleanse the Roman populace who beheld them. She would hold beautiful dance festivals to which she would invite all of Paris to renew their spirits at her "temple of dance."

Fifty comely little dance aspirants were recruited (one later to become the popular English comedienne Elsa Lanchester). Isadora dressed them in pastel colors and taught them to skip and leap in rhythm, a fetching sight that attracted artists with their sketch pads. But the idyl was short-lived. It was interrupted first by Isadora's advancing pregnancy — she had conceived a child by the Italian sculptor. Then came war rumors. The children were dispatched to Singer's English estate, while

Isadora awaited confinement. She was convinced that one of
her dead children would be reincarnated in this new birth. But
the baby, born with defective lungs on the day France noisily
mobilized for war, lived only a few hours.

The rainbow dream of Bellevue vanished in the smoke of
World War I. Singer donated the abandoned school for a war
hospital, and Isadora, shattered anew, resumed her search.
Wandering to the seaside resort of Deauville, she had an affair
with a doctor. Her school at Bellevue was her last systematic
attempt to inject permanence and order into her life. Another
dichotomy now wracked her; one part of her fought to maintain
a hold on existence, the other courted destruction. Her attempted suicide at Deauville was only the overt manifestation
of this urge.

Over the next five years she wove a tangled course, as she
circled on ill-managed tours over Europe, North Africa, South
America and the United States. Trailing debts and scandal,
she displayed marked contradictions toward the most important
elements of her life. There was her treatment of her pupils.
Proud of them and generous in their upkeep when solvent, she
nonetheless was almost criminally negligent of their well-being.
To shield them from war, Singer sent the children from both
her Paris and Berlin schools to New York in Elizabeth's care.
Joining them there, Isadora, although short of money, rashly
decided to take them back to war-torn Europe. She seated the
children on the New York dock and sent out an appeal for
funds. When a fan paid their passage, she took them to an
Italy mobilizing for war, then into refugee-swamped Switzerland. Depositing the girls at a pensione, she departed on tour,
leaving insufficient funds. The stranded children had to be rescued by their parents. In her autobiography Isadora spoke of
her pupils as resembling a Pompeian freize, and as objects she
seemed to regard them.

No more logical were her efforts to open another school.
When she expressed the wish to establish a school in New York,
Walter Lippmann asked the mayor to permit use of an aban-
doned armory for a studio. Isadora was elated at the prospects.
But when Lippmann brought the mayor to see her students per-

form, Isadora was rude to the mayor and declined to have her pupils dance. Later, Singer took an option to buy Madison Square Garden for Isadora's use as a studio-theater. When he proudly announced his move to her before friends, Isadora, in a perverse mood, haughtily spurned it.

Her attitude toward Singer was contradictory in the extreme. Overjoyed to find him in New York when she returned from South America, she hoped to make their reconciliation permanent. Singer, equally pleased, schemed to delight her. He gifted her with an emerald bought from a maharajah, and to launch her professionally engaged the Metropolitan Opera House and invited the cream of New York to a gala free concert. A successful engagement followed, but Isadora ended her performances with haranguing curtain speeches in which she tossed barbs at the rich, seeming to aim them especially at Singer. When he threw a party in her honor at Sherry's, she, well knowing his aversion to her tangoes, executed a shocking tango with a handsome youth, so enraging Singer that he seized a tablecloth and swept china, crystal and flowers to the floor.

Ambivalant too was her treatment of her mother. Isadora loved her mother and regretted that her affairs had caused her pain. She wanted their San Francisco reunion at the time of her 1918 West Coast tour to be happy. Yet, she quarreled with her mother, and during her visit pursued a romance with a married musician.

Her career vacillations were notorious. While pressing her manager for tours, she frustrated his efforts. In South America she invited cancellation of her engagements with pre-concert cavortings and anti-government statements. While the United States was still a war neutral, she criticized an audience for not supporting France and performed an inflammatory "Marseillaise." Yet, she followed that concert with an all-German program that infuriated the French. She was forever letting her drapery fall. In some cities police were posted in the wings to watch her shoulder straps.

The one solid, unsullied strand in her frayed existence was her art. She never doubted its worth. All else might fade, but the dance, its meaning for her, her respect for it, remained

inviolate. She never compromised it. Nor did she neglect practice, nor cease to create new works. The fire of her genius, her
marvelous urgency remained undiminished. Indeed, tragedy
brought her work new depth and intensity; stripped of sentimentality, it was less "pretty." The serious critics found her
dancing more profound than before, while audiences found it
more electrifying. When she danced the "Marseillaise," which
depicted man's eternal quest for freedom, she could rouse an
audience to a frenzy, regardless of nationality.

Her hummingbird path found her dancing in London early
in 1921 and feeling low. With creditors pressing, Singer now
indifferent, and her latest lover stolen from her by one of her
comely older pupils, she seemed to have reached a dead end.
Alcohol was a daily necessity. She still made curtain appeals
for a school, but without conviction, as a condemned man will
make one final plea. In the audience one night sat a visiting
Soviet trade official, who listened attentively. Afterward he
went backstage and told her his government might be willing
to offer a teaching contract. Eagerly she assured him no contract was necessary, that she would go to Russia on faith. When
a telegram from the Soviet confirmed his invitation, she tele-
graphed acceptance.

Taking along one of her older adopted pupils, Irma Duncan,
she departed, giddy with anticipation. Her sophisticated wardrobe was left behind, under the assumption she would wear a
red flannel blouse among comrades similarly dressed. Politically
innocent, she believed the new regime had banished all inequality, that all was love and happy self-denial.

Moscow, in the third year of the revolution, was far from
idyllic. The upheaval had been cataclysmic. The artistic set
welcomed Isadora, but she was appalled to find them scram-
bling for luxuries. She upbraided them for backsliding. Still,
how disappointing to find the ordinary people dubious of her
project. To them a government dancing school seemed a foolish
frill.

A confiscated mansion was relegated for her school and she
was allowed to select a confiscated fur coat. Although the
mansion lacked heat, she opened it for classes in December,

1921, admitting fifty pupils. Soon after, the government adopted its New Economic Policy, reinstating private enterprise, and it was ruled her school could not receive subsidy; she would have to support it with proceeds from her concerts. It was a cruel disappointment.

Of course, she numbed it with a love affair. Although neither spoke the other's language, it was instant mutual infatuation when Isadora, then 44, met Sergei Essenine, 26-year-old "poet of The Revolution." Stocky, flat-featured with a tangle of flaxen curls bobbing over fathomless pale-blue eyes, he was every bit as complex as Isadora. Torn between allegiance to the peasantry he sprang from and to the Moscow intelligentsia that had annointed him, he was morose and hyper-excited by turns; moreover, he may have had epilepsy.

Although unable to read his poems, Isadora pronounced him "another Robert Burns" and wished him to share her chilly mansion. But Essenine, who already had married and divorced two wives, cherished his wild bachelor existence as head of a pack of brawling, hard-drinking literary hangers-on, who idolized him and were set against surrendering him to Isadora. Isadora brawled along with them, scheming to get Sergei to herself.

Only a few months after arriving in Russia, she began dickering to leave — with Essenine. She arranged an international tour, and Essenine was eager to accompany her, but Russian officials feared for the safety of their tempestuous bard in the climate of anti-Bolshevik America. Reasoning that as Isadora's husband he would be protected, the government stipulated as a condition that they depart Russia married. The couple hastily exchanged vows and, leaving the school in Irma's charge, boarded a plane for Berlin.

There, in the spring of 1922, Isadora began her last major concert tour, a venture that in its degree of failure surpassed anything in the way of an international wander since the Children's Crusade. Her trek through Germany, Belgium, France and the United States roused all her destructive tendencies and some others learned from Essenine. Both these gifted artists had in common an acute underlying unhappiness; subconsciously each courted oblivion. Isadora had blamed Essenine's brawling on the influence of his friends, but he had brought the tendency along with his fur hat and Cossack boots. Acutely sensitive, he reacted violently to slights on his nationality, and from the outset, as symbols of the controversial new regime, they drew them in abundance. Essenine's frequent response was to desecrate their hotel room, breaking up the furniture and doing battle with whomever dared object. At first Isadora tried to restrain him, but soon she was joining in. Besides the emotional release, concerted crashing was a way of communicating with Essenine with whom she had to talk in a kind of pidgin English.

The obstreperous pair were ejected from hotels and attacked by newspapers; not infrequently Essenine was hauled off to jail. Having become a national scandal, they moved on to the next country — if admitted. England excluded them; France barred them, then relented. The United States admitted them after subjecting them to a political inquisition at Ellis Island.

Humiliation goaded them to new excesses. In the United States, Isadora carried their political offensive onstage, waving a red scarf, while Essenine provoked sidewalk altercations in his spectacular Cossack costume. There were reports of heavy drinking and of domestic imbroglios; Isadora sometimes danced with blackened eyes. Many concerts were cancelled, and when they were not, police sometimes stood by to control the riots that sometimes occurred. The country breathed a sigh of relief when they at last departed on steamship tickets bought by Paris Singer.

They landed back in Moscow broke, nerves frayed, and through with each other. The rumors were true: their marriage was finished. Tired and heartsick as she was, Isadora opened at the Bolshoi Theater and danced enchantingly for eighteen sell-out performances. Her art remained a transcendent wonder. Even amidst the furore that attended her American tour, her genius shone undimmed. Famed dancer Helen Tamaras, who attended Isadora's last New York performance, recalled her moving interpretation of the "Pathetique," at whose finish "everyone was crying, and I was crying too . . ."

Undertaking a strenuous tour of the Russian provinces, she rode third-class amid lice and disease between small towns, each more forlorn than the other. Her audiences were depressingly small and stolid. The workers felt she should dance free of charge, while the bourgeoisie sniffed at her morals. In her lonely, loverless state, she found the privation almost unbearable. Returning to Moscow, she found nothing there to hold to. Irma, who had worked to establish the school, considered it hers.

In 1924, she wandered to Germany with the vaguest of plans. Elizabeth had opened a school at Potsdam, enrolling pupils for pay, but she made it plain she didn't need Isadora. Investigating tour possibilities, she learned that the wreckage of her last tour had closed all doors. It was a cruel blow to find her art unwanted. With neither love nor career to charge her fierce energies, she sank into melancholia that was near catatonic. She had loved Essenine and over their romance had hovered a dream of recaptured youth. Now, it had dissipated, leaving her an aging woman beset with abscessed teeth and stomach trouble. She only bestirred herself to write brooding letters to friends threatening suicide and begging money. A sum arrived and she migrated listlessly to Paris.

After inhabiting headlines for two decades, she spent her last years in obscurity. Not that she went into seclusion. She ran with a crowd of young bohemians, not unlike the "flower children" of the 1960s. Dilettantes and failures, they migrated between Paris and the Riviera, lolling in sidewalk cafes by day, in seedy cabarets by night. Their small cadges they shared, Isadora's coming in the form of monthly checks from Augustin's actor's pay and handouts from Raymond, who made and sold togas and sandals. She squandered all without a thought for tomorrow or mounting bills. Dressed in billowy tunics of peony hues, her hair died flamingo and heavily made up, she appeared to the others a campy relic from the Art Nouveau period. And she knew it; she made jokes about herself in self-defense. But her young friends made her laugh, some of them made love to her, and they kept her from being alone, the one thing she couldn't bear. When alone she sobbed quietly and sometimes attempted suicide.

On the promise of writing her memoirs, Isadora had obtained an advance from an American publisher. But she shrank from the task. The crowd encouraged the project, as additional small payments were given in exchange for pages of manuscript, and a payment always meant a celebration. Occasionally she settled down to dictating, perusing yellowed newspaper clippings. She hated it, for it made her look backward, and there were present reminders that she was writing a tragedy instead of a success story — the auction of her Paris house to satisfy a claim, the news of the suicide of Essenine, the inconstancy of her 22-year-old lover. Her scrapbooks made her remember how much she missed her lost career, and she would pick up her dingy blue curtains and tearfully kiss them.

Sometimes her friends persuaded her to dance for them, and she would give a concert at her cluttered Nice studio made from an abandoned garage. In indolence she had grown fat and ungainly and no longer really danced. Rather, she stood almost stationary, making splendid arm movements and freezing into sculpture-like poses. The painter Francis Rose recalled, in *Vogue* magazine, an incident at one of her last studio concerts at which she danced to gramophone music while the audience sat amidst empty bottles and soiled clothing. "Isadora, rather drunk, was changing from her ordinary red garments into white stage draperies behind a rickety screen, which almost toppled over each time she lurched against it. A candle, placed at the wrong angle, threw her shadow against a wall, and everyone saw her struggling tipsily with a corset and removing her underclothes. When she finally made her entrance her toga, which had become entangled in the lock of an old straw clothes basket, dragged it in behind her."

At the end of the unraveled Riviera summer of 1927, when she was 49, something pierced her apathy. Staring across a cafe table at the street, her eyes focused upon a passing red sports car driven by a handsome young Italian. The vision excited her as nothing had for a long time. Afterward, she talked of nothing but the car and its driver. In her elation, she seemed the old Isadora. At length she learned the young man owned a repair garage and that the sports car was for sale. A sizeable check was in the offing (she had finally finished her memoirs), and she resolved to buy the car as soon as the check arrived.

But she couldn't wait for the check. One day in mid-September she arranged for the young man to come take her for a trial drive after dinner. Happily awaiting with friends his arrival, she wound up her gramophone and danced a tango. When the car pulled up she tossed a long red scarf around her neck and, waving to her friends, called gayly in French, "Good-bye friends, I'm off to glory!" A moment later she was dead. The fringed end of the scarf had fallen outside the low car and tangled in the wheel spokes. The wheel's first revolution had broken her neck.

Within hours Isadora was back in world headlines. She had died as she lived, it was said. But she also made editorial pages, as thoughtful writers assessed not what the world had done to Isadora, but what she had done for the world. She was called a daring and brilliant pioneer who had contributed more to the art of the dance than any other and who had given humanity an immeasurable gift of beauty. A Copenhagen newspaper eulogized, "In the realm of the arts she now belongs to the great fallen ones." More than 10,000 mourners gathered at Père-Lachaise Cemetery in Paris where she was cremated. Their tears mingled with a gentle autumn rain, and as the small puff of smoke went up from the high chimney there rose from the crowd a feeling murmur. "Good-bye, Isadora."

Julia Morgan before Notre Dame Cathedral when a student
at the Ecole des Beaux-Arts of Paris. (— *North Collection*)

Julia Morgan

Architect with Empathy

DURING THE 1920s and 1930s when William Randolph Hearst's mountaintop retreat at San Simeon was the world's most dazzling court, invitations to his house parties were snapped up by kings and presidents, playwrights and movie stars, super-celebrities of all sorts. Scores of them at a time. To the mystification of the sophisticated throng, there often moved among them a quiet little woman—grey-suited, bespectacled, make-up-less — whose every soft-spoken word claimed the attention of the awesome host. Who in the world was she? What was *her* priority with the world's most powerful editor and publisher?

Regulars hastened to inform that the retiring woman was Hearst's architect, Miss Julia Morgan of San Francisco. She journeyed down each weekend from her busy drafting rooms to confer with her client on his vast, continuing building program. She had designed the splendid towered castle and its ring of palatial guest houses, plus numerous other mansions and buildings for the Hearst family. Some regulars knew she had also designed hundreds of other residences and institutional buildings in this country and abroad.

But few of that crowd knew her full distinction — knew against what odds she had broken into a jealously-restricted profession to become the first successful woman architect in the United States. Or that she had been the first woman to graduate from the Ecole des Beaux-Arts of Paris, and the first to be granted an architect's license in California. Or that as a style pioneer she had figured prominently in the architectural history of the West. There was nothing in Julia Morgan's appear-

237

ance or her manner to brand her an extraordinary person. In the words of a fellow architect who admired her greatly, "She looked like nobody." Which was precisely as she wanted it. Indeed, so pronounced was her shyness and modesty, one wonders if she would not have preferred invisibility.

Throughout her career Julia Morgan shunned publicity as aggressively as her chief client courted it. This was not due to shyness alone, but to her concept of her profession. To her the proper role for an architect was the one filled by the medieval master builders, the anonymous coordinators of artisans — the stonecutters, woodcarvers and masons — who together were led to transcend themselves and give the world the great cathedrals. Her rapport with construction workers and craftsmen was the envy of her colleagues. Personal glory was distasteful to her. So assiduously did she court anonymity she would not even allow a sign bearing her name to appear at a building site. As a result she remained something of a mystery to the public, and only her fellow professionals knew that the quiet woman who looked like nobody was one of the great creators of her time.

Not merely did she eschew publicity, just as conscientiously did she avoid creating a personal style, a certain look by which her work might be identified. She believed human requirement should give form to a house or building, not some preconceived design. Therefore, she built from the inside out, starting with interior planning to meet the client's need for space and use. Massing and exterior detailing were made compatible with the core.

Yet this very quest for anonymity led her, despite herself, into innovation. She recognized her clients' needs to be emotional as well as physical, and in the years following the San Francisco earthquake-fire, her neophyte years, she found clients preoccupied with fire danger. Inexpensive redwood was still the logical material for residences, but to assist fire-fighting she left exposed such structural members as studs and rafters. Her imaginative handling of this functionalism came out as handsome treatment, and put her in the avant-garde of architects who used structure as part of design. Further questing for fireproofing, she experimented with reinforced concrete, employing it as a means of architectural expression. Pioneering in cement work, she naturally gravitated to the reputation of the foremost cement expert on the West Coast. Handling these practical solutions and others in a way all her own, she inadvertently created her own distinctive style and became a pacesetter in her profession.

But ego is a requisite for high achievement. If to her public Julia Morgan seemed to function without one, appearances deceived. Her ego simply flourished elsewhere — its habitat was her family. Her proud, clannish, self-sufficient family, presided over by a highly moral matriarchal mother, the strongest influence in her life, mattered greatly to her. Her seeming insouciance to fame was in reality indifference to what outsiders thought.

Julia Morgan was born January 26, 1872, in San Francisco in comfortable circumstances. Her small, dapper father Charles Bill Morgan had his hand in a variety of ventures, including Hawaiian sugar. But none was successful — the money came from his wife's side. Eliza Morgan's father, Albert O. Parmalee was a Maryland native who had become a millionaire speculating on pre-Civil War cotton. Half of each year he rumbled through the Southern plantation country in a horse-drawn surrey, cooly speculating hundreds of thousands of dollars on the outcome of the year's cotton crop. Sometimes his guesses proved wrong, but more often he judged correctly. And since he had the foresight to transfer his headquarters to New York, his fortune survived the war and established his family in style in Brooklyn.

His strong-minded daughter Eliza insisted on marrying an amiable young man of good Connecticut family but of vague ambition, who on a whim soon carried her off to California. For several years home was a San Francisco hotel, even after they acquired a son Parmalee and daughter Julia. Julia was still an infant when they set up housekeeping across the Bay in the fashionable suburb of Oakland. Charles Bill Morgan daily ferried to his disappointing enterprises in San Francisco. In the mid-1870s they built on a wide leafy Oakland street a large and opulent frame house that was an unabashed mixture of two of the latest Victorian styles and overlaid with exuberant wooden ornament.

The rich design could scarcely have failed to make a strong impression on the future architect, but at the time Julia's enthusiasm was for athletics. She was small and frail and her family endeavored to treat her as an invalid, bundling her in superfluous sweaters and doctoring her inflamed ear. Julia rebelled against all the swathing by becoming a tomboy, tagging after her three brothers and ignoring her sister Emma, two years younger. She was forever running off to the stable to swing daringly on the rafters and sneaking workouts on the gymnasium equipment set up for her three brothers. Stoically she endured the punishment — extra violin practice. She was as stubborn as she was fearless.

The athletic energies subsided, and the diminutive child became engrossed in school work and religion. The Morgans were backsliding Presbyterians, but a Baptist church just across the street attracted Julia with its stained-glass windows and ardent hymn singing. She became a regular Sunday school attender, collecting Awards of Merit and taking the Prohibition Pledge administered there. Proudly she wore the white ribbon boutonniere that signified abstention from alcohol. At school she awed her classmates with her scholastic prowess. Emma too was a grinding scholar, and the sisters vied for the approval of their mother. The three women had inherited the steel of old Parmalee. The Morgan men, but for the youngest, Gardiner, were all easy-going.

As they approached maidenhood, the Morgan girls solemnly weighed whether to study law or medicine, or perhaps train to practice architecture like their mother's cousin, the eminent Pierre LeBrun of New York City, designer of the Metropolitan Life Insurance Tower. Eliza Morgan interestedly followed these discussions, this at a time when most mothers were single-mindedly steering their daughters toward the altar. Most Oakland girls in their social set were nurtured as carefully as the hybrid blossoms in the private conservatories, to be exposed at the elegant winter cotillions and on tours abroad in quest of aristocratic suitors. But the Morgan girls chattered only of careers! No one was much surprised, however. The self-sufficient Morgans had always been slightly eccentric.

In the fall of 1890, Julia was one of about two dozen co-eds who newly enrolled at the University of California. "Cal" campus was a cluster of stone mansarded buildings on an almost barren hillside seven miles north in the sedate town of Berkeley. Julia commuted to classes in a neat coatsuit and ribboned sailor hat via horse-drawn streetcar, accompanied at her parents' insistence by her brother Parmalee. Male students were still trying to discourage females from invading what they considered *their* precinct. Self-sufficient Julia hadn't looked at a boy in high school, nor did the taunts of the black-suited-and-hatted collegians disturb her businesslike demeanor.

Midway through her sophomore year she decided to become an architect, even though the university had no architecture curriculum. It had a College of Engineering, however, so as grounding for architecture study elsewhere she followed the civil engineering curriculum, which included many subjects taught in schools of architecture. Taking her seat, the lone female, in the sacrosanct engineering lecture hall, she directed herself to such problems as analyzing building materials and structural stresses. One of her paper topics was "A Structural Analysis of the Steel Frame of the Mills Building in San Francisco."

Of joists and trusses Julia was learning, but the aesthetics of building were lacking until her senior year. Then an unlikely instructor appeared on campus. He was Bernard Maybeck, who soon would take the lead in creating a new style of domestic architecture, but who as yet was hardly weighted with accomplishment. Son of a Swiss woodcarver in New York's Greenwich Village, he had studied architecture at the Beaux-Arts, but success had eluded him in New York, in Florida and in Kansas City. When still in his twenties he brought his free-spirited approach to his profession to San Francisco, where he picked up drafting work from local architects. Now the university had engaged him to teach technical drawing to a class of engineering students that included Julia Morgan. The bearded, rather odd young man soon was also teaching a private class in architecture in his Berkeley living quarters. Julia Morgan is said to have been among those who gathered there.

For Julia it was a swing from prose to poetry. Maybeck was dazzlingly gifted with a sketch pencil, and Berkeley exhilharated him. He was fascinated with the native redwood and the tilted terrain. Soon he gained scope for experimenting with both through modest commissions, mostly residences for faculty members. He delighted in designing for a precipitous "goat lot," making his houses "climb the hill" and become part of the landscape. Julia was entranced with his unconventional designs. Maybeck in turn focused special interest upon his precocious pupil. He had firm advice for her when she received her engineering degree in 1894, and she was ready to follow it. It was: Go to Paris and study at the Beaux-Arts.

On May 30, 1896, "Roxy," the popular Oakland society columnist informed her readers: "Miss Julia Morgan, daughter of Mr. and Mrs. C. B. Morgan, sailed from New York on Wednesday. Her destination is Paris, where she will spend a year in close study . . . Oakland will expect and receive much in the future along architectural lines from so thorough and good a student."

It was like the dreamy Maybeck to have neglected to prepare Julia for a most pertinent fact. The Beaux-Arts was far from anxious to enroll women. The French government had only recently lifted its ban against foreign Beaux-Arts students, and the prospects of a female foreign student filled school officials with dismay. Caught without an express rule barring women, they advised the persistent little American that even if she passed the strenuous entrance examination she couldn't expect to graduate, nor to practice architecture. Architects had to mingle with artisans and climb scaffolds to inspect work. Of course, a woman could do neither. This was disconcerting to hear after traveling halfway around the globe. Defiantly, she took the entrance exam. She wrote long and determinedly, her thorough grounding in French coming to her aid. And she passed.

Then followed long delays in admitting her. Weeks lengthened into months, and the money she had brought for a year's study was fast dwindling. Moreover, she was homesick. The student quarter on the Left Bank was a startling place for an ex-Sunday school scholar. The sudden arrival of Maybeck in Paris must have seemed providential. The University of California was conducting a competition for a master plan to develop the campus and had sent Maybeck abroad to drum up entries.

The competition was being funded by Mrs. Phoebe Hearst, patrician widow of Senator George Hearst and mother of the budding publisher. When Mrs. Hearst came to Paris to confer with Maybeck he introduced her to Julia. Mrs. Hearst was so taken with the ambitious young woman that she offered to finance her schooling. Proud Julia, who would not ask her family for additional funds, declined Mrs. Hearst's offer. But she did accept Maybeck's help in finding employment. She went to work as a part-time draftsman for a Paris architect, solving her financial problem.

Then homesickness vanished with the arrival of her brother Avery, the next to the youngest Morgan. Avery was a small, gentle young man whose personality was as tentative as Julia's was decisive. Architecture study had enticed him too, or at least Paris had, and Julia encouraged him to come over and join her.

In 1898, the 250-year-old school finally admitted its first foreign female. Happily, Julia immersed herself in its rich traditions, its planning logic, its vast knowledge of ornament and classical detailing. She was advanced to the top class a year after admission and completed the course requirements within two years, much better than the school average. When the Ecole perversely withheld her certificate, she determinedly re-enrolled and also entered an important architecture competition for students. After the judges awarded her first prize, the school was embarrassed into relinquishing her certificate — the first it had ever vouchsafed a woman.

Julia was 29 when she got home in 1901. It had taken not one but five years to attain her goal. but she had not a doubt that it had been worthwhile. During her absence, her sister had graduated from college, married a lawyer, Hart H. North, and shortly thereafter became a lawyer herself.

Julia's credentials promptly won her a job working under the most talked-of architect on the Coast. He was young, elegant John Galen Howard, who had come West from New York to direct the University of California's building program and to establish a department of architecture. Howard's entry in the master plan competition had come in fourth, but when the winner, the French architect Emile Bernard, declined to come to California (afraid of Indians scoffed American newspapers), Howard was invited.

Howard's first campus commission was designing the mining building Mrs. Hearst had financed as a memorial to her husband. Assisting him, Julia drew the elevations and designed much of the building's classical detailing. When the benefactress came to inspect the plans, she was delighted to find the young woman she had met in Paris. Mrs. Hearst's high praise of the renderings probably influenced Howard to make his new assistant supervising architect of the next Hearst gift to the campus, the Hearst Greek Theater; he also trusted her with much of the design. Julia's Beaux-Arts training served her excellently when designing the amphitheater along lines of the theater at Epidarus, Greece, but with Roman overtones.

Julia found Maybeck happily engrossed in the experiment of "turning houses wrong side out" by making support members visible on the exterior. But he was also making sketches for a quite different project. Mrs. Hearst, who had a keen scent for architectural talent, had asked him to design a large vacation home for her at Wyntoon on the McCloud River. Maybeck invited Julia to assist him. Together they designed a castle of native rock with raftered halls and mammoth fireplaces.

With that project still on the drawing boards, Mrs. Hearst asked Julia to completely remodel a hunting lodge near Pleasanton, south of Oakland. It was for her residence, and she wanted room for large-scale entertaining. Julia designed a rambling stucco multi-towered mansion in the Spanish-Moorish style with grilled balconies and airy with inner courts and arcades.

While supervising this construction in the summer of 1902, Julia had her first meeting with William Randolph Hearst. The

Hearsts' only offspring had come West for his annual visit with his mother to whom he was deeply attached. Then thirty-nine, he was a handsome blond six-footer with piercing blue eyes and a shy but imperious manner. Already he had thriving newspapers in San Francisco, Chicago and New York, moreover was a political power to reckon with. Soon he would marry a pretty brunette dancer, Millicent Willson.

Julia was surprised to find her client's son so knowledgeable about architecture. They had long conversations, and he told her that later on he would have a commission for her. Although hardly crimped for money, Hearst was less affluent than he had expected to be on the edge of forty. George Hearst, concerned at his son's spending habits, had left his fortune to his wife.

In 1905, Julia left Howard's employ and opened her own office in San Francisco. She was probably encouraged by Mrs. Hearst, and she probably was goaded by the story going around in architecture circles that Howard had boasted he had a wonderful designer who he "didn't have to pay anything because she was a woman." But she was also anxious to try her hand at designing frame houses.

Modest commissions, many in Berkeley, were forthcoming from family friends and University acquaintances. From the first she showed an aptitude for residence design. While following Maybeck's use of redwood and shingles, she gave her houses as individual a mold as he. If less whimsical, she too was highly inventive.

This pleasant experimentation was interrupted by the shudders of the April 18, 1906 earthquake-fire. The catastrophe destroyed Julia's office, but established her reputation. With San Francisco in ruins, she was handed the major task of resurrecting the Fairmont Hotel. The new Nob Hill hostelry, one of the largest and finest in the world, was nearly finished when rampaging flames left it a shell of charred granite with buckled girders. Grounded in both Beaux-Arts classicism and engineering, she was equipped as no other architect in the West to handle the task of buttressing the six-story shell and rebuilding the vast interior. And to do it in a hurry. Rooms were desperately needed.

A woman reporter on the San Francisco *Call*, upon hearing a woman architect was working on the Fairmont, went to see for herself. Assuming Miss Morgan had been hired for the interior refinishing, the reporter posed questions concerning color tone and decoration. She was astonished to learn that the young woman, whom she described as "Quakerish . . . dressed in drab and severely hair-pinned," was directing all of the structural work. A New York firm held the contract for interior decoration. The mammoth glass dome had already been replaced and the rebuilding of the great staircases was under way. The reporter asked the foreman of a work crew, "Is the building *really* in charge of a woman architect?" The foreman brought her up short. "Now, this building is in charge of a *real* architect and her name happens to be Julia Morgan, but it might as well be John Morgan."

Ever after she was to have all the work she could handle, and always a varied program. Her enlarging staff pushed her out of her modest quarters into a suite of offices in the Merchants Exchange Building, for which she had designed the interiors. It would remain her address throughout her career, although she would twice change floors. Having proven her competence for big undertakings, she was sought for institutional work, much coming from women who took a feminist pride in her success. Designs for women's clubs, dormitories, sororities, girls' schools flew from her drawing boards, only to attract more and more clients.

In 1904, she had designed a Mission style bell tower for Mills College; now she was asked to plan the library, gymnasium and social hall. The YWCA heirarchy discovered her and commissioned a series of residence halls in cities throughout California. She also began the complex of buildings for the YW's Asilomar Conference Center in Pacific Grove, today a state property. Mrs. Hearst was instrumental in the Asilomar commission. Julia thanked her by letter for "your kindness since those Paris days when you were so beautifully kind to a most painfully shy and homesick girl. My mother's and yours are the greatest "faiths" put in me, and I hope you both know how I love and thank you for it."

And there were her early churches. Perhaps the most notable was St. John's Presbyterian Church in Berkeley, now The Center for World Music, which through the years has remained one of her most popular designs. The simple frame building of post and beam construction with shallow gables makes a statement at once dignified and dramatic.

Meanwhile, she continued to design residences, everything from cottages to mansions. Her clients were now from throughout the Bay Area and beyond. Mrs. Hearst had her design a $100,000 music room addition to her Pleasanton mansion and a wing to house her grandsons (offspring of William Randolph and Millicent) when they came to visit. In the first dozen years her office executed more than 300 commissions, among them some of the best work being done in California. With astonishing swiftness she had built one of the most prestigious architecture offices on the West Coast and the largest in the country run by a woman.

Family and architecture filled her life; her work, the challenge and creativity of it, sustained her bountifully. She lived simply with her mother, who had been invalided from the shock of losing in succession her youngest and oldest sons and her husband. Julia kept protective watch over Avery, who had finished his architecture studies, but showed no inclination to practice. She tried to assimilate him into her office, but he quit after a few days. So she gave him a job as her chauffeur, driving her Hudson, a job he performed contentedly. She kept in close touch with her sister's household. The two strong-minded sisters, if not attuned were nonetheless attached, and Julia doted on Emma's lone offspring, a happy-natured blond youth who had been given the family name of Morgan. Her idea of a perfect evening was to sit on the fringe of a family group, quietly thumbing through a picture book on art or architecture, courting inspiration.

Since work filled her cup, she couldn't understand why it would not likewise suffice her staff. To a degree her family feeling extended to her staff, who she seemed to have regarded somewhat as cousins once removed, taking interest in their children and sending presents at Christmas. But she also showed affinity by expecting them to like overtime as much as she. What more could they want than an endless stream of drafting chores? She fired one talented young man because he talked baseball on the job, but rehired him after he convinced her he had reformed. Dorothy Coblentz, who worked for her at two different times, remembers: "The pressure was terrible. She didn't realize that people had private lives . . . time meant nothing to her. She went out of her way to hire women, but expected them to emulate her. She always hoped one of her female children would last the course, but I think none of us did." (Her accounts revealed posthumously that she also aided many young women with their college expenses.)

Despite the pressure, young architects of both sexes vied to work for her because of the expert training they got under her perfectionist eye. Mrs. Coblentz recalls, "She was so thorough you couldn't draw a line unless it meant something. She'd say, 'Think it out *first.*' It was hard work but every minute was worthwhile." After such discipline, her "graduates" could go anywhere. But another reason she was a popular employer was her generosity. Not only did she shower staffers with gifts, but shared her profits with them, retaining only enough to cover her personal expenses and office overhead. Money meant little to her. A bonanza in the form of an especially lucrative commission was divvied into a happy bonus for everyone.

Her passion for quality, no matter how small the commission, made her keep a tight rein. In her constant monitoring she sometimes treated grown men like children. Significantly, they referred to her in the executive manner as "J. M." She was simply and naturally the boss. Undoubtedly, that is why her one partnership, begun in 1910, with Ira Wilson Hoover, a former Howard associate, lasted only a year.

Similarly, she kept a captious eye on construction work. That Parisian who predicted she'd never be able to perform work inspections should have seen her climbing ladders and pacing scaffolding twelve stories above the ground. Walter Steilberg, long chief draftsman in the Morgan office recalled, "Nothing bothered her — she was fearless. She had a strain of steel I have never found in any other human being." Nothing but first-rate work gained her approval. Far more than most architects, she knew the mechanics of construction and could interrupt a workman, saying, "Do it this way, friend." (She often forgot names, even of her staff, and substituted "friend.") She would order faulty work ripped out, sometimes joining in with her bare hands. She got by with such firmness, because workmen knew she recognized skill and applauded it.

Likewise, all materials she used were carefully selected and, on delivery, meticulously examined. Mrs. Mary Tusher, Oakland YWCA administrator, remembered that when Miss Morgan was building the Oakland YWCA, whose exterior design includes fifty columns faced with small tiles, she sat down and lifted separately thousands of tiles, scrutinizing each. All imperfect tile was returned.

She was not merely turning out volume and satisfying clients; she was innovating design. Her residences partook of an original excellence that made her, along with Maybeck, leader of a new kind of domestic architecture that had become ubiquitous along the Northern California coast. These were simple shingle-surfaced houses with gable roofs and deep eaves which fitted into the landscape with an indigenous air. Characteristically, structural elements were integrated with design, both inside and out. They suited exactly the increasingly casual style of California living. The output of half a dozen or so architects later was to be branded The Bay Area Shingle Style. Louis Mumford called this work "the first designs that put California aesthetically on the modern map." They served as precursors of the present-day distinctive San Francisco Bay Region Style of domestic architecture, which also contains elements of the California ranch house.

Despite her avoidance of personal style, certain qualities in her residences stamped them "a Julia Morgan house." There was her distinctive, always unostentatious detailing. In her quietly elegant door and window treatments classic ornament served as suggestions not as models for copy work. Then there was the personalization of her designs. She had a knack of planning a house that suited her clients exactly. This came from genuine solicitousness of their needs and desires. Unlike

the independent Maybeck who started with exterior design and
sometimes cut short an objecting client with, "But this is what
I *see* for you," Julia started her planning with interior requirements and preferences. The result was convenient houses.
Sometimes the result was also some odd feature, such as the
gadget made to satisfy a client's desire to control his heating
system by reaching under his pillow. Further her floor plans
jettisoned the long hallways of the formal Victorian house,
while still permitting entry to rooms without passing through
others. She accomplished this with an entry hall variously at
the front or side of the house that opened into major rooms and
to upstairs. Opening to one another, her rooms also opened up
to the gardens and views.

At the same time she was deep into another architecture
trend, Spanish Revival. Impractical Mission Revival had been
short-lived, yet the burgeoning interest in California's past created favor for Spanish motif, and the newly available inexpensive cement made it economic. Julia's Beaux-Arts training
equipped her excellently to work in this mode; her work in
Spanish and other Mediterranean styles was among the best
being done. The elegant simplicity of her grilled villas and
residence clubs was a far cry from the toothpaste Spanish of
Southern California. Especially handsome were her serene
designs suggested by the vernacular architecture of Andalusia.

She didn't know it, but by experimenting with Spanish and
cement she was boning up for the most challenging commission
of her career. Her client-to-be, on the contrary, had been quite
consciously preparing. For decades, William Randolph Hearst
had known he would one day build upon his favorite camping
spot, a height overlooking the Pacific on the sprawling family
rancho midway between San Francisco and Los Angeles. A
shimmering castle rising from that sun-kissed hill had been the
most insistent dream of his childhood. As an adult he had returned frequently to the site, and after marrying he took his
young family there to camp elegantly in striped tents with
floors and rugs and bathrooms. Through the years he had been
collecting furnishings and art works for his castle and storing
up building ideas galore.

Steilberg recalled that late one afternoon in the spring of 1919, after most of the staff had gone home, Hearst presented himself at Julia Morgan's San Francisco office. Calmly she showed the famous visitor into the most imposing room, the library lined with shelves of architecture books. Through the open door, Steilberg heard the thin soprano voice of Mr. Hearst: "I'm a little tired of camping out on the campground on the hillside. I want to build something a little bit more comfortable . . ." He said he wanted her to design a residence that would accommodate his art collection. Cost, he made clear, was no object. Phoebe Hearst recently had died of influenza at Pleasanton, and newspapers had reported her bequest to her son to be something over $11,000,000.

It has been facilely assumed that the wand of Hearst's commission transformed Julia Morgan's office from a shoestring operation into a success. When he dropped by that afternoon she was working overtime on a jam of work. In 1918 *The Architect and Engineer* had devoted an entire issue to her work. No doubt, she initially considered this commission to be not so unlike others she had executed. In later consultation with her client, she must have been astonished to learn that the art collections she was expected to incorporate into a castle and three sizable guest houses included not merely art works and furniture, but *architectural sections!* Waiting in far-flung warehouses to be strung together like widely assorted beads were such items as huge staircases and doorways, towering columns, enormous mantlepieces with chimneys, as well as extracted rooms of palaces and monasteries, complete from floor to ceiling. They ranged in time from the Pompeiian era to present-day.

Yet, characteristically she did not hesitate. Hearst was determined in his plan, and she knew that her engineering training and her Beaux-Arts study with its grounding in the classical was the best preparation an architect could have for this unprecedented commission.

But other surprises awaited. Weeks later on a hot summer day Hearst took her to inspect the building site. Alighting from a train at the village of San Luis Obispo, she was driven sixty miles in a Buick touring car, first over washboard roads until the road disappeared, then bounced across fields and farm lands to the foot of desolate Camp Hill. Alighting, they hiked the 1600-foot summit.

The top was a dry knob, barren and rocky, but for one earthen spot where grew four large oak trees. A glance told her the knob would accommodate the castle only; the guest houses would have to be hung upon the steep slopes. While she walked about taking measurements her mind grappled with a myriad of questions. Without roads or port how were building materials to be delivered? Not to speak of the contents of those warehouses. Where was water to be had? Hearst meanwhile, oblivious of obstacles, talked happily of terraced gardens and groves of orange trees.

Plainly, she had been commissioned to execute no mere housing order — she must fill a psychic need. Not merely Hearst's childhood dream insisted, but an adult wound. After he had served as Congressman from New York, a series of political defeats had shattered his hopes of becoming United States President. Of course, he was now a publishing giant with eight magazines and newspapers in eight cities, but a prime purpose in building his media empire had been to gain political power. Still, all was not lost. He might yet attain greatness — by building a beautiful monument and filling it with the world's greatest collection of art.

It was principle with Julia Morgan to serve a client's emotional needs, but satisfying a complex man like Hearst was the ultimate challenge. Since she never invited staffers to sit in on design conferences with clients, none of her employees knew exactly and neither she nor Hearst ever told, just how the castle design was arrived at. But it was the impression of one of her draftsmen, Louis Schalk, that Hearst always let her come up with an initial suggestion in sketch upon which he oversketched changes, often in profusion.

The design she arrived at was a two-towered scheme reminiscent of Romanesque cathedrals, but with High Gothic ornamentation. That was the facade. The rear of the building wrapped around a three-sided court with a prevailing motif of gay Venetian Gothic. The requirement that the main dwelling provide lounging and dining areas for all occupants of the complex (143 rooms in all) dictated the size of the Refectory and Assembly Hall. The Refectory, lined with 400-year-old Spanish choir stalls, gained its elongated form from a narrow dining table from a medieval monastery.

The guest houses, varying in size from ten to 18 rooms, were to be built first. Eager to get construction under way Hearst from New York prodded via mail and telegram. Top floors of the guest houses were designed to open at the castle level with three or more floors reaching down the mountain sides. White-walled and red-roofed, they were variously in the Moorish, Italian and Spanish Renaissance styles. Hearst named each according to its view: La Casa del Mar facing the sea, La Casa del Monte facing the mountains, and La Casa del Sol looking toward the setting sun.

While Morgan the architect was pursuing aesthetics, Morgan the engineer was coping with thorny technical problems. Technical problems bored Hearst. His attitude was: "Do whatever is necessary. I'll pay the bills." To gain access to the site, she constructed a road to connect with a wharf for bringing in heavy supplies by sea. Earthquakes had cracked the knob's surface rock, and it was necessary to blast to bedrock for foundations. The four oak trees were in the way, but Hearst wanted them saved by transplanting them. One he wanted placed so that a certain branch overhung the approach drive. The difficult transplants were accomplished by encasing tree roots in vast concrete tubs and hoisting them to an area sodded with soil carted up from below. Water was piped from a mountain spring five miles away.

By summer, 1921, the first guest house was ready for Hearst and his family when they arrived for their annual visit. The hill vibrated with activity. Dozens of masons and carpenters busied themselves on the other guest houses, while a group of skilled artist-craftsmen created staircases and panels and cabinetry. One expert only bored worm holes. Cargoes of lumber and cement were arriving by coastal steamer. Art shipments were uncrated and stored in the warehouses Miss Morgan had constructed in the village at the foot of the mountain. She

inspected each arriving crate and must have been astonished
to find so many voluptuous nudes in the collection of a man
who banned nude art from his publications and required gym
suits to be painted over photographs of scantily-clad athletes.
She came down on the Southern Pacific each week, a trim
figure in a tailored suit with white collar and cuffs under a
wide-brimmed hat. Eschewing a regular purse, which would en-
cumber her hands, she utilized suit pockets to carry necessaries.

She had enlarged her staff to 16 architects to permit handling the Hearst work while continuing her regular practice.
At this time she turned down an invitation from the YWCA to
direct their world-wide building program. She explained she
could not live apart from her family. Her mother was now bed-
ridden and her mind failing, but she wouldn't hear of giving
up her Oakland home. Julia thought it too large for just the
two of them and finally maneuvered a move, sans argument.
One Thanksgiving Day she drove her mother to the North
home in Berkeley, where they enjoyed a happy family dinner.
She had just finished building, next door to the Norths', a small
house which contained one room exactly like her mother's room
in Oakland. That evening Mrs. Morgan was carried out to the
car and driven several times around the block, then carried
through semi-darkness to her new room. She never knew, or
admitted she knew, that she had departed Oakland.

With completion of Hearst's guest houses there began that
era of fabulous entertaining that attracted an endless file of
famous visitors. By day between horseback safaris and champagne picnics, guests wandered about watching the wormhole
borer and admiring busts of Roman emperors and Della Robbia
reliefs lying in the grass awaiting installation. Hearst was in his
element playing host while watching his visions assume physical form. His happiest days were those when his architect was
on the hill to confer with him. Ordering that they not be disturbed he secluded himself with her for hours in the board-and-
batten shack that served as her San Simeon office. Together
they pored over sketches and blueprints, working and rework-
ing them. She seems to have accepted change as integral to this
singular commission. Underlying her sympathetic patience

with Hearst was her deep affection for his mother. But she frankly admired his refusal to admit the impossible — a quality she shared. The constant challenge he threw out exhilarated her.

Despite the many changes Hearst ordered, he placed the highest value on Miss Morgan's ability and on her character. His chief biographers have rated her one of the four most important women in his life, along with his mother, his wife and film star Marion Davies. Hearst is reported to have said she was the only person who had never tried to take advantage of him. Because San Simeon's building costs ran to astronomical figures, what with incorporating dismantled palaces and cathedrals, she did not charge the standard ten per cent of construction costs for her fee. Instead, she computed a fee based on her expenses plus a profit which must have been reasonable indeed. Her accounts showed she never during her entire career drew a salary of more than $10,000 a year, even though her work for the YWCA and for Hearst were multi-million dollar operations. Hearst's total outlay for construction ran into the millions. Had she charged the usual commission, she would have been a millionaire herself.

By 1925, the lord was ensconced in his castle. It wasn't completed, but ready to accommodate his frequent visits was the grand fourth-floor Imperial Suite with its enormous carved canopied bed and adjoining Gothic Study which commingled under its vaulted ceiling the artistic expression of five centuries and more than a dozen countries.

By now orange trees were thriving in holes blasted in rock and packed with topsoil. Flower beds and lily ponds abounded. Nowadays film folk were often among those invited to luxuriate amidst this splendor, for Hearst had acquired a film company as a showcase for Marion Davies. Guests gathered in the Assembly Hall with its stunning mantle works from a French Renaissance chateau (by way of Stanford White's estate sale) and sipped the one cocktail per person Hearst dispensed before dinner. When Miss Morgan was on the hill she was placed near Hearst at table. Walter Steilberg recalled a dinner party of forty, including Marion, when Miss Morgan was seated "directly across from him. . . . They were talking back and forth, and gesturing, and he was drawing things, and she was drawing things. The rest of us could have been a hundred miles away. They didn't pay any attention to anybody . . ."

Perhaps to reward his architect for her patience, Hearst, in 1925, dealt her a commission beyond his censor. As a memorial to his mother, he endowed a women's gymnasium for the University of California with the proviso that his mother's favorite architects, Julia Morgan and Bernard Maybeck, collaborate on it. The two old friends were happy to be united again. Shrugging off acclaim, Maybeck had remained as professionally cavalier as ever. He rarely maintained an office, preferring to operate out of his small home on a Berkeley goat lot; often he set up his drawing board under an oak tree. Perhaps Berkeley's most spectacular eccentric in those pre-hippy days, he affected a waist-length beard and a strange wardrobe of his own design that included voluminous side-fastening trousers that reached to his armpits. The bearded bohemian and the brisk little woman worked in perfect harmony to create a monumental gymnasium that was as poetic as it was utilitarian. Inside it glistened with white marble, while its exterior was stately with classical columns and detailing.

That the building has remained admirably functional to this day was due to the practicality of Miss Morgan, in whose office the blueprints were prepared. Maybeck is said to have been so oblivious of what might be preferred by college women as to propose communal showers. According to Edward Hussey, a draftsman in Miss Morgan's office, the labyrinth of the vast structure remained mysterious to Maybeck. Hussey recalled: "When they had the grand opening of the Hearst Gymnasium, Mr. Hearst was there and he wanted to know where the men's room was. Mr. Maybeck, the architect, couldn't tell him. He had to get somebody else to find out where it was."

What befell Julia Morgan in late 1928 would have dealt a major setback to one of ordinary mettle. An emergency mastoid operation on that much-doctored ear of her childhood required removal of the complete inner ear. It left her equilibrium severely impaired; further a slip of the scalpel cut a facial nerve with an effect similar to that of a stroke. One side of her face was distorted and her speech affected. Quickly returning to work, she dispelled predictions that she would no longer be capable of work inspections. She insisted on climbing ladders and walking scaffolding as always, bracing against structure and gripping workmen's pockets. She suffered falls, some requiring stitches, but she refused to concede.

Her attitude toward this irreparable injury revealed another character trait. The taskmistress who could scold a draftsman for an error was remarkably tolerant in matters outside architecture. She took pains to assure the young surgeon who made the error that she held him blameless. To convince him she made a singular gesture. Learning his wife liked orchids, she placed an order with a florist to have her receive each New Year's an orchid bouquet. She seems not to have had a jot of self-pity. Her imbalance, which gave her a weaving gate that required her to walk close to walls and fences she turned into a joke. She once regaled a friend with a demonstration of her efforts to avoid a similarly weaving drunk.

The years following the maladroit surgery were among her busiest. Hearst had her build a gift for Marion, a Colonial style beach house in Santa Monica which incorporated many art treasures. He also commissioned a hacienda on a corner of his San Simeon estate. In Berkeley, she designed a handsome club-hotel, the Berkeley City Club, whose detailing echoed San Simeon, but was highly functional in its use of structural necessities as part of the design. In recognition of her distinguished career the University of California in 1929 conferred on her an honorary doctor of laws degree.

More than ever work absorbed her. Often she forgot to eat, subsisting on coffee and chocolate bars. Steilberg remembered, "I've seen her so tired her head was on the table from fatigue. But she'd be up and at it again." In the mid-1920s she bought two adjoining Victorian houses in San Francisco, remodeled them and converted them into apartments. She moved into one and daily rode the cable car to her office. Probably her most relaxed moments were spent with her nephew Morgan, the apple of her eye despite his indifference to architecture. Once when she showed him the sanctuary of St. John's church, he cocked an eye at its exposed rafters and teased, "Aunt Julia, where's the hay?" Still happy-natured, he was preparing to become a mining engineer.

Meanwhile, San Simeon kept growing like a tropical vine. Taking shape were the vast recreational complex and the marble Neptune pool with its Roman temple for a cabana. Hearst still expected his architect to come down weekly. But she now declined invitations to join his dinner parties, explaining in wry reference to her facial aspect, "An architect should never appear asymmetrical."

Soon she was also making trips north. In 1929 fire destroyed the Wyntoon house she and Maybeck had designed for Mrs. Hearst, and Hearst plunged into rebuilding plans. He wanted no less than another castle with guest houses. Not long before he had asked her to design a mansion for a site overlooking the Grand Canyon. To oversee these far-flung operations she leased a plane and hired a pilot. Her eagerness to depart in any weather for any improbable landing strip worried her family and staff. Steilberg recalled that right after World War I when flying was unknown to ordinary people, she once paid a stunt pilot to take her up and satisfy her curiosity as to "what it's like up there." There remained in her something of the daredevil who had swung from the stable rafters. Those pacings about on twelfth-floor scaffolds went beyond the call of architecture duty. She was highly admiring of the keeper of Hearst's private menagerie, a swashbuckling type who kept a leopard for a pet and fought bulls in the Mexico rings.

The keening pine forest at Wyntoon reminded Hearst of the Bavarian forest country. Would his architect go abroad and garner ideas for designing a Bavarian village? Julia Morgan sailed from New York in 1931 on her first trip to Europe since her student days and was met at Naples by a limousine and chauffeur who had been instructed to "take Miss Morgan anywhere in Europe she wishes to go." They motored through dark German forests, she filling notebooks with sketches of medieval mansions and castles. Later, she visited Paris to look up old Beaux-Arts friends, and finally traveled through Spain.

Returning to California, she designed for Wyntoon three storybook cottages, Cinderella House, Fairy House and Bear House. So delighted was Hearst he asked for but minimal changes. He and Marion would find a cozy haven at Bear House during World War II. But the castle and his Grand Canyon mansion were never built due to a depression-induced crisis in his publishing business that required him to shelve his building program.

Neither the Hearst cessation nor the Depression much affected the Morgan office. Hers was one of the few San Francisco practices which didn't have to retrench. Her expertise with large steel-reinforced concrete buildings gave her a choice of institutional work, including a commission to build part of the new Principia College in Illinois. She was recognized as one of the most versatile architects in the West and was probably second to none in technical knowledge. She had a thorough understanding of carpentry, masonry, plastering, iron work and sheet metal, mostly gained by close observation. She knew construction from proper window balance to the recipe for concrete, and she kept vigil to see that high standards prevailed. A client whose Russian Hill residence she remodeled during the mid-1930s remembers her climbing on her hands and knees an unrailed skeleton stairway in order to check its proportions.

There was always a new YWCA on her drawing board. Eventually her chain of stunning Ys, among them the Hollywood Studio Club, was to spread throughout California and to Utah, Hawaii and Japan. Many of the elegant touches of her palaces found their way into these egalitarian buildings via such economic substitutes as molded cement, redwood and local tile. Grace notes were provided by wrought iron grillwork, at which she knowledgeably directed craftsmen, having observed the technique in Spain.

Steilberg has said "she regarded each job as the important one. There was no rating of priorities." Great or small, the commission claimed her whole attention, for each plan had to meet her ideal of fitting structure to use. Her dedication to occupant is well illustrated in her series of San Francisco Ys.

Not for a moment did she forget she was designing for young working women — not for the privileged matrons on the Y boards who engaged her.

Mrs. Henry Marcus, then a member of the San Francisco YWCA board, recalls the consternation on the board when Miss Morgan disclosed her plans for the YWCA Residence Club near San Francisco's downtown. Miss Morgan informed the board: "My idea is to have one or two little private dining rooms with little kitchens so that the girls can invite their friends and cook a little meal." Several women protested that working girls didn't need such frills — they weren't used to such things. To which the architect quietly responded, "That's just the reason," and went right on to say she planned also a sewing room, a self-service beauty parlor, and a laundry. "You're just spoiling these minimum wage girls!" one woman exclaimed.

The architect did not back down. "She so quietly got her way," Mrs. Marcus recalls . . . "in a soft little voice — you had to try hard to hear her speech. . . . There was never any excitement about her, just this wonderful quiet power." The minimum wage girls got besides three handsome living rooms and a garden. The Residence Club, which has since gone co-ed, remains beautiful and functional today. Mrs. Marcus remembers the architect lavished similar care upon the neighborhood Ys. "When she did the Chinatown Y, she did Chinese research and put in some things that were very sacred for the Chinese."

World War II brought labor and materials shortages, and institutional work almost ceased. Julia Morgan reduced her staff to a skeleton force. Now seventy, she was resigned to phasing out her practice. The new so-called "International Style" had swept in with its sterile geometry and she felt alien to it. One of her draftsmen recalls, "She would work in any style but modern."

A new relationship and a hobby helped fill the gap. Her nephew Morgan went off to war in the South Pacific, leaving behind a young wife Flora and a fledgling printing business. Miss Morgan and her nephew's wife became close friends, drawn not only through loneliness but a marked affinity of temperament. Flora, who had assumed management of the printing business, also had a touch of steel. While the temperance pledger still spurned cocktails, she delighted in Flora's wine-laced cookery. Her hobby — the first she had ever permitted herself — was mastering Cantonese brush calligraphy, which had long intrigued her in her walks about Chinatown. After her work was done she would open a book *Introduction to Colloquial Cantonese* and paint the graceful figures with quick deft strokes. She liked copying the letters, she said, simply because "they are so beautiful."

At this time Hearst glimpsed a new beginning. His publishing empire had survived the Depression and was fattening on the war boom. He was anxious to resume building. Summoning his architect he asked her to draw plans for an additional wing for the castle and for another guest house to occupy Burnett's Peak behind San Simeon. But Hearst's five sons had assumed positions of power in the business and they opposed further building. Hearst, now nearly eighty, had a heart problem which at any time might confine him to an invalid's bed. While they did not veto the building, they did effect delays. He was permitted to construct his wing, but by various ruses was hobbled to a slow pace.

The leisurely building program left time for Miss Morgan to pursue her long-planned travels abroad, and the pending work conferred purpose upon them. Progressing from country to country, she busily made sketches and took measurements, gathering ideas for the Hearst commissions. Architect and client exchanged correspondence stuffed with sketches and suggestions.

She returned often for conferences with Hearst and visits with her family. Always she arranged to be with Morgan and Flora for the Thanksgiving and Christmas holidays. Now the parents of two children, they pleased their aunt by purchasing one of her Berkeley designs, a 1924 stucco. But with her office closed, idleness wore heavily and she would be off again — to Italy, or Spain or Greece, filling her notebooks. She who had never wasted a minute in her life enjoyed these scouting trips far more than had her travel been pointless. Hearst's autumn dreams, which largely remained unrealized, nonetheless sustained both of these very active mentalities during their declining years.

Julia Morgan remained active, creative and contented throughout her seventies. Tired of touring, she replaced it with ocean cruises, preferring tramp steamers. She confided a wish to die at sea, but gradually her activities were centered to San Francisco. In 1951, after a series of small strokes, she was confined to her home in the care of a nurse. Used to constant activity, she chaffed at confinement. One day she eluded her nurse and crossed the bay to Oakland to visit the neighborhood where she had grown up. For several anxious days Morgan searched everywhere for her, before locating her in an Oakland hospital where she was being treated for injuries suffered in a mugging. Evidently she had put up a fierce fight against a thug. She recovered from that, but never ventured so far again. She died in San Francisco in 1957 at the age of 85.

Her will, which named Morgan to be executor of her modest estate, requested that her burial be "a quick tuck-in with my family and no fanfare." Hearst had died six years earlier. He had corresponded with her until the end, but had never permitted her to put a permanent roof on the castle, for he would not concede that it was finished.

The shy woman who shunned publicity and supposed she worked anonymously would be astonished at how well she is remembered. Architecture students at the University of California are aided by an endowment fund admiring friends established in her name. Architecture scholars honor her pioneering work in unifying structure with design and her contribution to today's Bay Area Style — those pleasing uncluttered dwellings which blend into the coastal hillscapes and are much copied in locations of similar terrain. Moreover, her work remains a force in the real estate market. Not merely her luxury residences but those small experimental houses built sixty to seventy years ago. When one rarely comes up for sale it goes for many times its original cost. Her sincere houses with their muted detailing have proven timeless, removed from fad and fashion. A "Julia Morgan house" has cachet that makes its owner envied. They are coaxed to open them to architecture buffs for Sunday afternoon tours.

And at San Simeon her name is evoked hourly by tour guides who shepherd ever-waiting crowds of visitors about the castle and grounds. Since 1958, San Simeon has been, as Hearst wished it to be, a public monument. His sons presented San Simeon and its contents to the State of California, and it has proven enormously popular, attracting more than 600,000 visitors annually. If San Simeon annoyed some critics who thought it too opulent and diverse for a residence, hardly anyone has denied its audacious, commanding beauty. The truth is Julia Morgan never conceived of San Simeon as a residence. She told Morgan North it was for Hearst's use only temporarily; eventually it would be for everybody. Ever her most insistent goal was to design her buildings for use. And just as she designed the Residence Club for the minimum wage girls, so did she design San Simeon for you and me. That we might freely wander its inviting halls and draw sustenance from priceless art treasures that span two thousand years. Who can deny that she did so with éclat?

Bibliography

BOOKS

Angel, Myron. *History of Nevada*. Thompson and West, 1881, Berkeley: Howell-North, 1958.

Anthony, Susan B. and Ida H. Harper. *History of Woman Suffrage*. Rochester: 1902.

Atherton, Gertrude. *Adventures of a Novelist*. New York: Blue Ribbon Books, 1932.

Bernheim, Bertram M. *The Story of Johns Hopkins*. New York: Whittlesey House, 1943.

Bluemel, Elinor. *Florence Sabin, Colorado Woman of the Century*. University of Colorado Press, 1959.

Bridgman, Richard. *Gertrude Stein in Pieces*. New York: Oxford University Press, 1970.

Cummings, Ella Sterling. *A Story of the Files, A Review of California Writers and Literature*, 1893.

Desti, Mary. *The Untold Story, the Life of Isadora Duncan 1921-1927*. New York: Liveright, 1929.

Doty, Robert. *Photography in America*. New York: Random House, 1974.

Douthit, M. O. *Souvenirs of Western Women*. Portland: 1905.

Duncan, Irma and Allan Ross MacDougall. *Isadora Duncan's Russian Days*. New York: Covici-Friede, 1929.

Duncan, Isadora. *My Life*, New York: Boni and Liveright, 1927. *The Art of the Dance*, New York: Theater Arts, Inc., 1928.

Duniway, Abigail Scott. *Path Breaking*. Portland: James, Kearns & Abbot, 1914.

Egan, Ferol. *Sand in a Whirlwind, the Paiute Indian War of 1860*. Garden City: Doubleday, 1972.

Flexner, Eleanor. *A Century of Struggle*. New York: Atheneum, 1970.

Gabe, J. *Portland, Its History and Builders*, Vol. 3.

Gallup, Donald. *The Flowers of Friendship, Letters Written to Gertrude Stein*. New York: Knopf, 1953.

Grimes, Alan P. *The Puritan Ethic and Woman Suffrage*. New York: Oxford University Press, 1967.

Harrison, Gilbert. *Gertrude Stein's America*. Washington, D. C.: Robert B. Luce, 1965.

Hart, James D. *My First Publication* (Gertrude Atherton). *San Francisco:* Book Club of California, 1961.

Hodge, Frederick W. *Handbook of American Indians North of Mexico.* New York: Pageant Books, 1960.

Holbrook, Stewart H. *Dreamers of the American Dream.* Garden City: Doubleday, 1957.

Howard, O. O. *Famous Indian Chiefs I have Known.* A D. Worthington, 1908. *My Life and Personal Experiences Among Our Hostile Indians.* A. D. Worthington, 1907.

James, Edward T. and James, Janet W. *Notable American Women, 1607-1950.* Cambridge: Harvard University Press.

Johnson, Jalmar. *Builders of the Northwest.* New York: Dodd, 1963.

Josephson, Hannah. *Jeannette Rankin, First Lady in Congress.* New York: Bobbs-Merrill, 1974.

Luhan, Mabel Dodge. *European Experiences,* New York: Harcourt, Brace, 1935. *Movers and Shakers,* New York: Harcourt, Brace, 1936.

Lyman, George D. *The Saga of the Comstock Lode.* New York: Scribner's, 1934.

MacDougall, Allan Ross. *Isadora, A Revolutionary in Art and Love.* New York: Thomas Nelson, 1960.

Magriel, Paul. *Isadora Duncan.* New York: Henry Holt, 1947.

Mann, Margery. *Imogen Cunningham, Photographs,* Seattle: University of Washington Press, 1970. *Imogen!* Seattle: University of Washington Press, 1974.

Mellow, James R. *Charmed Circle, Gertrude Stein & Company.* New York: Praeger, 1973.

Murray, Ken. *The Golden Days of San Simeon.* Garden City: Doubleday, 1971.

Nevada, *A History of the State from the Earliest Times Through the Civil War,* Glendale, California: Arthur H. Clark Co., 1935.

Nevada Historical Society Papers, Vol. I, 1913- 1916.

Norman, Dorothy. *Alfred Stieglitz, an American Seer.* New York: Random House, 1973.

Phelan, Mary Kay. *Probing The Unknown: The Story of Dr. Florence Sabin.* New York: Thomas Crowell, 1969.

Powers, Alfred. *History of Oregon Literature.* Portland: Metropolitan Press, 1935.

Richey, Elinor. *The Ultimate Victorians of the Continental Side of San Francisco Bay,* Berkeley: Howell-North Books, 1970. *Remain to Be Seen, Historic California Houses Open to the Public,* Berkeley: Howell-North Books, 1973.

Ross, Nancy W. *Westward the Women.* New York: Knopf, 1944.

Sabin, Florence R. *Franklin Paine Mall, The Story of a Mind.* Baltimore: Johns Hopkins Press, 1934.

Scott, Lalla. *Karnee, A Paiute Narrative.* Reno: University of Nevada Press, 1966.

Seroff, Victor. *The Real Isadora.* New York: Dial Press, 1971.

Shumate, Albert and Oscar Lewis. *Homes of California Authors.* San Francisco: The Book Club of California, 1957.

Smith, Helen Krebs. *The Presumptuous Dreamers* Vol. 1. Lake Oswego, Oregon: Smith, Smith & Smith, 1974.

Sprigge, Elizabeth. *Gertrude Stein: Her Life and Work.* New York: Harper, 1957.

Star, Kevin. *Americans and The California Dream.* New York: Oxford University Press, 1973.

Stein, Gertrude. *The Making of Americans.* Paris: Contact Editions, 1925.

Stoddard, Hope. *Famous American Women.* New York: Thomas Crowell, 1970.

Sutherland, Donald. *Gertrude Stein: A Biography of Her Work.* New Haven: Yale University Press, 1951.

Victor, Frances Fuller. *The Women's War On Whiskey, Or Crusade In Portland.* Portland, 1874.

Wheat, Margaret M. *Survival Arts of The Primitive Paiutes.* Reno: University of Nevada Press, 1967.

Wheeler, Sessions S. *The Desert Lake, The Story of Nevada's Pyramid Lake,* Caldwell, Idaho: Caxton Printers, 1969. *The Nevada Desert,* Caldwell, Idaho: Caxton Printers, 1971.

Wickes, George. *Americans In Paris 1903-1939.* Garden City: Doubleday, 1969.

Winnemucca (Hopkins), Sarah. *Life Among The Paiutes, Their Wrongs and Claims.* New York: Putnam's, 1883.

Wright, William. *The Big Bonanza.* San Francisco: A. L. Bancroft, 1877.

Yost, Edna. *American Women of Science.* Philadelphia: Frederick. A. Stokes Co., 1943.

MAGAZINES

American Heritage, April, 1973. "It All Began in Wyoming," by Lynne Cheney.

American Institute of Architects Journal, May 1957. Julia Morgan obituary.

American Journal of Anatomy, September 1909. "The Lymphatic System in Human Embryos," by Florence R. Sabin.

American Literature, January, 1957. "The Quality of Gertrude Stein's Creativity," by Allegra Stewart.

American Mercury, August 1948. "No Doll Was Abigail," by Sibyl Walter.

American West, September 1972. "Victims of Justice, Tragedy at Carson City," by Ferol Egan.

Aperture, 1957. "An Experiment in 'Reading' Photographs."

Architect and Engineer of California, October 1907. "Woman Architect Who Helped Build the Fairmont Hotel," reprinted from *San Francisco Call,* by Jane Armstrong.

Architect and Engineer, November 1918, "Some Examples of the Work of Julia Morgan," by Walter Steilberg. April 1923, "Reflections on Houses," by Irving F. Morrow.

Bookman, February 1924, "Gertrude Atherton: A Personality," by Isabel Paterson. July 1929, "Atherton versus Grundy — The Forty Years' War," by Lionel Stevenson. September 1931, "The History of Their Books — Gertrude Atherton," by Arthur B. Maurice.

California Monthly, May 1957. Julia Morgan obituary.

California Historical Society Quarterly, March 1961. "A Brilliant California Novelist, Gertrude Atherton," by Henry J. Forman.

Coronet, March 1949. "Colorado's Little Doctor," by Katharine Best and Katharine Hillyer.

Critic, July 1902. "That 'Affair' of Mrs. Atherton's," by J. P. Mowbray.

Forum, September 1911. "The Renaissance of the Dance," by Etscher Gaspard. November 1917. "My Types — Gertrude Atherton," by Pendennis.

Georgia Historical Quarterly, Spring 1974. "Jeannette Rankin in Georgia," by Ted C. Harris.

Independent Woman, December 1940. "Who's Who in the Elections," by Juliette K. Arthur.

Independent, April 2, 1917. "The Lady from Missoula," by Donald Wilhelm.

Journal of the Society of Architectural Historians, Vol. X, No. 3. "Domestic Architecture of the Bay Region," by Elizabeth K. Thompson.

Kappa Alpha Theta Journal, Spring 1967. "She Built for the Ages," by Flora D. North.

Ladies' Home Journal, August 1917. "What We Women Should Do," by Jeannette Rankin.

Life, September 16, 1957, letter to editor about Julia Morgan by Allan Temko. March 3, 1972, "At 91, Jeannette Rankin is the Feminists' New Heroine," by Elizabeth Frappollo.

Literary Digest, November 25, 1916. "The Member from Montana."

McCalls Magazine, January 1958. "Three Women of Courage," by John F. Kennedy.

Modern Photography, May 1951. "Imogen Cunningham and the Straight Approach," by Christina Eerding.

Montana the Magazine of Western History, Winter 1973. "Montana Women and the Battle for the Ballot," by T. A. Larson. Summer 1974. "Women's Role in the American West," by T. A. Larson. Summer 1967. "The Lady from Montana," by John C. Board. Summer 1974. "Mother Was Shocked," by Belle F. Winestine.

Nation, May 31, 1917. "The Lady from Montana."

Nevada Highways and Parks, Summer 1972. "The Mountains of Nevada," by John Schilling and Philip Hyde.

Nevada Historical Society Quarterly, Winter 1971. "Sarah Winnemucca," by Patricia Stewart.

Oregon Historical Quarterly, December 1949. "Reminiscences and Anecdotes," by Oswald West. March 1951. "The War on the Webfoot Saloon," by Malcolm H. Clark, Jr.

Outlook, November 22, 1916. "The First Woman Elected to Congress."

Overland Monthly, June 1916. "A Mother of Suffrage in the West," by Fred Lockley. October 1932. "Gertrude Atherton," by Cyril Clemens.

Pacific Northwest Quarterly, January 1964. "The Montana Woman Suffrage Campaign," by Ronald Schaffer.

Pictorial Review, January 1930. "Dr. Sabin, Scientist," by Genevieve Parkhurst.

Popular Photography, June 1957. "West Coast Photography: Does it Really Exist?"

Publishers Weekly, June 26, 1948. Gertrude Atherton obituary.

Ramparts, February 1968. "A History of the Rise of the Unusual Movement for Woman Power in the United States," by W. and M. Hinckle.

Saturday Review of Literature, May 28, 1932, "Mrs. Atherton's Life." August 21, 1971. "Liberation of Gertrude Stein," by Frank Gervasi.

Survey Graphic, February 1947. "Dr. Sabin's Second Career," by Albert Q. Maisel.

The New Yorker, January 1-22, 1955. "The Lakes of the Cui-ui Eaters," by A. J. Leibling.

U. S. Camera, August 1955. *"Interview with Three Greats,"* by Herm Lenz.

Wilson's Photographic Magazine, March 1914. "Imogen Cunningham — an Appreciation."

World's Work, February 1926. "Dr. Florence Rena Sabin: A Woman Scientist of Great Achievements," by Frances D. McMullen.

NEWSPAPERS AND OTHER JOURNALS

California Alumni Weekly, October 23, 1915. "Julia Morgan '94 Makes Name in Architecture."

California Historical Courier, April 1975. "Julia Morgan's Buildings Grow Old Gracefully," by Bernice Scharlach.

Carson Daily Appeal, November 12, 1875. "A Colony for Indians."

Chemawa American Bulletin, April 25, 1928. "Sarah Winnemucca," by Robert Hall.

Christian Science Monitor, April 1, 1936, "I Would Vote 'No' Again," by Jeannette Rankin. October 1, 1959. "Years Add Camera Skill," by Bernice S. Decker.

Congressional Record, December 8, 1942. "Some Questions about Pearl Harbor," by Jeannette Rankin. June 22, 1970. Speech on Jeannette Rankin by Lee Metcalf before U. S. Senate.

Johns Hopkins Hospital Bulletin, May 1920. "Presentation to John's Hopkins University of the Portrait of Florence Rena Sabin."

New York Times, June 15, 1948. Gertrude Atherton obituary. May 6, 1973. "Cunningham, Still Going Strong, by A. D. Coleman; and "Imogen Cunningham at Ninety, a Remarkable Empathy," by Hilton Kramer.

Oakland Saturday Night, "Roxi's Column" (on Julia Morgan), March 28, 1896 and May 30, 1896.

Oregon Daily Journal, October 11, 1915. Abigail Scott Duniway obituary.

Portland Oregonian, February 4, 1945. "Abigail Scott Duniway; She Won Freedom for Women of the West," by Margaret Thompson.

Reno Evening Gazette, October 27, 1882, November 16, 1882, April 10, 1883, June 26, 1885. Reports on Winnemucca family.

Reese River Reveille, November 15, 1886. "Sarah Winnemucca's School."

The New Northwest, Abigail Scott Duniway, editor. 1871-1887.

DOCUMENTS AND UNPUBLISHED MATERIAL

"Backgrounds and Beginnings in Domestic Architecture of the San Francisco Bay Region," by Elizabeth Kendall Thompson. San Francisco Museum of Art Catalog 49.

"Culture History of Lovelock Cave, Nevada." University of California thesis by Gordon Leonard Grosscup.

Dedication Ceremonies of the Florence R. Sabin Building for Research in Cellular Biology, December 1, 1951.

Diary of Abigail Scott Duniway, 1852. Oregon Historical Center.

Diary of Amelia Stein, January 1878 to September 1886. Bancroft Library.

"John Galen Howard and the Beaux-Arts Movement in the United States," M.A. thesis by Joan Draper. University of California, 1972.

"Julia Morgan, Some Introductory Notes," research paper by Richard W. Longstreth. School of Environmental Design Library, University of California, Berkeley.

KPFA Radio transcript. "Imogen Cunningham," by Marilyn Hagberg.

Letter from Leo Stein to Annette Rosenshine, February 1947. Bancroft Library.

"Life's Not A Paragraph," manuscript concerning Gertrude Stein by Annette Rosenshine. Bancroft Library.

"Notes on Some Paviotso Personalities and Material Culture," Anthropological Papers No. 2, by Robert F. Heizer. Carson City: Nevada State Museum, 1960.

Oral History Project, Bancroft Library. Jeannette Rankin Transcript. Julia Morgan Transcript. Imogen Cunningham Transcript.

"Reminiscences," transcript of a tape recording concerning Gertrude Stein by Therese Jelenko. Bancroft Library.

Sarah Winnemucca letter from Camp McDermitt, Nevada, written April 4, 1870 to Commissioner of Indian Affairs. Bancroft Library.

Index

Clockwise this page: Julia Morgan, Florence Sabin, Abigail Scott Duniway, Jeannette Rankin with John Kirkley, Imogen Cunningham.